Before, During and After the Falklands War

Richard Stevens

Before, During and
After the Falklands War
Richard Stevens

ISBN 978-1-909660-76-2

A CIP catalogue record for this book
is available from the British Library.
Published 2017 Tricorn Books
131 High Street, Portsmouth, PO1 2HW

Printed & bound in the UK

I would like to dedicate this book to Toni for the computer expertise and stress counselling and to Caris and Liam to remind them of their heritage.

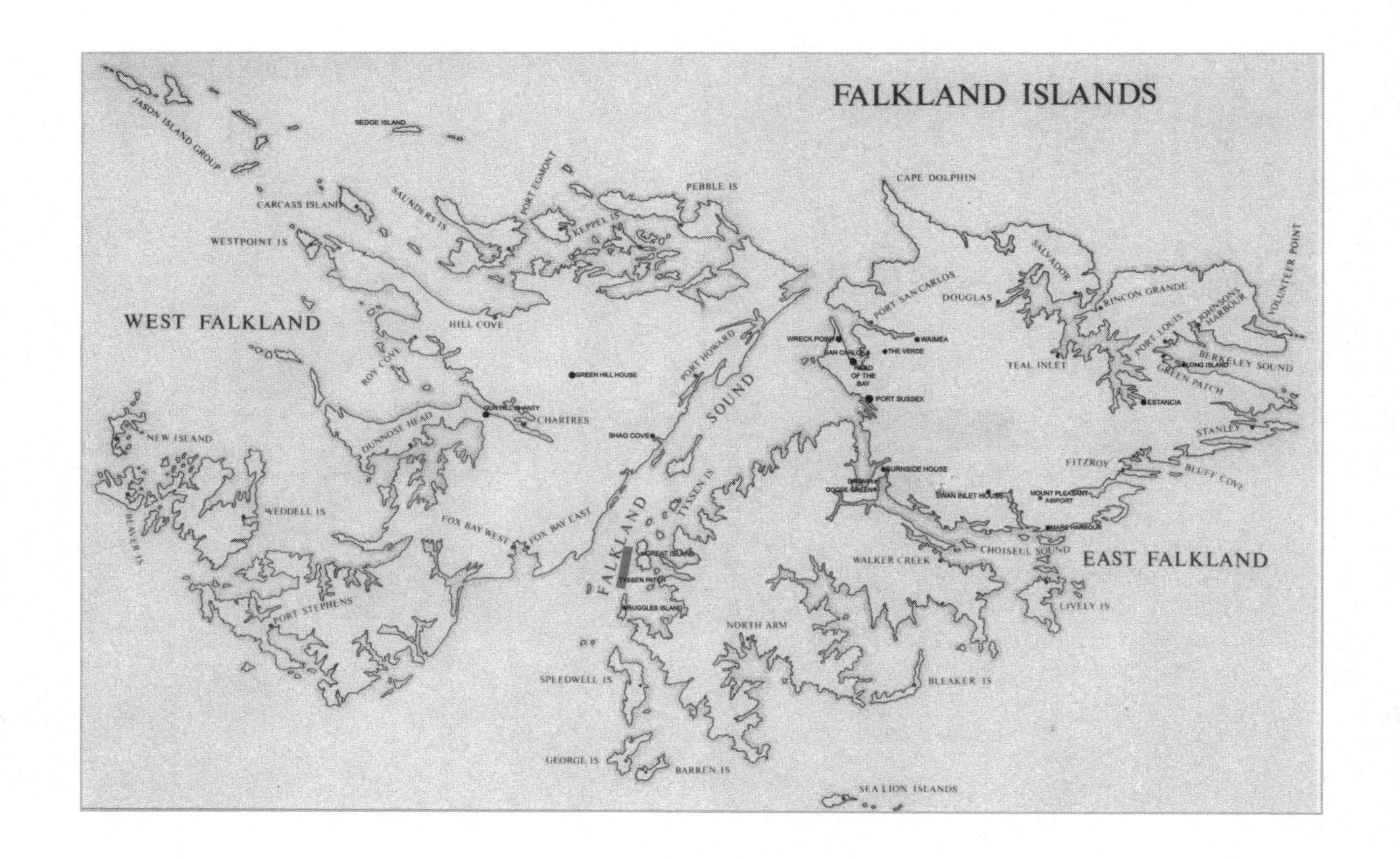
FALKLAND ISLANDS
WEST FALKLAND
EAST FALKLAND
FALKLAND SOUND
JASON ISLAND GROUP
SEDGE ISLAND
CARCASS ISLAND
WESTPOINT IS
SAUNDERS IS
PORT EGMONT
KEPPEL IS
PEBBLE IS
HILL COVE
ROY COVE
GREEN HILL HOUSE
PORT HOWARD
CHARTRES
DUNNOSE HEAD
NEW ISLAND
SHAG COVE
WEDDELL IS
BEAVER IS
FOX BAY WEST
FOX BAY EAST
PORT STEPHENS
TYSSEN IS
GREAT ISLAND
RUGGLES ISLAND
SPEEDWELL IS
GEORGE IS
BARREN IS
NORTH ARM
BLEAKER IS
SEA LION ISLANDS
CAPE DOLPHIN
PORT SAN CARLOS
WRECK POINT
WAIMEA
THE VERDE
HEAD OF THE BAY
PORT SUSSEX
DOUGLAS
SALVADOR
RINCON GRANDE
JOHNSONS HARBOUR
VOLUNTEER POINT
PORT LOUIS
LONG ISLAND
BERKELEY SOUND
GREEN PATCH
TEAL INLET
ESTANCIA
STANLEY
FITZROY
BLUFF COVE
BURNSIDE HOUSE
GOOSE GREEN
SWAN INLET HOUSE
MOUNT PLEASANT AIRPORT
CHOISEUL SOUND
WALKER CREEK
LIVELY IS

Contents

Introduction

I was born in Plymouth and brought up in a small village in Kent. I was educated at a small village primary school in Cobham and then moved to a secondary modern in Longfield.

I didn't know what I wanted to do when I left full time education.
My father had commuted to London all the time we lived in Luddesdown (Kent)but I didn't fancy spending hours of my life doing the same.

I wanted to do something exciting so I worked for Kimberly Clark to earn enough money to do a professional diving course. I did six weeks of boot camp at Fort Bovisand in Plymouth where ex military divers bullied us through explosives, cutting with Kerry cable, (flexible thermic lance) underwater welding, a 50 metre dive and much more. I was too young however to work for any reputable firms in the North Sea oil industry.

I then worked on farms with a friend doing anything that was legal for money. We managed to rent a sixty acre field and grew barley but because we were so young, no bank would loan us the money for seed or fertilizer. A farm that we did work for loaned us the seed and fertilizer and we paid for it by working. This led to us working on farms all day and trying to do our land at night. I did a few nights ploughing in a cables tractor. There didn't seem to be a happy ending in sight.

Somehow I ended up working for Securicor, which offered me a career, a dog at some locations and promotion opportunities. When a job was brought to my attention about working 8,000 miles away in the Falkland Islands, I couldn't get my application off quickly enough.

I hand wrote all the adventures that I have had living in the Falkland Islands a few years ago. I then took a while to type them out and even longer unravelling some of the overlapping themes. I have tried to compile a light-hearted but informative narrative covering 40 years of living in the Falkland Islands

Hopefully readers will realise what an amazing place the Falkland Islands is to live in, with huge personal freedom, very special and approachable wildlife and plenty of adventures and excitement, including raising children, to be had.

Camp Education

1. FALKLAND ISLANDS 1977

Arrival

We approached the Islands from the air. A huge blanket of thick cloud covered the Falklands and as we dropped through it we could imagine the propellers of the aircraft plaiting it into lengths behind us.

Descending through such immense cloud disorientates me and I was soon beginning to think that we should have seen the ground. Another couple of minutes dawdled by before we eventually came out of the cloud and you could see the temporary airstrip made from hundreds of sheets of aluminium planking about 150 feet below. The runway didn't look that big.

The aircraft, a F27, came in from the east and I felt the plane touch the runway while the wheel I was sitting by was still a few feet in the air, bearing testament to a strong cross wind and a competent and very skilled pilot at the controls.

The aircraft operators were LADE, which was the Argentine air force that flew into the Falklands once a week. It was definitely an air force plane because the seats were thin, uncomfortable and canvas and disconcertingly, in the middle of the plane, was a huge life raft secured under a cargo net.

The trip over from Comodoro Rivadavia, Argentina, had been fairly unmemorable apart from the walk out to the plane in staggeringly strong winds and the flight catering and customer service (which even in today's climate of reducing everything to cut costs, has yet to be equalled in my experience for awfulness). The in-flight snack were those sugar-free dog biscuits in multiple shapes and colours. Circular, diamond, oval and square. These were washed down with the grimmest orange drink ever, made by adding water to orange-flavoured dust.

I wonder to this day whether someone in the chain of procurement was taking the piss. Was it the airline itself? 'We'll give these British sorts dog biscuits because they are too ignorant to know what they are eating and we can all have a laugh behind this curtain.' Or was it the bursar who convinced the Argentine air force that this product, with a dog on the box, was what the animal-loving Brits liked eating most on short-haul flights on antiquated turbo props.

'Excellent safety record,' my father said after I wrote home to record my flight.

So despite dog biscuits and foul orangey liquid, here I was in the Falkland Islands surrounded by rippling white grass and darker stuff which turned out to be diddle-dee, a low growing shrub. Outcrops of rock stretching back to the west becoming part of low-lying mountains.

I mean no insult to say the arrivals lounge wasn't that flash. It was a presentable Nissan hut with 'Stanley Airport' painted on the roof and without any frills like a conveyor belt for luggage. It was all pretty cosy and delightfully low tech. What was special was how passengers and customs officials alike were greeting one another. I was one of the only people on the plane who wasn't known and even I was given a warm welcome as the new 'schoolie'.

My duties as a peripatetic teacher were to move around the settlements and isolated houses, that had children, and do my best to educate them. Ideally I would have three places to work at, staying two weeks at each location before starting all over again. I was to work within the Camp Education Department, managed by a senior teacher and a secretary who worked out of a small building in the grounds of the senior school. Their responsibilities included deciding the teachers beats, booking the flights and sending out material.

All was very cheery and good-natured until one of the Royal Marines who was on the flight –part of a detachment of about 40 that were here to protect us – suggested that he was smuggling a woman back into the Islands in his suitcase. A joke shared by his mates and others who recognised the shortage of woman to the many keen and deprived men living in the Falklands. Looking at the luggage, she must have been incredibly small, but the chief customs official didn't take this into account and certainly didn't appreciate the quip. The boot-neck's sense of humour had cost him dear and he was still there after I had left. The last image I had was of him turning out his pockets surrounded by the contents of his suitcase.

A new airport had just been built, with a small but modern arrivals and departure lounge, but it hadn't yet opened. A company called Johnsons Construction had built it using a lot of local labour, which had given plenty of blokes, including many working in the rural sector, an opportunity to do something different and earn reasonably good money.

The timing of this new airport couldn't have been better, because on one very windy night, shortly after my arrival, the temporary airstrip blew away.

Stanley

I was met by the acting Superintendent of Education, Frank O Riley, who was a short and energetic type of man. We walked to his Series 3 leaf-sprung Land Rover and put my belongings into the back. I had a huge red trunk which had all my worldly possessions in.

We set out on the track weaving from side to side as we avoided potholes full of water and vehicles coming the other way avoiding the same potholes. We were soon on some tarmac and heading into town. I was asking about my new job as a peripatetic teacher but Frank was more concerned about whether I had played rugby before. I arrived at my lodgings knowing diddly about my job but with an invitation to play a game of rugby on Sunday at the Eliza Cove rugby pitch, against a team selected from the Royal Marine detachment.

As we rattled and bounced into Stanley the views of the wrecks of old sailing ships seemed to be in every direction. I felt as though I had fallen into a fantasy world of a ship's graveyard. Some vessels just graced the shoreline but others, with corrugated iron roofs, were part of jetties and were being used as warehouses. It was a spectacular sight. The Falklands had been the final resting place to many ships, as many battled round Cape Horn and the winds and currents swept them towards the Islands. Many were wrecked around the coast of the Falklands and some managed to limp into Stanley where costs of repair were exorbitant and many never left.

I didn't know at the time but Frans Axel Pettersson from Sweden, an ancestor of my future wife Toni, came to the Islands this way and was wrecked on the West Falklands. He had, not surprisingly, lost the appetite to further his seafaring career on the high seas and ended up settling in the Falklands. A number of other families originate from sailors that have left their ships for a life in the Islands.

The town itself sits on the northern side of the ridge overlooking the inner harbour of Port Stanley and sheltered from the cold southerlies. Most of the houses were brightly coloured, wooden framed and clad with flat iron on the sides and corrugated iron on the roofs. There were houses, clad with corrugated iron on the sides as well as the roofs, and there was also a peppering of stone buildings, including some substantial examples on the seafront like Crozier Place and the Upland Goose Hotel.

The interiors of most houses were made of hardboard fastened to wooden framing. Some of the stone buildings were plastered.

Cooking with peat

I was lodging with Mary and Laurie Goodwin and they made me feel really welcome. Mary gave lodgings to teachers and others, giving an extended group a midday meal.

In the 1970s, most people had a Rayburn stove or an equivalent and cut peat to fuel it. This heated the home, although only to any extent in the kitchen where it was situated. It also cooked the food and heated the domestic water. The smell of these stoves was rich and scented and was so different to the characterless oil-fired central heating and electric cooker that I was used to.

Mary, with many years experience, coaxed the very best out of her stove. I had never seen people cook eggs in a frying pan using a small amount of water rather than oil. I knew what poaching was but I thought the egg had to be fully immersed. Toast was made by waiting until the peat was red and then opening the damper on the flu and opening the fire door. You then use a long fork to get the bread close to the heat and your hand far enough away.

The peat stove had its advantages and as long as you were reasonably fit and able to cut 150 to 200 cubic yards this would keep most people, in a modest home, going for a year. It was free apart from the effort of cutting, rickling (turning it over and stacking in small piles to aid the drying process) and carting it back to your peat shed, throwing it in or stacking it. You then chopped it into smaller bits and filled 25-litre containers. These were taken to the back door where they were brought in one at a time to burn the contents at the stove

The ashes were then collected in the pan at the bottom under the fire. This had to be taken out in any weather to tip into an old drum with its top cut off. This was the most messy and treacherous job of all when it comes to burning peat. In windy conditions it is many an inattentive person who has had ash all over them.

2. TRAVELLING FROM THE UK TO STANLEY

Flying from the UK

As I sat in the warmth generated from the peat during my first night in Stanley, the Falklands' weather buffeting the outside of the house, I had time to reflect on my flight from the UK.

In fact, a few weeks before my departure, I had never even flown and so, with all these air miles looming, I thought I should go for a reasonably long flight to get a feel for my pending adventure.

My sister had also caught the wanderlust and had recently gone to Crete to work as a tourist rep so I found the cheapest bucket seat possible and left for sunny climes. I enjoyed a couple of weeks drinking Cretan wine and eating Greek food, then I flew back to the UK one day and left on a British Caledonian flight to the Falklands the next.

We came into Rio de Janeiro, on to Sao Paulo and then to Buenos Aires. Unbeknown to me, South Americans break into spontaneous clapping on landing. I was petrified when it happened this first time. I thought the back of the plane was ripping off!

I was pretty knackered after the long flight after very little, if any, sleep. Fortunately, I was met at the airport and taken to a hotel.

Buenos Aires

The first thing I noticed in Buenos Aires was that the rules of the road were open to interpretation. If traffic lights were red and it looked as if you could get across before being hit by another vehicle you chanced your arm. The other thing – and I suppose this was not surprising – was that every vehicle had a dent or scrape and most of them had both and many of them.

Coming into the city there was a thick band of shanty towns that surrounded the clean and modern European-looking centre. There was a huge difference in the communities. The first looked a far-from-comfortable existence, in fact very grotty looking. The European part had most of the sophistication that you would expect in any European city.

Most people that have visited Buenos Aires know that the centre is very cosmopolitan. An air of busyness prevails with a feeling of energy and bustle. Supporting this bustle was the amount of chrome on lorries and buses. More chrome than at a Hells Angels convention. It made the buses in UK look decidedly drab in comparison. Imagine this scene of vehicles weaving in and out of one another, ignoring any kind of driving protocol, with horns blaring as if the drivers were slumped onto the steering wheel. People would be jumping on and off moving buses with many others taking their lives into their hands by crossing this multi-laned, traffic chaos.

I arrived at my hotel and crashed out in my room and slept for twelve hours. The next day I was ready to explore but first I had to have breakfast.
The first meal I had in the hotel was interesting and a lesson. The room was large and badly lit with tables sprinkled through the room in no recognisable pattern. On the tables were the usual stuff apart from right in the middle of the table was a tall glass with pesos sticking out of them. Waiters only earned a living wage through the added income of their tips. These displays were there as pointers to help people realise what was needed.

I can remember the service of that first meal vividly, with a cheery soul putting everything into providing for my every need, all with a Latin flourish.

I can't recall what I had as a main course but it would probably have been a steak. When I left the table my chair was pulled back for me.

The next meal was very different. I sat down at the table and the waiters came together in a huddle at the far end of the room before the most junior man was dispatched to serve me. He moved towards the table in a slow and reluctant walk. I suffered service with attitude. I had obviously cocked up with what I had thought was an extravagant tip on my first meal. It was, in my defence, very difficult to judge the value of the Argentine peso. There were new and old and regardless of this you needed tens of thousands to buy anything.
My first night at the hotel was consumed by the total sleep of someone who was exhausted, but from that night on my sleep was disturbed by the chiming of a clock, which seemed to be right outside my bedroom window. I was told later that it is a clock that the people of Britain gave to the people of Buenos Aires.

Part of my time in Buenos Aires was taken up by securing a picture for my white card, a document all people from the Islands had to have if they were travelling to and from the Falklands.

I was soon leaving Buenos Aires, driving through streets of dented and scratched vehicles. As we approached the airport uniformed people had stopped a car. They were giving the vehicle a thorough going over. There was a strange atmosphere in the car between my guide and the taxi driver and there was some mention of terrorists. I didn't realise that this was probably part of the dirty war where thousands of Argentines disappeared and were murdered by their own people.

I flew south on a Boeing 737 down to Comodoro Rivadavia, a town that was surrounded by large areas of bare clay with a smattering of nodding donkeys slowly cranking over, pumping oil to the surface. The next flight was to the Falklands.

Difference between UK and Falklands

The Falklands were as different a community to anything that I had witnessed in England, and as a child we had travelled with my parents and sisters the length and breadth of the British Isles – including visiting the Isles of Skye, which was probably the closest.

I came from a small village in Kent where everyone knew one another, but there wasn't the warmth that I felt as a complete stranger walking these Falklands streets. Everyone would look you in the eye, from the very young to the old and say at least hello, and many would comment on the weather past and present.

As a child in the UK you are taught that you don't talk to strangers and if an adult stranger approaches you, you wonder what they are up to or think straight away that they must be after something.

Here there was also a strong sense of community where people would barter skills. A mechanic might do some work on a vehicle and get paid with a sack of potatoes. A bottle of spirits or a case of beer was popular currency that in many ways seemed to be disproportionate to the job. I would often think why would someone do all that for a bottle of rum? I had a lot to learn.

Most houses had a vegetable garden, which was the only way to put vegetables on a regular basis onto the table. Even the hospital had a gardener who tended a vegetable garden, which supplied the patients with veg.

People would come to the house where I was staying for a cup of tea and a chat. Not just woman and children but men and whole families. Over the first three years, I saw many sides of this. An evening visit or during the weekends, a tot would be bought out in many households which would always liven up the conversations.

One of my lasting memories of living in Stanley for those first few days was the smell of the town, especially on the cold, still, winter nights. It was one of peat smoke as it wandered lazily along the streets of Stanley, hanging nearly motionless above the town. It was a very appealing, exotic smell to my senses and one that you only occasionally smell from the one or two peat fires that still burn today.

3. ARRIVING AT CHARTRES

Port San Carlos

So I left Stanley for the first time in the Beaver float plane and flew to Port San Carlos via San Carlos. It was great to see the countryside and the colours of the land and sea. On a sunny day the blues and greens of the sea were amazing and some of the tarns in the mountain landscape had a deep blue that was rich and colourful.

I got out of the plane at San Carlos where the manager, Adrian Monk, harangued me about the long absence of a teacher at their farm. It was a bit of a surprise considering that I was only a lowly travelling teacher with no influence at all. I said I was happy to go wherever my masters sent me. I did return six months later for an enjoyable period. Seven years later, Toni and I bought a piece of San Carlos when it was split up into a number of family-sized farms.

My destination was Port San Carlos, which is next door to San Carlos. Both farms were in San Carlos Waters, northwest of the East Falklands. With the names being quite similar many visitors or short-term workers get confused between the two places. The local names are far easier to remember. San Carlos was called JB or Bonners after Jack Bonner a one-time owner, and Port San Carlos was called KC after Keith Cameron a previous manager/owner. These distinctions made it a little clearer for everyone.

I spent a week with a settlement teacher, Carol Miller, who was the manager's wife at KC and who taught the farms' children around a table in her kitchen. It didn't seem too difficult even though the children were all ages and many abilities.

So a week later it was on to the Beaver and off to Chartres which is in the centre of West Falklands. Chartres is on a point that comes down to one side of a creek that is opposite Mount Chartres. The sea comes in through a narrow neck and then opens out into a bay into which the Chartres River feeds. A lovely settlement when the tide was in and the gorse was out, and which ran along the road that was in front of the settlement on the sea side of the houses. Chartres was part of my beat for two-and-a-half years of my three-year contract.

Community at Chartres

At that time, John and Candy Blackley lived in the cook's house, with their baby son Shane, and Jimmy and Avis Duncan lived in the next house followed by John and Betty White. Then it was the 'Big House' where the manager and his wife and their son Stephen lived, and behind them lived Roy and Ann Murphy. The next house housed Jack and Muriel Harvey. Marshal and Deidre Barnes lived in the next house with their four children Susan, Marie, Trevor, and Paul. The last house housed the Marsh family who had recently moved in from the outside house, The Green Hill – Frank and June Marsh, with their three sons Alistair, Gavin and Leon. Robin, a fourth son, was working on the East Falklands when I arrived and Leon still had a few weeks of school but left after only one visit.

All the settlements in the Falklands were self-contained communities where the peat was cut for everyone and carted to each house. On some farms this was a community activity carried out by all able-bodied men with spades, but other farms were starting to cut peat with a McConnel arm, an articulated arm with a bucket at the end. This was connected to the hydraulic arms of a tractor and operated by one man assisted by another, on foot, who cut up the bigger pieces of peat with a sharp spade. Most farms paid someone to cart peat on contract.

Provisions

Farm workers received meat as part of their pay. The farms' mutton was killed by a couple of shepherds for each household and the cookhouse weekly. Beef was killed in the winter once it became too cold for flies. The beef would arrive at a house in quarters and the mutton usually whole and a member of the household would do the butcher's job cutting it up into what was required. The mutton and beef were given free to residents although I think there were limits with a household having one mutton a week.

Non-treated water would usually come, gravity-fed, to each house from a small reservoir fed from a spring but sometimes from a watercourse. A small generator provided power, which in the medium-sized settlements were usually about ten kilowatts. This seems ridiculously small but it powered the lights and peoples' washing machines, but how if they were all running together I don't know, but I can't remember any debate on staggering use. The manager's houses on the bigger farms had their own generator. If you wanted fresh vegetables you had to have a garden and spend significant time in it to reap the best rewards.

Everyone had hens to supply eggs which were needed for cakes, buns, and biscuit cooking. You also needed a rooster so that you could replace your hens as they got older.

Provisions that couldn't be generated by the people were brought by the two boats, which serviced all the settlements in camp from Stanley, the only town – *The Forrest*, which was the government vessel, or the coastal shipping ship *The Monsunen*. The latter did the majority of the work. I think on average *The Monsunen* would be seen once every three months. All hands in the settlements that I visited, would work the boat because it could be an arduous job, particularly when wool was leaving the farm. The plane was used occasionally to bring lighter freight to the farms and to deliver the ordinary mail.

Most farms had cowsheds where the women of the settlement milked cows by hand for their families. Each farm had different ideas, but most had designated cows supplied by a senior woman. Many families had separators, which would be used to take the cream from the raw milk, and then this cream would be used as a luxury on cereals and desserts but most was made into butter. There were a few farms that decided to employ a dairyman to milk cows and supply milk to the settlement, arguing that this centralisation was a much better use of cows and grazing resources.

Milking cows can be surprisingly and incredibly competitive in a large settlement, with individuals vying to be the first to the cowshed each morning. At one large farm this reached new heights with people in the middle of summer arriving at the cowshed at dawn which is around 3.30pm. Tempers began to get a little frayed with too many early mornings and with two particularly strong-willed ladies unable to become a clear winner as to who was the first to the cowshed. One thing led to another and words were exchanged and the two protagonists, after going to all that effort, ended up sloshing their milk over each other.

Hierarchy on the farms

There was a hierarchy in these settlements, which started with the manager who was the boss. His word was law and the authority trickled down through other senior members of the farms. Managers would, in severe circumstances, sack people and give them just hours to remove themselves from the farm.

Farm managers had their own cowman gardener and domestic staff in the 1970s but this was slowly disappearing. The cowman gardener milked the cows to supply milk to the manager's family and also did the digging, planting and weeding in the garden. Many of the cowman gardeners were old men but there were young men that did these jobs and would contribute to the overall effort of the farm. For example, during the shearing season once the manager's requirements for the day were fulfilled the cowman gardener would go and shear sheep on contract.

People like the settlement mechanics were also important members of the community and often single-handedly kept the generators going, plus all the other important mechanical tasks such as keeping the manager's Land Rover in working order.

Many of the managers left the Falklands during the winter, some went each year and so it was important to have a strong and responsible team, even in the quietest farming months, to keep the farms functioning.

The foreman would have probably been the next man down from the manager, organising the navvy gang and running the business of the settlement such as delivering meat or carting rubbish and ashes away. They would also maintain roads and cut the hedges in the winter when the shearing season was over. The navvy gang used to congregate in one of the buildings at 'turn to' to receive their instructions for the day.

The shepherd boss would be a near equal to the foreman and have the shepherd gang under his authority. He would manage the stock, moving sheep in and out of the settlement during the season to have them shorn and then take them back to their pastures. Other jobs like putting the rams out with the ewes at the correct time and managing the cattle and horses were also part of their responsibilities.

Some farms had tussock islands which they used for horses and cattle during the winter. Some islands would be accessed by walking or driving stock onto them at very low tides. Some farms needed and used motorboats and scows to access islands. These islands were a good resource and helped some of the stock through the hard winter. Again it would be the shepherd boss that would decide, with the manager, which horses or bullock needed to go.

Each shepherd had his own troop, each horse was allocated on a seniority and need basis, i.e. manager, shepherd boss and those having been shepherding the longest, and then the colt tamer having a small claim over the ordinary shepherd. The worst place to be was the last shepherd to arrive, especially if there had been a gap before your employment, because on some farms the best horses would be relocated and you would end up with all the 'hard cases'. Another very important member of any settlement was the store keeper

There was a main store day on the farms that I visited, although most farms had an understanding storekeeper who would go to the store at any civilised hour. It paid to keep in with them.

One of the things that really struck me was how provisions came to camp, especially the volumes, which I was not used to. For example, flour and sugar came in sacks and people had flour and sugar bins in their back kitchens that could hold a whole hundred weight sack of each.

4. LIVING AT CHARTRES

The bunkhouse

I got off the Beaver at Chartres onto a ramp that was wheeled into the water. The whole of the settlement had turned out to see the new schoolie as I came ashore. Three of the men had Klondike full beards and looked quite imposing and then there were other single men and women of many ages.

As I got off, members of the Triggs family – who had lived at an outside house called The Saddle House – got on the plane and left the farm for good. The Saddle House was then not lived in by anyone until it was sold as part of a farm to Dave Dunford sometime in the 1980s.

I was taken to my room in the bunkhouse. The bunkhouse was where all the single blokes that worked on the farm lived and it had its own rules and regulations.

The bunkhouse/cookhouse was usually one of the biggest buildings on a farm and often the galley was an integral part. Here the cook would conjure up their culinary delights. There were some fantastic cooks who made jams and pickles and kept the costs of living in the cookhouse down, although the latter also depended on how dedicated the residents of this humble abode were in their gardens. There were some awful cooks too, most if not all were old single blokes who couldn't navvy or shepherd anymore.

Most bunkhouses had a senior person who had the room downstairs off the dining area and absorbed the heat from the galley and any fires lit downstairs. The settlement chaps had the rooms upstairs, over the galley, which kept them warmer than the rooms on the back of the bunkhouses where the newest arrivals – men from outside houses and the travelling teacher – had a room.

The Chartres cookhouse became one of the most infamous cookhouses on the West, and probably on the Islands, as all the mature members moved out and a young gang grew.

My first cookhouse experience was like walking into the Wild West, but with fewer cattle and six guns. My room was the first on the left upstairs and regularly visited, even though the door was usually locked to allow the patron a feeling of privacy. In truth it wasn't even a feeling because most nights at the weekend if I turned in before the end of the frivolities I would be woken by having my door booted in.

Many of these friendly drunks that kicked the door in would sit at the end of my bed discussing the lack of women and other such worldly topics. One chap, in comparison to most, wanted to discuss the problems he was having with his current girlfriend. It was pointless asking any of these friendly folk to leave you alone, as they poured beer over your bedspread and spilt their finer feelings about life, the universe and everything.

Sometimes, although to be fair not on my first visit, high spirits would have the protagonist tipping you out of your bed and sometimes you would end up on the floor with the bed on top of you. It was interesting times but I was only just 22 and could take it.

It was at times like this that I realised why it was me that got one of the two jobs out of the 130 that had applied to be a peripatetic teacher in the Falklands.

I had been working as a night watchman for Securicor in the new Bromley Library and I had gone home and then headed up to Victoria and Stagg House where the interviews were held.

There were quite a few other individuals waiting for their interviews and as time passed people got talking and I became aware that I was probably the least qualified in the room for any teaching post. Everyone seemed to be incredibly qualified, to such a degree that I wondered what I was doing there and as the time started to disappear and my next shift at Bromley Library drew nearer I was considering leaving. I was thinking, well what's the point?

I did get to my interview, but I was totally relaxed because I didn't think I had an earthly chance. I was asked whether I could entertain myself because people in the Islands weren't great talkers. Alan Hague who was to become my immediate boss was at the interview. He was employed to construct a tape library for Camp Education, but also managed the department.

I think this feeling that I didn't have a chance allowed me to express confidence, friendliness and resourcefulness without fear of saying the wrong thing. Coming from a small village in Kent also seemed to get a good response from the interviewing team.

Once in the Falklands I found nearly everyone to be friendly and talkative and many were incredibly well informed, not just within the Islands but about world affairs.

Back in the cookhouse environment, being young I could participate in these high spirits and eventually I was to return the favour in kind, although it wasn't how I expected it to go. Just as the annual sports event (a celebration of the end of the shearing season) in February at Chartres began I received a Dear John letter. In fact, I received an invitation to the wedding. It was a bummer and so I had a consoling drink followed by another and another and…

It suddenly felt like a cool idea to return the favour of the main abuser of my door. But a push and a shove followed by a few kicks on his door had no effect. This kind of assault on my door would have had it open in no time. Next it was a couple of shoulder charges that hardly had the door quivering or the lock giving in.

The doors in the cookhouse used to be opposite one another in a long central corridor that ran the length of the building, so you could stand against the back wall of the room opposite, run through the open door, take to the air in the passage and bring an awesome shoulder charge to bear on the opposite door. This door could have graced the doorway of some minor fortification, however after the fourth or fifth flying shoulder charge the door finally gave but not at the snib. The doorpost that housed the hinge and four planks from the wall fell into the room. It wasn't what I had intended but I had had my turn and the results were more than impressive.

Entertainment in the cookhouse

For many in the cookhouse the weekend began by visiting the store on a Friday night after knock-off, where a bottle of spirit and a case of beer was purchased. Booze was rationed on most of the farms that I visited to one bottle and a case a week, apart from at shearing when you could have six cans a night. Most farm managers had worked out that to get the most out of his gang, a bottle and a case could be consumed on Friday night, Saturday night and then Sunday with enough time to give a sufficient recovery period for a hangover. The workforce could then turn up for work on Monday morning and be productive.

Entertainment was very frugal in those days – limited radio of four or five hours a night, and World Service if you had a reasonable radio and were prepared to put up with background noise that nearly overwhelmed speaking and music. In winter at some places on the West, medium wave became impossible to listen to apart from the most dedicated listeners.

There was a film library where 16mm reels would be sent from farm to farm to be shown in cookhouses Island-wide. There were some good old classics like *Cat Balou* and *Butch Cassidy and The Sundance Kid*. Regardless of what was showing most people would come and watch and the entertainment was in the whole production.

After the film was shown the reels had to be rewound. Some films had a number of reels and because some of were old they broke or would jam and the light would burn a hole in the film and it had to be repaired. All these things led to occasional confusion and reels were put back in the wrong order and so you saw a film out of sequence or they hadn't been rewound so started backwards or a splice was in back to front.

One of the funniest things I saw was at Chartres when too much commotion on the couch at the back drove two rats to make a run for it up the main room as we were watching some epic.

Most farms used the transport available to move the films on to the next place and each farm ticked themselves off a list once they had seen a particular film. Some farms worked harder amongst themselves to get the films on to the next place. Two individuals, Bill Pole Evans from Saunders Island and Bernard Betts from Pebble Island, used to use their speed boats to meet halfway between their islands to exchange films. This kind of cooperation would have sped up the number of films seen by these smaller communities considerably.

So entertainment was usually a case of beer and a bottle of spirit and to sleep it off over two days. No one had heard that one glass of wine is the recommended number of units of alcohol per day and that saving up your units, to drink them over one day, wasn't recommended, as this type of drinking is binge drinking and the worst possible way to consume alcohol. I can only imagine that the people that have come to these conclusions would frown on the act of consuming a year's supply of sensible units, most weekends.

I'd never drunk the larger cans of Tennants, the Scottish lager, until I lived in the Islands. The cans were tall, sky blue and had pictures of women on the back. These women were probably taken from the factory that canned it because I think it was only Sandra that wasn't going to damage your eyesight. One of the lonely souls at a particular cookhouse had put in a lot of drinking effort into collecting every woman on these cans and had them like cups and trophies on one of his cupboards – even in those days he was looked upon as a bit of a loser.

Horse riding

So on the first weekend at Chartres a young lad enquired about my horse-riding skills and did I want to go for a spin. The schoolteacher had a horse named Quane and he had been well tamed and mouthed by a chap called Billy Duncan. He would let you get both feet in the stirrups before moving off and once on board he would turn effortlessly in any direction. The Falklands' horses were trained to steer over the neck with one hand that gave you the other hand free for a whip or to lead a second mount or for other tasks.

The teacher also had horse gear that I felt had been well picked through but was adequate for one to gear up and ride your animal on a short, irregular basis. The gear was very different to the tack that I was accustomed to riding on in England. The saddle I had was described by those that knew as a military saddle but it was a one-piece seat with a slight rise at the back. Unlike UK gear there wasn't a girth attached to the saddle but a chinch made up of a hide spreader which was in contact with the horse's ribs and a length of hide which went through a metal ring on the spreader to a metal ring on the piece of hide on the other end. So it was ring, hide, spreader, hide, loose end. So the cinch went all the way round and you threaded the plain end through the rings a couple of times and pulled it tight and then fashioned a slipknot or jammed it under the piece that you sit on. It is a knack to get it in the right place, or it could mean the hide could rub on your legs. After the saddle and cinch, a sheepskin goes over the top and that is held in place by a small cinch. It is important to get everything just right and get the knots under the sheepskin and away from your legs. Needless to say, put on well, it was very comfortable.

This gear is wider than the English equivalent. All working horses had a bosal (head collar) and *cabresta* (leading rein) as well as the *cabesada* (bridle). When working with horses in a shepherding or travelling capacity one often needed to bring a spare so the *cabaresta* was essential. Many jobs in the camp, like skinning sheep, were done with a foot on the *cabaresta*. The well-trained horses would stand when all the reins were dropped but because of the distances between places one had to be sure. A horse running home could promote great mirth with your workmates, but didn't necessarily raise your spirits if you had to walk many miles back. Most shepherds that I knew had *manares* (hobbles) which were put on two legs to stop the horses you were unsure of, leaving you stranded.

I found gearing up horses a very individual task, which varied from farm to farm, and sometimes between individuals on a single farm, but each person swore that their way of gearing up was the proper way. The biggest difference was whether you put the end of the main cinch back under the *bastos* (saddle) or tied another slipknot to finish off. Another first for me was the use of tie-downs, which was a bit of strong cord tied between the stirrups. I was taught to make a hands-width gap between the horse and the stirrup when applying the tie-down. This handy piece of equipment was very useful when you were riding a spirited animal and when it inconsiderately started to buck. The idea was to turn your feet out tightening the tie-down which would help to hold you fast into the gear. As long as you could keep your feet in the stirrups and the gear stayed on, so would you. It was a good aid but there were no guarantees.

Quane's one downfall was his fear of riding down the road at the front of the Chartres settlement, because in his distant past a pig had rushed out of a yard and frightened him, so it was always wise to come in behind the houses.

Brian rode the manager's horse, an animal named Hurricane who was very spirited. My riding experience wasn't too bad but I had never ridden more than for two-and-a-half hours continuously. Ever.

So off we went out to the *manada* (mares in a troop for breeding) and drove them into a corral. Quane was great turning this way and that at speed as we followed them in.

Once the horses were in the corral Brian felt that he should warn me that we should not speak to the manager about this.

On the way home I rode Hurricane and it was just great to be alive. We must have been in the saddle for eight hours. The next four or five days my legs were so stiff and sore I could hardly walk. I looked like a cross between John Wayne and a child who had crapped itself.

Brian would remember my gait and discomfort with great mirth for over 30 years – bastard.

Games in the cookhouse

There were a number of activities that the blokes in the cookhouse used to get up to in the name of entertainment during the weekends. Like 'going through the broom'. This entailed holding a broom at each end, with your knuckles facing forward, stepping over the handle between your arms and bringing it up over your back and ending up at the beginning without letting go of the handle. At this point your knuckles are pointing behind you. You then take one leg and take it out around the corresponding arm, down through the middle and onto the floor. You then have to be a contortionist to pull the broom up and over your back and end back with the broom in front of you and your knuckles pointing forward again, all without letting your hands off the broom. 'Pulling the broom' was a test of strength, where two people sat facing each other on the floor with their feet touching and a broom in the middle horizontally. Both parties would grab hold of the broom and on the count of three pull. Whoever pulled the other up and over was the winner – the bulk of the contestants featured quite highly in this game.

'Going around the table' was another popular pastime. The idea was to start on the top of the table and then go under and up the other side, coming back to the top without touching the ground.

Another such activity was to stand with your heels against the wall holding two beer cans. You then had to go down and put one can out as far as you can in front of you, supporting your body weight on the one remaining can, and returning to the upright position without touching the floor. It sounds pretty easy and one in which the tallest individual should always win, but that was not the case. Many smaller people could hold their weight on the second can at a greater distance and have the ability to get back to the wall.

You had to be very supple to go through the broom, and fairly agile to go around the table or place the beer can. Most of these activities happened after a few drinks so many skills deteriorated. It helped to keep everyone's minds off girls.

Boredom and booze is a bad combination but most of the behaviour was good-natured. I remember a sheep-drafting demonstration in the Chartres cookhouse with a few pet sheep and their followers. They came in one door and then into the galley or main room. Drafting sheep is when they come up a narrow race that has a gate, usually on each side, where you can take off different sheep. It seemed bizarre that someone that had been working with sheep all week would want to draft them into the bunkhouse in their leisure time.

One chap had a memorable party trick and when really pissed, late at night, he would go over to the cook's henhouse and pinch her rooster, feed it rum and then march around the cookhouse pretending that he was a pirate (I think). On one occasion the rooster was so pie-eyed that he fell off the chap's shoulder and dropped to the floor without even flapping his wings. On such occasions I was always interested to see how the cockerel was the next morning, but there he would be each morning with his hens, showing no visible signs of his night out.

A great favourite with the younger chaps was to try and get their motorbikes up the bunkhouse stairs and I was an interested bystander to many attempts in my three years. In fact, I lie. I did have the odd turn. The rather difficult feature at Chartres was that the stairs had been inconsiderately built to go around a corner, which was challenging to even the best riders.

Two stroke trial bikes, especially Suzuki 250s, were very popular but they did create a serious amount of smoke. Confined in the cookhouse, after some epic attempts to reach the landing, it was impossible to breathe let alone see.

There were some sterling attempts and some memorable failures. You had to wiggle the handle bars to get passed the doorposts and then lift the front and give the bike some power, although not too much so that the bloody thing would come over backwards on you. A few riders got three-quarters of the way around and I did see a bike on the landing but I am sure it wasn't driven there, but I would love to be corrected.

The greatest failure was when someone on a donor bike rolled backwards and pinned the rider's hands on the doorpost. Much derisory, raucous laughter ensued, mixed with cries for help before this poor soul was rescued with no sympathy and plenty of cutting remarks about his ability on a bike, at work, at play and as a human being.

Wheelies in the main room were not unknown. It nearly always resulted in the rider falling off and the bike hitting the wall. On one occasion the bike actually bent the tin on the outside wall. The billiard table and a few posters would be tactically moved to hide the damage.

One night I returned from having supper with Deidre and Marshall, and as I approached the cookhouse I could hear a bike ticking over. When I opened the door into the cookhouse there was a bike running in the main room with nobody about. The whole building was full of two stroke smoke. Not only that but the big table which the gang sat at for meals was on its side and whoever had been riding the bike had been wheel spinning through all the pickles and sauces that had ended up on the floor. The mess was considerable, with broken glass everywhere and the pickle spun onto the walls and ceiling.

Whoever had carried out this act wasn't very quick to brag about their exploits because all the condiments belonged to individuals living in the cookhouse and not many, if any had survived this onslaught.

Usually even the worst excesses eventually come out over time but I didn't hear who the villain of this piece was.

Other bike sports were dares – I bet you wouldn't ride up the road in your underpants – and, you've guessed it, eventually naked. In the Falklands there might be a handful of days when it would be deemed suitable by anyone remotely sane to accept this sort of challenge but fortified with six Tennants and the same number of spirit chasers and there were an equal number of days that were unsuitable.

Of course you still had to stay on the bike from the bunkhouse to the clay road up the four hundred yards and back. With the rider hyped up for the challenge, many a ride started with a huge wheelie and swerving all shapes, but riders didn't seem to fall off.

The rider's report was always sought after and who were we to question the validity of why it always seemed to be the manager's wife that was shocked by a naked drunk, lightly veiled in two stroke smoke, flying by. No one felt able to enquire of such people whether a) the manager's wife enjoyed a little colour in her otherwise humdrum life, or b) if she had been mortifyingly offended as reported, why the manager hadn't arrived and sacked the entire cookhouse complement for displaying such discourteous behaviour? Most of us were probably ungenerous enough to doubt, on sober reflection, the 'gospel' of the moment.

Riding in the cart

Unfortunately, I arrived after the period where the horse did absolutely everything including carting the peat. Most, if not all, of the people involved in carting the peat would have welcomed the tractors and trailers that carted the peat home with much bigger loads and at a far greater pace.

There was still the odd horse that had been trained to the cart and the gear was still to be found collecting dust in sheds around the farms. There were still many people that could put the horse, the gear and the cart together and have it all in working order.

The usual weekend entertainment was; shall we drink ourselves to oblivion? Scare the manager's wife? Plant or tend the garden? Wait quietly for another ten years plus for TV and an episode of *The Bill*? Or something else?

After a few beers: let's get Dobbin in and put him in the cart.

I never realised how uncomfortable and rough one of these cart things was to travel on. No suspension, wooden wheels shod with iron, wooden boards to sit on. I had more of a romantic notion of trotting off into the countryside with a picnic basket in the blazing English sun.

In reality we had a happy, original weekend followed by a thorough check for loose fillings and damaged vertebrae that may play up in later life. Of course the manager's wife wasn't shocked and waved to every passing passenger. She came out to the gate on every run, all 200 times in one weekend.

Boats

I stayed two weeks at each place on my beat. My beat was always changing but it was supposed to be made up of three locations. At first it was Chartres, Keppel Island and Shag Cove, an outside house belonging to Port Howard. But things got a bit out of hand with a shortage of camp teachers. On one circuit I did Chartres, Keppel, Shag Cove, San Carlos and the Verde, an outside house belonging to San Carlos. An incredible ten-week beat but then factor in the days the Beaver couldn't fly and a three-month turn around was not unheard of.

By the time I had been around my beat and back again the horse and cart had had its moment and was never exercised while I was there again. The gang had returned to drinking and wondering what else would come along.

And along it did come. While I was travelling around on my next circuit a couple of the lads invested in some boats. An inflatable and other frail craft powered by asthmatic, powerless Seagull outboards. I think one of the boats had a modestly sized Yamaha of 15 or 25 horsepower.

So after a few drinks the weather seemed ideal for mucking about in boats and everyone was soon zipping, chugging and wheezing about in the sea, encouraged by shouting and yelling from those in the boats and the supporters on the beach.

The Falklands is renowned for its small boat fatalities and there are many tales of individuals coming to grief in small dinghy-type vessels because of drink. People's memories seem to block this out after more drink and they in turn put themselves at risk. It is not a Falklands' phenomenon, it happens all over the world.

One day there was an episode where the gang were tearing about in their boats and one stopped. Unbelievably one of the participants had to put some extra effort into pulling the starter cord to get the outboard going and threw himself over the side of the boat and into the water. I wasn't there but many who were, told me that one of the people, on one of the boats, reached down into the water and caught hold of the chap's hair and pulled him to the surface.

One of the responsible members of the farm community went down and cut the small inflatable into ribbons so that it would never float again.

Everyone went off boats but the fascination with water continued. The next craze, fuelled with the internal heat generated by a couple of rums, was to dive from the jetty for those that could swim (and there weren't that many). I could swim and so I had the chance to be centre of attention. I dived from here and there but usually off the side of the jetty. Trust me when I say that to enjoy water sports in the Islands you have to have consumed a fair amount of rum, whiskey, vodka etc. To fancy diving into the freezing waters you do need a bit of fortifying. Even when totally trollied it still takes your breath away. Probably my best feat in this weekend activity was to dive off the end of the Chartres jetty at the lowest of low moon tides. As I launched out into space I remember thinking the water seemed a long way down. As I went in I opened my eyes and I could see the bottom but there was still a reasonable amount of water for such a feat.

Again near disaster ended this period of tomfoolery. I ran back up the jetty and dived over someone and into the sea. As I opened my eyes I saw an anchor chain and the bottom looming up. I bent my body to try and avoid both but hit the bottom hard with my chest. The chain was a side brace to the jetty that I hadn't thought about. Sober, I would have never dreamed of diving into unknown territory like that. I had survived another adventure.

Tractors

I was off on my rounds when things came to a head. After some casual intake of booze, the lads wondered how to beat the excesses of boating, nude motorbike riding, suicidal swimming and diving. Let's break into the tractor shed.

I'm not entirely sure of the finer details and I am not sure who all the protagonists were, but the tractors were taken out on a little jaunt one night. I can imagine the roaring round and the feeling of daring and risk-taking, but something went wrong. It was poor judgement in many areas. Firstly that you would break into the tractor shed in the first place, secondly that you think that it was a good idea to take a couple of tractors. Thirdly that you think you had the hand-eye coordination to drive around without crashing in to one another, and finally to be able to do it and not get caught. They did crash into one another causing some expensive damage. The door of the garage was also damaged on the way in or out.

Everything was tidied up and the tractors put away but no one was able to hide the damage done to the tractor that had its hydraulic arms hanging down at a funny angle.

If there had been little damage perhaps just to the doors, and it is debatable, the individuals involved would have only suffered a severe reprimand. As it was, there was some parting of the ways and Bill Luxton, the manager, had to let some people go.

Geese

Chartres had loads of tame geese, the ones you see in farmyards in the UK and Europe. After a successful breeding year there must have been forty if there were a dozen. Eating grass, foraging at the end of the sewer pipes on the beach, and honking and hissing for hours on end in a four square mile radius. They were noisy and messy things too, leaving piles of muck wherever they had spent the night.

One night in the middle of winter the geese decided to shelter on my side of the cookhouse. They whistled and they honked all night long. Geese honking continuously can grate on your nerves. One goose would honk and another would answer it, which would build up to them all honking and being unsettled until it gradually calmed down to nothing. There would be a small hush and then it would start again with a whistle or a honk.

The first night I hacked it but lost some important sleep but hey! It happened a few more times when they were sheltering from a very cold wind. I was beginning to feel slightly victimised. There was plenty of other shelter such as buildings, gorse hedges and peat stacks but they chose below my window.

I'm not sure if it was an autumn grump or what but I had had it with these bastards interrupting my eight hours sleep and so I began to plan my revenge. In a premeditated campaign I took the lead out of a few shotgun cartridges and replaced it with a little bit of coarse salt. Nothing happened during those two weeks but as night follows day the subsequent visit had the gaggle of geese camped out outside the back of the cookhouse. The usual cacophony of whistles, hisses and honks ensued. I got dressed, picked up my single-barrelled shotgun and my few doctored cartridges, sneaked downstairs and outside, with the idea that I would scare them down towards the beach.

I peered around the corner of the cookhouse in a lull of honks and I could just make them out in the dark. I had already slipped a cartridge into the gun because opening and closing a shotgun cannot be done quietly.

In the dark, a three-foot flame shot out of the barrel with a loud and impressive bang, followed by a second as quickly as I could get another cartridge into the chamber. Pandemonium. The geese ran this way and that making enough noise to wake the dead and everyone at Chartres. The geese spent the rest of the night honking and whistling in the sea making an awful racket.

A goose's memory must be good for up to two years because in the rest of my time at Chartres the geese didn't shelter behind the cookhouse.

Sitting around the fire

Many things were done for a laugh without any thought of the dangers or consequences. Why people didn't get hurt when they got up to such things is probably against anyone's comprehension.

Not every cookhouse had an open grate. Chartres didn't but in some it was a place where everyone congregated to listen to the local radio or perhaps read Ranfurly library books. Most books, for the ordinary folk in camp came from the Ranfurly library in England. Today many people would be appalled at the treatment metered out to the younger guys by the older members of the cookhouse but many a person that had done the same journey a generation before saw the new regime as soft. Many of today's adults that went through that system reckoned it stood them in good stead for the future.

Many of the old hands had got the best seats around the fire, whether it was closest or the most comfortable they had got it because they had been there the longest. Sometimes, for a number of reasons, an upstart took a chair that belonged to the cookhouse hierarchy. It might be a genuine mistake because the person whose chair it was was thought to be visiting friends somewhere else in the settlement or it could be that a youngster felt ready to challenge for one of the better seats.

One of the methods of reclaiming one's seat was to throw a few rounds of .22 gun ammunition into the fire. God knows, once again, how no one was killed or hurt but people would just run for their rooms or for cover or both as the rounds went off. The aggressor would stroll seemingly unperturbed by rounds going off in the hearth, to reclaim their seat. I am told .303 rounds have been used in this way but I have never witnessed it.

In the cookhouse, amongst all the single men, was one thing, but this type of activity was known to happen under other circumstances. At the Flats Shanty, in the 1970s, the San Carlos shepherd gang were working away from the settlement for a few days. This would mean many family men amongst the contingent. These shanties were never that big and the Flats Shanty was a two-roomed building with a very small porch, a living room with an open grate with a bedroom with bunks. In these days there were so many folk that the sleeping arrangements included someone, the boy, sleeping under the table.

So in this very cramped environment the gang were finding space to sit around the open grate and, according to one of the gang members, there was a problem with the seating arrangements. Into the fire was thrown a handful of .22 bullets, which had everyone scattering in the direction of the porch and the outside door.

A small debate ensued, considering how many bullets were thrown so that the shepherds could calculate when it was safe to return to the warmth of the fire.

On the return, some of the more mature members of the crew were grumbling because ash from the fire had covered the food and had to be scraped from the butter.

There was a pecking order in the main room of the cookhouse. The senior chaps were unmolested although not immune to the challenges of the young chancer. The new members of the cookhouse were referred to as the boy or boys. They were at the bottom of the pecking order.

The Ranfurly library was Book Aid International founded by Lady Hermione Ranfurly in 1954. She was prompted to set up this service after witnessing a shortage of books in the Bahamas where she lived with her husband who was the Governor General. Her first efforts were to encourage friends and acquaintances to donate surplus books, which she would distribute to schools and libraries.

By the early 1960s she was distributing books to many places in the developing world. Over the next 50 years 25 million books were sent all over the world including the Falklands. Ranfurly books would come to the farms in tea chests and folk used to pick through them usually for the cowboy books like Louis Armour and J.T.Edson.

Cookhouse chores

'Doing the peggy' was when it was your turn, your week, to do the cookhouse chores. For instance, if the cookhouse had central heating, it was your responsibility to fill the wheelbarrow or buckets with peat and stoke the boiler. There were also open grates or other stoves in some cookhouses that needed tending to. This job also involved taking the ashes out.

Bunkhouses were big buildings catering for the needs of many men and to get enough hot water for their needs and to have the heating working well the person doing the peggy had to be fairly energetic. These stoking duties in a well-regulated bunkhouse were kept to a high standard and if things slipped, everyone made the slacker aware of their shortcomings. Some bunkhouses couldn't care collectively and so the hot water and central heating could be a bit hit and miss.

The person who was doing the peggy usually had time off farm duties on Fridays to sweep and scrub out, fill peat buckets and have the communal areas shipshape ready to hand over to the next person.

5. KEPPEL

Keppel was the first Island farm that I went to and the second place on my beat. It was a family unit with around 3,000 sheep and it was owned and run by Sam and Hay Miller. They lived there along with their children Andrew and Julie, although Andrew was at the Darwin Boarding School during term time.

Keppel was fantastic and had many points of interest, not least of all the history of the SAMS (the South American Missionary Society) and their attempt to Christianise/civilise the Indians of Terra del Fuego from a base in the Falklands.

I flew to Keppel, landing in a southeast-facing bay with the settlement to the north sitting under the lee of the mountain behind it. The little settlement was made up of a modern house of the long sloping back type, a design to which many camp houses built in the 50's were built to. Then there were many old stone buildings, including the old stone shearing shed which had become the bale shed, which was attached to the more modern shearing shed.

Not only did it have all this history but it also had amazing wildlife. Gentoo penguins to the east, with sand grass and sand dunes, plus two big ponds that always had something of interest in, such as grebes and ducks. I once saw a big heron-type bird, which had obviously blown in from the South American mainland. As if that wasn't enough there were black-browed albatross, rock hopper penguins and king cormorants in abundance on the north coast.

During the summer the Royal Navy ice patrol vessel *the Endurance* was travelling round the West with the Falkland Island Governor. Governor Parker and his wife were flown into Keppel for a visit on the ship's wasp helicopters. I am sure it was pleasant for them to visit different settlements outside Stanley and enjoy the hospitality of people in camp.

Life on Keppel

Keppel Island was a fantastic place for food both from the garden and foraged from the land. On one of my visits, Hay and Julie went out and picked a huge amount of tea berries, little white and pink berries the size of a small fingernail that sit in prickly rough grass and are not that easy to pick. Imagine picking berries from within a nailbrush to understand what it is like to harvest them. For pudding we had a large bowl full of these berries with fresh cow's cream that was too thick to pour. I troughed mine back and had a second helping of both berries and cream.

I did over do it slightly and after a while felt a little bit queasy. I have never really warmed to them since that occasion. The closest I have come to eating and enjoying them is in a pavlova that Toni makes that has a teaberry filling and top.

Keppel was a grand place for reading books because Hay and Sam belonged to a book club and the titles were about people sailing down south. I remember reading a book called *Ice Bird* by a chap called Tristan Jones. This man sailed to the Antarctic in a boat more suited to a shallow bath. It was tiny. I would be just as keen to go to sea on an airbed as a boat of that size.

I gave up smoking during 1978 and visiting Keppel used to put my resolve to the test because Sam and Hay always smoked at the times that I enjoyed a cigarette most. On the other hand, it was a good place to stop because there wasn't a store to go and buy more.

A number of years later Sam and Hay decided to sell Keppel. The opportunities that people have today just weren't there back then. Today the garden at Keppel could probably make a living on its own with carrots at £3 a kilo and cabbages at £5+ each, in the stores of Stanley. Every discerning tourist would have to visit not only the wildlife but also to witness all that unique history.

It is incredibly sad that today very few people are able to see this wonderful island because an absentee landlord owns it. If Keppel was in local hands it would be without doubt one of the jewels in our tourist industry's crown.

6. EGGING

People had harvested wild bird eggs since the beginning, even the eggs of the black-browed albatross. People had been doing it for years and in the 1970s there didn't seem to be a problem. In the 1990s however there was great concern about the birds and their mortality rates in our fisheries, especially in connection with the long-lining operation. There was concern expressed by conservationists about the penguins as well. In the 1990s legislation went through controlling the collecting of wild birds' eggs. It became illegal to take albatross eggs. It may make the conservationist shudder but the fact is that albatross eggs were a good food source. The contents of one of these eggs would fill a normal frying pan and be a hearty meal.

There is an art to robbing these birds. You gently walk up to them sitting on their pots of mud and put the bucket between their powerful beaks and any part of you. You then reach under them and take the egg and pop it into the bucket. They don't usually fly off. It is like taking an egg away from a domestic hen.

I feel slightly guilty to write that the albatross egg was one of my favourite eggs out of all the wild eggs I have tried. The ones I have eaten haven't been strong just a pleasant fish kind of taste. You would have to have a good appetite to want two.

Many different eggs were taken in the Falklands, but today all the eggs, which you are allowed to take, are only removed under licence. There is one exception and that is the upland goose.

Man has taken penguin eggs, I should imagine, ever since they arrived in the Islands, as a good, storable source of protein. Penguin eggs will last for a long time especially if you keep turning them. Many farms used to send a couple of men up to a rookery to collect enough eggs for a settlement. They would rob hundreds each year to satisfy that demand. The more discerning farms would rob different parts of the same rookery each year. Some with sufficient choice might even rob different rookeries.

I haven't got a huge appetite for penguin eggs but I do like a few each year. I like mine boiled for ten minutes which is usually enough to leave a little moisture in the yolk. There is an art to getting the shell off which many people do by cracking the shell then holding the egg in a tea towel and peeling it off. I then like them with salt, pepper and vinegar. Others prefer them fried and crispy. The whites of the gentoo egg make good meringues.

A gentoo egg is probably most peoples' favourite and many years ago sailing cutters used to bring thousands into Stanley. People would go down to the jetties and pay so much a hundred and carry them home in buckets. There are a few pictures in different books about the Falklands showing this practice but unfortunately I didn't witness this.

I have seen people fill a tea chest with eggs and pop them into the back of their Land Rover.

The 'white' of a gentoo penguin egg stays opaque and when it is boiled and out of its shell you can see the orangey, red yolk within. Some people see them as a red eye sitting on your plate. The well-boiled gentoo egg has a modest bouncy feel to it and is quite unlike a conventional hen egg in consistency.

Rockhopper eggs are smaller than the gentoo and you probably need two or three to have a decent meal. The consistency of these eggs is very different from the gentoo because it doesn't matter how long you boil them for, the contents that aren't the yolk do not solidify. The taste is okay but it is a bit disconcerting eating what looks like snot. These guys didn't give up their bounty easily and although they are the smallest of all the Falklands' penguins they defiantly defend with sharp beaks and slapping flippers. You need special equipment, in the shape of tall rubber boots, to guarantee that you come away unscathed. It is completely unconnected to the few rocky eggs that people took in the past but sadly this 'cheeky chappie' of penguins has been drastically reduced in some areas of the Falklands although there are still some big colonies scattered around.

Finally, in the egg stakes we come to the magellanic penguin, locally called 'the jackass' because of its continuous braying noise. These penguins live in a burrow that they dig along the shore, going inland for many hundreds of yards in some places. Some of these burrows are many feet deep going back into the ground at a very gentle angle. To rob a jackass is quite a performance compared to the other penguins. Only a born-again idiot would put a bare hand down into a jackass hole to collect their eggs, as the sharp and powerful beak is more than capable of inflicting a serious wound.

Most people used to put a loop of metal onto a stick of two feet or more. The band would have to be at least an inch and a half deep and big enough to encircle the egg. The idea then was to reach down into the burrow put the loop under the penguin and over the eggs, then pull the bounty to the top. Some penguins have an awkward streak and as they see their eggs disappear they peck a hole in them. The mark 2 stick, designed by the thriftier collector, has a tin at the end. Same operation, but once the tin is over the egg there is little that can go wrong and one's efforts are always rewarded with eggs in pristine condition.

In today's world of conservation people question this practice of collecting gentoo eggs, which still goes on in a much-reduced fashion under licence. But I feel that the small amount of effort of a few people collecting them has never affected penguin populations. It is the bigger things that have this potential, like global warming, changing sea current patterns and even large fishing operations. These in my opinion have the might to create radical change, not a few hundred or even a few thousand eggs being lifted each year.

The older members of the community confirm that penguins will lay again. In fact, they will lay a number of times and in many cases the first eggs aren't always fertile. They do go on to say that the subsequent eggs, if robbed repeatedly, do get smaller. It's clear that robbing to this extent would not help those birds because a smaller egg must mean a smaller and less viable chick and egg laying must coincide with a food source and a chick that is too late might miss that peak.

There is a bird that hasn't been afforded any protection and is seen as a pest by many – especially the farmers – and that is the upland goose. In the spring, the adults pair up and there is usually a bit of gander testosterone floating around with the mature males swaggering around with their wings slightly down, stretching out their necks and whistling insults at one another. The strongest males chase off all comers, but when there is a difference of opinion that can't be politically resolved with some extravagant posturing, physical violence is resorted to. The protagonists wade in and really whack each other with their wings. They are hefty blows that you can hear clearly from some distance away. Eventually the stronger male will prevail. Unbelievably these birds will and do kill each other on occasions.

Throughout the breeding period pairs are very territorial and when geese are squeezed into each others' territory, for whatever reason, the strongest gander often kills the goslings of the weaker parents. I have often seen the males fight until one is exhausted and then the victor murders the goslings of the vanquished gander.

So once the males have proved their dominance over partner and territory, the goose scratches out a nest and lays usually seven eggs. It is once the eggs are laid that the goose will add some down and feathers and settle down for the incubation period. On the outer-lying Islands, geese usually lay a little earlier and many are laying in September but there are probably one or two that start before that.

Goose egging used to be a national sport and even today there are many people that enjoy this pastime. The idea is to find the goose once she has a nest full of eggs, but before the goose has started to sit on them for any period of time. Once the goose is sitting on the nest to lay and eventually to sit to incubate, the gander stands guard and his job is to confront danger. With humans and other predators his job is to lead them away from his mate and their nest. We call this 'laying off'. Some ganders are really good at laying off and don't give you a clue as to where the nest is.

It is a funny situation, because him standing sentinel tells you that a goose is sitting nearby. Yet I suppose a predator would see him and this takes the focus away from looking for anything else. There are many tactics employed by people to find eggs. One is weight of numbers where you turn up with plenty of people or with your dogs and ignore the gander and just cover a piece of ground. Some people have trained dogs to find them by their sense of smell.

The purists, and they seem few and far between, find the goose by interpreting what the gander is doing. For instance, some people think he will always stand down wind of the nest. I have found that there are few hard and fast rules. I liked to circle the gander first to see what he would do. If he just walked aimlessly away it was very hard to interpret but if on that circle he started to pretend to eat grass or become agitated, it usually meant you were in a straight line between him and the goose. It could be behind you or behind him or by sheer luck you could be close to her. Then you would walk that straight line. Even then a find was far from guaranteed because the goose is exceptionally hard to see and she will remain motionless even when you are feet away. If a goose sticks to her nest until you are just about on her you can be fairly certain that the eggs have started to grow goslings.

Most people enjoy egging where there are lots of geese which makes their territories small and their nesting possibilities few. If you get this congestion on coastal greens you have the best opportunity of all because there are no hiding places. A small tuft of grass, a sheep track or a small undulation does not afford the goose an adequate hiding place and nesting site.

Once you have found your goose and its nest and eggs you then have to determine whether they are good or not. Meaning whether they have started to become a gosling and be unpalatable to most people's taste. Looking at the nest is a good pointer because if there is a lot of down and goose feathers it usually means she is sitting and the eggs won't be edible.

If it is a nice sunny day you cup your hands together with the egg held between your thumbs and forefingers and hold it up to the sun. Holding closely to an eye you try to see through the egg as you slowly turn it. If you can see the light through the egg it is good but if you can see a shadow of any size then it has turned. This is a fairly foolproof method if it is bright. You can use the headlights of a vehicle but I have found this a little more hit and miss.

The goose is exploited or persecuted during every phase of its life. During the months of September through to November people look for goose eggs. Although most geese usually lay at the end of September and the beginning of October, if they are robbed they will lay again later.

When there were many isolated shepherds' houses, a lot of effort was put into egging during the spring as the shepherd went about his shepherding duties. The family would also enjoy going out and looking for eggs on a pleasant spring day. Some people have suggested, scurrilously I'm sure, that many shepherds were far more interested in goose and duck eggs than they ever were in how much camp wool they could collect, ewes they could help, or lambs they had seen.

It is not that many years ago that the bigger farms saw the goose as a competitor to their stock and paid a bounty for goose beaks. Wages weren't high and so for some this was a way of getting a bit of money. Some individuals would throw themselves into this pastime with great enthusiasm threading many goose beaks onto pieces of string. Young lads would get a box of 500 .22 bullets and spend the weekend murdering geese. It encouraged good shooting to ensure maximum profit from this endeavour.

People took it to extremes and would round up shedders (geese that are moulting and cannot fly) with nets and then wring their necks. The real entrepreneur or fanatic would flick the beaks out of a well-developed egg to earn their reward. I have never witnessed this last act and it might have been a one-off that was designed to get everyone talking, i.e. people say that some people would skin a mouse if they thought it would make them money and so someone could have said 'They would flick the beaks out of an egg to make a few pennies.' It does seem extreme and rather hard work for the return.

There used to be an egging week holiday that has sadly disappeared. I thought it was great and so individual to the Falklands. We still have peat cutting Monday but more people continue to egg than cut peat.

So back to the goose calendar of exploitation and with September and October behind you the goslings have started to appear, from the ones that you couldn't find followed a few weeks later by the ones that you did who are now playing catch up.

Bad timing in the case of the goose but convenient for all those that like a feed of gosling, the young are feathered up and big enough for the pot around Christmas and the new year. The art is to catch them just before they can fly or fly well. It sounds barbaric but the goslings run for it when you chase them and when they are far enough away from you they lay down and unless you have seen where it is very difficult to find them. So there can be seven goslings scattering in every direction with you running after them. The clever ones stay by the coast and take to the sea and get away. The ones out in camp usually have a sanctuary of water that they run to. It depends how determined you want to be but if it's a big pond most people say sod it. If it is a small water course you can get in to catch them. Goslings at any age can dive and the bigger ones for some distance. So it is a case of trying to guess where they are going to come up. Some techniques utilise a rope that you use like a deadly skipping rope from either side of a bank.

In the time of outside houses and numerous children on the rampage many goslings were bought back for the pot in this way. This kind of heavy attrition didn't seem to affect the geese populations in any way.

I prefer the older bird, within reason. I think it has more taste but many like the tender meat of the gosling as a roast. Gosling legs in breadcrumbs are also considered to make a worthy meal.

From the late 1900s to the present day many farmers have invested a lot of time, money and effort into growing grass in reseeds and this has brought people and geese into even keener conflict. A reseed is made by rotovating the pasture that is already there. Once this has dried the farmer burns all the trash from the area leaving the soil exposed. He then plants some finer grasses usually with some fertiliser. It is true to say that once the grass starts to grow in these areas the geese, from surrounding countryside, converge on the new grass to gorge themselves. It is annoying enough to see them eating your precious grass but totally beyond it when they pluck the seedling out of the loose soil causing terminal damage.

There are other birds whose eggs are worth taking. The logger duck (flightless steamer duck) lays an egg of equal size to the goose and it doesn't taste too strong. You can still collect these eggs under licence but not many people collect and eat them. They are harder to find than a goose and the duck sits very tightly even when you are feet away. The drakes are in the general area but in a creek it is hard to judge which side the duck is sitting and he doesn't give a lot of pointers. Dogs can be trained to find them and a good dog can find hundreds during a season. There is a logger duck every few hundred yards along the beaches in the Falklands and so there would have to be thousands of good dogs to endanger them and also you would need an army of people to eat that many eggs.

There are some strong eggs that are an acquired taste for a small minority. Shag eggs are in that category. The kelp goose eggs are in the category of hardly anyone, if anyone, can stomach them. They taste of strong, fishy kelp. The goose is a dark colour with flecks of white and she has a brown skullcap. The gander is snow white and stands out for miles. The nest is easy to find because the gander often sits alongside or only spitting distance at most. It's no wonder really because they can be quite assured no one will bother to take any eggs.

We were giving a neighbour a lift to town a number of years ago and he was bemoaning the fact that you couldn't do this and you couldn't eat or rob that. We somehow got on to black-necked swans and how they must be the biggest flying bird in bulk in the Falklands. No one had heard of anyone killing a swan to eat although we had heard of people eating a swan that flew into power lines at North Arm. So we were mulling over this fact when a voice from the back of the Land Rover said: 'I know you're not meant to kill a swan but the eggs are good chay.' (Chay is the local name for mate. The South American Indians of Patagonia used the word for friend.)

Shepherds duties at an outside house

My first beat had a little bit of everything. A settlement, an island and an outside shepherd's house. All the large farms had houses out in the sheep grounds where a shepherd and his family would live. The shepherd would be employed to look after the sheep that needed that extra care like hogs – sheep in their first year – and ewes especially during lambing time. The shepherd would go around the camp skinning dead sheep or plucking them and bringing the wool back to the house and eventually this would go to the settlement. They would also rescue orphaned lambs and at many an outside house in spring a token lamb or even two would appear, although in my travels I can't remember more than a couple at any one house. Because most people milked cows there was something cheap to feed them on. Today with colostrum and Lamblac at extortionate prices it is hard to justify raising a lamb unless it is something pretty special. (Colostrum is the first milk that a mammal produces which is full of antibodies and goodness and you can buy this formula for orphan lambs. Lamlac is the powdered milk formula for lambs). During the summer months the shepherd also had to pull his weight either shearing or performing other tasks in the shearing shed.

I think living at an outside house during the sheep shearing period could be hard because you could do a week's work, which ended on midday Saturday, and then ride home and kill mutton and dog's meat and all the other chores before having to ride back to the settlement to turn to in the shed at 6am Monday morning. If you were close to the settlement it might not be too bad but some of these shepherd's houses were hours away on horseback.

7. SHAG COVE

Getting around

My first outside house was Shag Cove at Port Howard. Ron and Wendy Buckland lived here with their two girls Patsy and Linda, who I was sent to teach, and a son called Colin and later a baby son called Peter.

On my first round I flew from Keppel to Port Howard. Here they had a long platform thing with iron wheels at the end. It was a big settlement and a few people used to come down to the plane and pick up their mail and to view the new schoolie for Shag Cove.

I'm not sure how it happened but Tony and Liz Burnett somehow got saddled with me during the time it took me to move, especially when I was waiting for the Beaver to take me to my next place. They were incredibly kind to me for several years, putting me up and feeding me and letting me treat their house like home. They had two children, Emma and Jonathon, who didn't seem to see my presence as anything unusual.

My first journey to Shag Cove was late in the afternoon. Ron was taking the potatoes that he grew in the settlement, back home in a trailer pulled by a tractor. I was in with the spuds.

Everything was so new that it didn't take long before we were at Shag Cove. Ron seemed to be pleased that I was on the trip because I was able to jump out of the trailer and open and shut the gates. On his own he would have had a double task of opening getting back in to drive through before getting out again to shut them.

Shag Cove was a modern bungalow with central heating powered by a peat-fired boiler that sat in the porch. Most of these outside houses had small Lister diesel generator sets to provide lighting and power the washing machine. A lot were only 1.5 kilowatt but this one was 3.5 and so could manage the lights and the kettle but only just.

Shag Cove was a picturesque place where the sea comes in through a gap in the coast ridge and forms a small and shallow inlet below the house.

Two weeks seemed to fly by and it was time to return to Port Howard to catch the Beaver. Ron materialised from somewhere to show me the horse track which we rode together back to Port Howard. In those early days in the Falklands my brain was still in UK mode and attuned to finding my way by prominent buildings or pubs or old oak trees etc. I should have looked back, I am told, which helps you get your bearings. On arriving in Port Howard I had little idea where I had been.

To help prompt my memory on my return from the rest of my beat there was a horse and its gear but no sign of Ron.

I think it is fair to say that a shepherd never left his best horses or his most comfortable gear for the travelling schoolteacher. In fact, I swear that many bits of virgin or neglected gear was softened on my arse during my time riding to various outside houses.

My first solo ride back to Shag Cove, after my one ride in in the opposite direction months earlier, was interesting. Everyone told me the horse knew the track and that it would take me about two hours. Try as I might to recollect the track I hadn't got the foggiest. But I knew that if I stayed on the west side of the coast ridge I couldn't miss it.

Once I was more experienced I realised that all these horses could trot all day without too much effort. Unfortunately, I had been indoctrinated at Joan's Riding School in rural Kent where to trot for more than 100 yards at a time is likely to break a horse's wind and ruin him forever and you to be labelled a horse killer from that day. So on this first trip I walked and trotted on and off, mile after mile and hour after hour. It began to get dark and I did begin to think there were a few flaws in this itinerate teaching lark. I was just about to stop and search through my *maletas* (big canvas saddle bags) for a pen and paper to write a last note to my family in England when I saw the light of the house. Although this is a slight exaggeration about pen and paper, it made me try a lot harder to remember tracks and to master the skill of navigation in the Falklands.

Ron didn't ever ride with me again to 'fine tune' my track skills. I think I just got a little better on my own but not before a few meanderings away from the recognised track. Once ploughing through a muddy creek fearing that I was going to get bogged I was so relieved to get back on the ground, but the camp also had its obstacles especially if you strayed from the track. These obstacles were usually boggy ground or ditches but there were other things as well.

I remember a tall colt called Sadat. Either he hadn't been taught to stand, was naturally impatient or he just liked to see me rise to a challenge. There were a number of gates on the way to Shag Cove where I had to get off, open the gate, lead his nibs through, shut the gate and then get back on. The minute the gate was shut he was ready for off. I would keep the nearside reign fairly tight, put a foot in the stirrup and then the minute that other leg was starting its journey up and over the back of the horse and down for your foot to find the other stirrup, he was off like a bullet bringing you to the verge of a whiplash injury in his eagerness to get home.

A horse heading home can always find something extra but not with the same enthusiasm Sadat showed. This horse excelled in the complete opposite when it was time to make the journey back to Port Howard. He would need much coaxing to get him to leave the corral and then on the journey he would continuously pull one way or the other. If he were given his head he would do a complete circle and head for home. Every gate was a battle to get him through, obstinately standing in the gateway, only moving by pushing and shoving. On reflection it doesn't surprise me that Ron left him for me. I wouldn't want to ride the retched thing all day either.

On the positive side, this horse improved my mounting technique. Most shepherds mount in one fluid motion, which I tried to emulate and was such an asset in riding a number of horses which had been generously called 'tame'. If I see riders get onto a horse in this one movement action I know that they are good riders.

I must have improved Sadat to such an extent that eventually there was another renegade. I went to put the gear on the horse that had been left for me but it wouldn't let me and would try and cow kick or bite and be genuinely awkward. He was too many guns for me but fortunately there was a young girl called Lisa of around thirteen years who happened to see my dilemma (and probably thought how pathetic I was). Most young people in the Falklands were more than proficient in getting their own way with horses.

Lisa didn't need any assertive training classes. She went up to this stroppy horse, lashed its head to the stall with the leading reign and put its gear on. She then undid the leading reign and the reigns and handed them to me. Another important lesson learnt. A contrary brute, that was allergic to horse gear and anyone being near or on him. Actually that is slightly unfair because I can't remember it bucking with me and trying to get me off.

I did get fired off a horse at Sea Lion Island, of all places, because I didn't have to ride there and it was just a trip for pleasure. So here was Sovereign, the children's tame horse, and as I swung my leg up my foot never reached the stirrup, even though I had perfected that fluid motion by then. As I was going up this rotund, under-exercised animal he cut into a series of bucks and I went over his head. If I had been ready, I would have been okay because once on you would have had to roll twice to reach the side. This gave everyone a good laugh and returning to a common theme it was only my pride that was hurt after such a demonstration of my horse-riding abilities.

Horse taming on the whole was pretty basic. You caught the horse by lassoing it and then got him down, and put a leather bit into his mouth. A number of you would pull until he kicked and then you let it up and the colt tamer would jump on. Then it was a battle between the horse and the tamer. There were people even back then that were doing things in a more humane way but I would say they were in a minority.

A lot of the horses were tamed on contract and so the word 'tamed' was used loosely with many of the horses. I think it was down to the animal's temperament to whether it turned out to be good and also to the individuals that worked them in their troops. If the shepherd was interested in horses, they would make an effort to ride all their horses and so the younger ones would get regular rides and develop. There were shepherds that only rode their best horses all the time and that could also be down to a number of reasons like they had been fired off too many times by some half-tamed horse or horses and had lost their nerve. It could be down to laziness as well because the tamer animals were much easier to catch in the morning and took less time to gear up because they were not fritting around. Sometimes the head shepherd would encourage their juniors to rest individual horses.

Make no mistake there were some very fine and noble animals throughout the Falklands but there was some total rubbish as well.

Fire!

Teaching at an outside house could be tricky because you would ride to the settlement a day before your flight but due to many things, mainly weather, the plane might not fly. For this reason, at Port Howard I would spend many days with the Burnett's waiting for the plane.

They never seemed to mind but there must have been times when they dreaded me coming and invading their home, eating their food, drinking their coffee. I took further advantage and also recorded some of their LPs onto tapes, like Chris Kristofferson, Bachman-Turner Overdrive and Cat Stephens, to complement the fare of the local radio through my one luxury I had, which was a large radio tape recorder with a speaker at each end.

One of the things that happened to me at Shag Cove was when I was nearing the end of my visits there. The bungalow was very modern for an outside house and the only one that had central heating. The peat-burning fire was in the porch as you came into the house. You couldn't heat a kettle on it because its sole purpose was to heat the house by way of heating water that ran to all the radiators in the house. On the inside wall of the porch were the pegs where you would hang your coats before you went into the house. There were coats as well as boiler suits and some of them Ron had been wearing when he was working on his Land Rover and so had a bit of oil and diesel on them here and there.

Colin was four at most when he decided that he was fed up with the girls in school all day and he needed some excitement. So he rolled up sheets of paper and shoved them into the top door of the peat stove. The flames crept out of the stove and up the rolls of paper, which bent over and set fire to the boiler suits and coats.

Wendy was understandably upset and started screaming, which bought me on the scene. Wendy and the children left me to it. The coats were beginning to get going and smoke was billowing into the house as I found some buckets and had the taps going flat out into the bath as I ran backwards and forwards into the porch and sloshed water onto the fire. I had felt it was pretty touch and go but it hadn't had time to really get going and I managed to quell the flames. Wendy, Patsy, Lynda and Colin came back into the house. Wendy pulled the kettle over and we sat down to a calming cup of tea only for it to dawn on us that during this few minutes of panic, Peter, the baby had been left inside the house in his pram.

I was a little surprised on returning to Port Howard how little interest these events had on people I spoke to who assured me that this house was made of fire-retardant material and wouldn't have burned down.

I am not sure if this reassured me that I was sleeping in a safe house on subsequent visits or pissed me off to find that I wasn't a super hero after all.

8. SAN CARLOS

In both the other outside houses that I visited from Chartres and San Carlos I also taught in the settlements and so any significant flying delay I would return to my room in the cookhouse or flat respectively and teach the odd days until the plane arrived. At Port Howard, Liz Burnett was the teacher and so there was nothing for me to do.

It wasn't long before my regulation three-place beat grew. There had been problems recruiting other peripatetic teachers so two extra places were stuck on to the existing teacher's beats. I gained San Carlos and one of its outside houses, The Verde.

San Carlos Water is now world famous because of the images of the Falklands war where many of the British ships were crammed in to execute a landing and the Argentines bombed them constantly for a number of days. San Carlos, a medium-sized farm of around 27,000 sheep, was situated near the southeast corner of the waters.

Under normal conditions I would fly to San Carlos and land in the sea below the settlement and then taxi to the jetty. The people working the plane, and there were usually quite a few, would fend the wings and tail off the jetty. If the wind were blowing onto the jetty with any kind of strength the Beaver would taxi to the beach.

For a medium-sized farm San Carlos was very forward thinking when it came to education. They had set up a flat and accommodation at one end of the farm's community hall. For me it was total luxury, with my own peat stove, peat buckets and ash drum. In this scenario I ate in the cookhouse with all the single men and the men from the outside houses if they were in shearing.

It was a shame really that with such good facilities San Carlos only had two children in the settlement compared, let's say, to Chartres where eight or nine children were shoe-horned into a small part of a run-down Nissan hut where the floor had broken through in the store cupboard.

It could be a bit intimidating as a complete and utter stranger, walking into the cookhouse and a room with a load of people you had never met. Certainly at San Carlos I had no need to worry because a chap named Ron struck up a conversation and broke the ice almost straight away and although I did not know it at the time Ron was to become a good friend. It never ceased to amaze me how well informed people were in the Falklands about world affairs, but Ron seemed to be especially knowledgeable. He talked of many towns and cities in the UK and he even knew Gravesend, my hometown, and the two cinema houses, which were there in the distant past.

Ron's knowledge came from a number of sources and like many young lads he had joined the local vessel *The Darwin* that used to ply her way from the Falklands to Montevideo in Uruguay. This boat would travel around the camp picking up wool (the main export in those days) and delivering stores to every farm. He then joined the

British Antarctic Survey (or Falkland Island Dependent Survey – FIDS) and travelled to the UK where the crew were laid off for several months before signing back on for the next season. In this downtime Ron lived in Southampton and visited other places. The ships of the FIDS also visited different ports in different countries when going about their business.

This was also a time when there were large gangs out on the farms and a large shepherd gang that would leave these different farms on mass with many horses and even more dogs. The shepherds would lead a second horse if they went to a far-flung area of the farm to round up sheep. These gathers meant the gang could spend days working from a remote shanty. For me it was a magnificent sight and would tickle my imagination once more with comparisons to the Wild West and to the James and Younger gang leaving the Hole In The Wall to rob another train.

The San Carlos cookhouse

I was privileged to see these times where not only were there large gangs in the settlements but also many people in the outside houses scattered around the camp. At San Carlos every outside house had a couple living in them. Sue and Mike Morrison lived at The Verde with their two daughters Carol and Ann, Johnnie and Cinti Morrison lived at the Head of the Bay, Johnny Wilson and his wife lived at the Wreck, and Ron and Iris Dickson lived at Port Sussex with their two sons Steven and Keith.

In the settlement Charlie Alazia was foreman, with his wife Freda and their son Keith who was one of my pupils. Henry Alazia was shepherd boss and he lived at the galley, which was attached to the bunkhouse, with Hazel who had the cook's job. Anita was their daughter and she was also a pupil at the school. Buster and Sheila Summers and Tom and Alva Keen lived in the double house. Gordon and Gloria Anderson were just moving out of the green-roofed house. Ray and Mary Berntsen lived at the cottage next to the big house, which was occupied by Adrian and Nora Monk. The cookhouse had Sid Berntsen downstairs and upstairs there was Keith Bonner, Ted Jones and Brian Jaffrey.

The San Carlos cookhouse had its characters but none probably eclipsed that of Keith Bonner. One popular weekend activity was to get shotgun cartridges and empty out the shot and then to replace them with small tightly rolled up pieces of paper. The idea here is that, so armed, one can lie back in your bed and shoot blue buzzers (blue bottles) a big fly that is everywhere in the summer. Aniseed balls could also be used but they were lethal compared to bits of paper. There are many important rules to this kind of recreation and one was to make doubly sure that not one piece of shot remained in the cartridge and not to get the doctored and the lead-loaded cartridges confused. Not a problem unless you have stunned your thinking skills with alcohol.

So, a few unfortunate flies got blatted and then 'whoops chay' the wrong cartridge is selected and a hole is blown out through your neighbour's bedroom wall and the side of the cookhouse. Today in the new century, the police with their yellow and black tape would have cordoned off the cookhouse, having arrived armed with pump action shotguns, a taser and riot gear. Back then, Adrian Monk, the farm manager at the time, walked down to the cookhouse and confiscated Keith's guns and kept them in his possession for a few months. Job done.

The John Shaw Press

One might get the idea that it was all hard drinking but with it came some very hard workers and a strong work ethic. During the week there was some unbelievably hard work going on. In the summer months the gang would turn to at 6am and shear for over eight hours with breaks for breakfast and lunch and smaller breaks mid-morning and mid-afternoon for a cup of something and a biscuit. This would all stop at five. Then some of the younger chaps, like Keith, would work on contract, baling up wool, until 9pm at night.

It is very hard to think of the old John Shaw Press once you have seen a modern equivalent. The whole thing started off at the bottom of an eight-foot trench in the floor of the shearing shed. In it sat a twelve-foot tall rectangular box with sides about three by four foot.

One chap would climb into the box and drop down to the bottom and then one, or there might be two, would bring wool over to the press and throw it in. The man in the press would stack the fleeces as tightly as he could, pushing as many as he could into each layer of fleeces. The idea of this was that stacked like this you should get a heavier bale than just jumping it down. The modern press does all the hard work with one operator feeding the wool into the front and a ram pushes it down until the ram can't push it down any longer and at that point the bale is ready to pin up and release ready for your next bale.

Back to the John Shaw. Once the box is full the man gets off the box and a sheet of bagging is placed over the top and the box is pushed along the rails and over the ram. Four large rods come from the bottom to the top of the trench and attached to the corners of a big heavy metal head. The ram fits neatly into the box at the bottom, and pushes everything up against the head, squashing that box of wool up to a three by four foot bale of wool. The box is then sprung open and pushed back ready for another bale to begin. With the box out of the way the operators connect five wire bands that have curved ends that lock into a figure of eight and this holds the bagging in place as well. The pressure is then taken off and the bale is rolled out onto the floor and off to the scales to be weighed. The ram in the meantime returns to the bottom.

It was hard work, particularly the box work. Compared to the modern press it was close to slave labour. But these guys did the work on contract to make a little bit extra. Come six the next morning these young men would be ready to bend over a sheep all day, hardly an easy job itself.

Off to The Verde

My time at San Carlos soon passed and so it was off to The Verde for two weeks. Unlike Chartres the teacher didn't have a horse or his own gear. Just like Port Howard the horse came from the shepherd's troop and also the gear.

Luckily for me my newfound friends were able to gear up for me and point me in the right direction. Little did I know – and I had to be told – that the rotten sods had put the gear on back to front. It wasn't that far but there were a few gates, which I managed getting on and off my steed. I solemnly plodded along wondering, as you do visiting a new place, what The Verde had in store for me, unaware of the lads back at San Carlos rolling around on the ground and slapping their thighs absolutely delighted at being entertained by such a complete ignoramus.

The Verde was an easy place to teach with the two young girls Ann and Carol. Carol was too young to come to school full time but she would join us to splash some paint round in the afternoon. Mike was never there, chasing or shearing sheep no doubt but Sue was good to chat to and like many women in outside houses ran the house with all that entails with very little effort.

Sadly, I only did San Carlos a few times but made some good friends and we still laugh at some of the pranks that they played on me. The horse gear was probably up there with the night after a bit of socialising, some rotter put some gorse in my bed. The settlement engine used to go off at night, which didn't interfere with a few beers but it was rather constraining when searching for bits of gorse in one's bed. Fortunately for the quality of education outside Stanley new recruits swelled the ranks and took the pressure off the rather beleaguered team that were at times just representing the Education Department with such long beats. The success or failure of the Camp Education system back then depended on whether the children did their homework. The odd child whose parents had the commitment, education and time, carried on doing the homework set by the teachers to be done by the pupil while they were away. Most didn't.

A successor at San Carlos

As San Carlos came off, Green Hill, an outside house at Chartres came on.

My successor at San Carlos was a big chap from Wolverhampton called Andy Clark who had a distinct Brummie accent. He was as strong as an ox and seemed to fit in well as a travelling teacher and be popular with most people.

Each year the Royal Marines used to come out from their barracks in Stanley to the sticks and give training to the young folk of the settlements. It was a chance for civilians to fire military rifles and on some occasions a machine gun.

Of course at night there was the obligatory drinking session. Marines and local lads could be very competitive. 'We are better than you.' 'Prove it!' Not surprisingly the marines were handy with their fists but the last to find a goose nest.

So add to all that testosterone, posturing and add an outside entity, a travelling teacher, who is not a local or one of the marines and you have an interesting mix.

So here were the marines at San Carlos in the drink stage of their visit and arm wrestling was on the agenda along with other power games. The marines were really miffed to find that Andy was as good if not better at these disciplines and they didn't warm to his company. At all. Andy unwisely dished out some cheek for good measure.

The evening ended with threats to Andy's wellbeing. If anyone had been sober they would have realised that these threats were pretty hollow as most of the drunken rabble were going to struggle getting home let alone throwing a punch at this stage of the evening.

The San Carlos residents dispersed back to the cookhouse and home and the marines staggered back to their ship, *The Forrest*, that was their transportation around camp. With the threats ringing in his ears Andy weaved his way back to the teachers' flat.

He hadn't been home long when he heard something. After the unpleasantness of the latter part of the evening, Andy, feared the worst (although in hindsight it was probably someone's milk cow scratching on the school) and hid in the school part of the building and waited.

No one knows or cared to admit what happened next, but Andy was sure there was some intruder inside the building and ended up falling through the rather large school window taking the frame and everything with him.

All farms were self-contained and ran with a large amount of normal glass, vehicle spares, stores, etc. Most other places in the world it would be a case of getting the glaziers in and paying to have it fixed. Here large panes of glass could be a problem. The supply line was extremely extended with a charter vessel coming from the UK every three or four months with provisions, and then the local vessel, *The Monsunen* usually, would load up with fuel, stores and come around to all farms every few months. The vessel couldn't manage the whole Islands on each trip and so these voyages would be split up into convenient areas. The ports in Salvador Waters would be one and the far west another. Port Howard was scheduled with San Carlos and Port San Carlos. Luckily for Andy and his class, the windows were going to be replaced and so the farm had everything on hand and the school wasn't open to the elements for long.

Keeping informed and in touch

The announcements for the Falklands community were broadcast every evening at the start of the evening's entertainment programme on the Falklands Radio Station. The radio would come to life with a signature tune and then straight into the announcements. The weather forecast was first followed by the flights. The announcer would say the name of the plane, let's say *Alpha Romeo*, followed by a list of destinations and the list of passengers. There was no mention of who got on and off at which stops as they do today.

Everyone listened to the announcements and any noisy inattentive individual would be hushed into silence if they hadn't heard the announcements come on. There would generally be silence as the announcer worked through the ten minutes of information, jobs, items for sale and who was selling them and then that person's name and telephone number etc. Occasionally people would be selling fish like mullet or smelt at the Working Man's Club corner. I always felt sorry for the poor sod that came on, on the night after a sweep draw and read out the results with number of ticket, name of winner or winners, and nom de plume.

Listening to the evening announcements, sitting around a peat stove in the depths of winter, had a therapeutic feel to it as if the routine of this daily event, meant that all was well.

In Stanley the radio worked differently, distributed through a rediffusion system and all houses had a speaker sitting somewhere in the kitchen, which came on in the morning as well for a couple of hours.

In the early days of my travelling teaching career I would listen to the flights carefully on the radio. I would then pack my case and be ready and waiting for the plane the next day. As I got more experienced, however, I would look at the weather and not bother until I knew the plane was at least near to my location. It also paid to listen to the weather stations, which broadcast through 4.5 radiotelephones to the radiotelephone operator in Stanley. This was a short but fairly detailed weather report, from a number of farms, first thing in the morning.

I found it strange in such a small country – even though we are three-quarters of the size of Wales – to note the different weather patterns. Fox Bay East seemed to be very windy compared to other west mainland settlements. Once I became accustomed to weather variations I could also detect when people wanted to fly or get a flight when wind speeds and adverse conditions at certain settlements were minimised.

I became a dab hand at getting ready in a couple of minutes and using the time hanging around when it is difficult to read or focus on anything. The packing used the same technique as a trolley dash but instead of rushing along supermarket shelves cascading all and sundry into the shopping trolley it was all the things I possessed into my suitcase.

9 CAMP IN GENERAL

Flying

FIGAS, Falkland Islands Government Air Service, was another important component of camp life at that time. Sadly, a year before I arrived in the Islands, a tragedy had befallen the service with a crash that had taken the life of a very popular, local pilot. It seemed that the pilot was trying to teach a doctor to fly the plane, when they crash landed. The doctor survived but sadly Ian Campbell did not.

This led to a bit of a dearth of pilots, with FIG countering this problem with a recruitment drive that resulted in some mature members of the aviation fraternity coming to fly the Beaver on contract. There is no doubt that these pilots were good airmen, but the challenges of flying a float plane in the Islands were many.

In essence, a pilot had to be good in the air, but also on the water, with the agility of an athlete to jump out of the plane and run forward to catch the mooring lines. Landing in some places could be a doddle if the winds were fair and the tide was full, but if the tide was running in or out with a wind from any direction, with no visible indications from a wind sock, the task could be challenging. Add to this the fact that with a bit of wind the Beaver could land and take off in a short space. If there was no wind and the sea was calm however, it took a long run to get the Beaver into the air.

Even the younger contract pilots had to be on their guard, as the ever-changing conditions sought to catch them out. I was on board with a pilot called John Ayres. We flew into Fox Bay East and landed into a modest wind with a textbook landing. Off went the mail, on came a passenger and then it was a short hop over the bay to Fox Bay West. In that small amount of time, the wind had disappeared and as we proceeded to land the plane we came down a lot quicker. John spanked on the power, but this time we landed quite heavily.

Looking back the pilots were amazing and the planes amazing. I think the worse landing I had was coming into a settlement called Roy Cove, where you landed in a deep-sided creek. It was blowing a hoolie across the creek as we came in to land. As we ducked down below the level of the land the wind was confused and the plane went some funny shapes. I must have been slumped in the seat looking pale and dazed and the pilot, John White, asked me if that had worried me. Before I could answer, he said 'Yeah, me too'.

At times it seemed that the need for pilots was so desperate that we would consider any option. The commanding officer of the Royal Marine Detachment, Major Willoughby, had a pilot's licence. He had hours of flying helicopters and also fixed wing, and so he was quickly recruited to fly for FIGAS. I am sure there was some kind of conversion training, but to the regular customer, the travelling teacher, it seemed rather rudimentary. I imagined the conversation went something like this:

'Can you fly planes?'

'Yes.'

'Would you like to try the Beaver?'

'OK.'

'Try some take offs and landings. Now how about some mail runs. You have done really well and got the plane back in one piece. How about flying some expendable people about, as your final test, like the odd camp teacher or two.'

Some unkind wag called him Willoughby the Wallaby, because some of his earlier landings tended to be a bit bouncy. He did conquer the Beaver and got better and better.

I did have a heavy landing at Port Howard with captain Willoughby. The plane picked me up from Keppel. Sam rowed out to the *Alert*, a boat moored in the harbour, and then as the plane came in, we rowed away from the *Alert* and alongside the plane. As we drifted across the bay, I passed my stuff to the pilot who stowed it in the plane. Port Howard had its issues, sitting between the Coast Ridge and Mount Maria. If the wind was blowing hard a certain way, it held the plane up in the air. This was one of those days and the pilot went through the procedures of landing. He lowered the flaps, feathered the propeller and lowered the revs. The Beaver could never be called aerodynamic but we didn't seem to descend. Then we seemed to just drop. On came the power but not enough to stop us hitting the water quite hard and doing a few ungainly skimming stones simulations.

On another occasion we were flying a chap, Fenton Hirtle, back to Golding Island and there was no one there to meet the plane, so we landed on the lee shore and drove towards the shore letting the wind blow us back. The idea was to get as close to the rocky shore as possible and then for Fenton to jump into the shallows, but obviously not for the floats to hit the rocks. We had a few practice runs and the Fenton was given the thumbs up and he went along the floats and leapt into the sea. I don't know if he could swim but I remember that it was pretty deep.

As a travelling teacher, we rarely got to Stanley and so when we did it could be quite wild. There used to be the Falkland Islands Defence Force Club on John Street. They had a permanent barman and if you wanted a few more beers after the pubs kicked out this was the place to go. So a fellow traveller called Robin Montague and I were having a bit of a last night on the town thing in the FIDF Club. We were sat back a bit from the bar, when a small party staggered in and someone got a round in. As the group were waiting for their drinks, one of their number fell back as if he had been shot. He hardly made any effort to break his fall. His chums pulled him up and they carried on partying. Of course the reveller, who had fallen over, was well known to Robin and me because he was one of the Beaver pilots! Robin turned to me and said, 'at least we know he won't be flying us tomorrow.'

Not four hours later, we are waiting at the Beaver hangar waiting to resume our beats on the far west. Wonders of wonders, here to fly us to our destination was the chap who had been imbibing at the FIDF Club and who had so dramatically fallen over backwards. Robin was outraged and threatened to march down and complain to the Governor. Of course we didn't and we helped the pilot stow our bags, clambered in, and waited for the ground crew to push us down the slip and into the water. They then took the wheels off and we floated back as the pilot fired up the big radial engine. One could not take off straightaway because the engine had to warm up and there was a dial that showed you the manifold temperature. Once the hand on the gauge reached the desired point, the throttle was opened up and we were on our way.

There was an episode when the plane few out to Sedge Island, a small island off the north coast of West Falklands. The plane landed to pick up passengers, but then could not take off. The pilot in question taxied from Sedge in the open South Atlantic, around Carcass Island and into the bay on the south side before taking off.

Sea Lion Island was the most interesting place I landed at. It was a small pond at the west end of Sea Lion Island I usually flew from Port Stephens. On one particular flight, I flew with Dr Summers after he had done an overnight visit to Port Stephens. We sat in a rowing boat in a small, sheltered strip of water coming off the main bay. Into the Beaver we got and off we went without any drama. Doctor Summers read his book for a few minutes and then bellowed to me, over the noise of the engine, that he was going to have a snooze and to wake him up before we got to Sea Lion Island.

This was usually an interesting flight going over the old Albemarle Sealing Station, and then over the picturesque Arch Islands on the way to our destination. I woke the good doctor up as we approached Sea Lion Island. His eyes widened as I pointed out where we were going to land. From the air the pond didn't look very big.

I felt sorry for everyone as Dr Summers carried out his visit at the end of the pond, far away from any creature comforts.

The pond, I am told, is 800 yards long, but being enclosed it never felt that big. When it was calm it took most of its length to take off. Even in a slight westerly, the pilots used to let the plane drift back into the mud and then use the suction to give it a cork-out-of-the-bottle effect to get going. It is true to say that in the summer the pond did shrink, and in winter there was ice to contend with. Having said this, with a bit of wind, pilots like Jim Kerr took off across the width.

The Beaver also carried out mail drops, which could be a bit fraught. The idea, which was successful most of the time, was to fly over the settlement and for the pilot to swoop down and hurl the mail bag out of a little side window in the pilot's door. Occasionally, though, things went wrong and the bag got hooked up on parts of the plane. The pilot would then fly over the settlement waggling the wings in an attempt to dislodge the offending mail bag. If all else failed, the plane would have to land and the mail bag be physically removed. Sometimes though things would really go pear-shaped and the bag of mail would come loose over the water and the mail might even be lost.

One of my favourite stories was about Jim Kerr, who was the senior pilot for a number of years. Toni was at Johnson's Harbour when he flew in to pick up a passenger. Toni was out in the boat with her Uncle George and was being allowed to pass Jim the rope from the dinghy. The plane landed, Jim switched off the engine, jumped out, went along the float, tried to catch the rope and fell off the float and disappeared under the water. Up he comes, his half-moon glasses still on his nose, Toni is mortified and thinks it must be her fault. The seriousness of the situation had been lost on her Aunty Jenny who could be heard on the beach roaring with laughter. Jim was not amused and flew back to town.

Camp radio

When I first went to camp I was struck by the lousy reception of the radio. Not just the BBC World Service, which one would expect, but the local station as well. The far west was the worst place where the signal would fade in and out along with the background noise. In fact, it was that bad I struggled to reason why people bothered. It was like listening to your radio in a big deep fat fryer, as fresh chips are first put in. However, strange as it may seem, over time my brain started to filter the background noises out so that I could enjoy the many varied programmes including live sport. World Service used to broadcast on Saturdays, the second half of a first-division match, which subsequently became the premiership. It was never quality listening but I got a lot more from the radio than I thought I would when I first heard it.

The thing that was totally amazing was the telecommunications in the Islands and how there was nothing outside Stanley. That is not entirely true because there was a single wire joining most of the farms on the East and another on the West. It was a fence wire going from post to post perhaps fifty yards apart. The posts could be metal angle iron in three sizes going from the biggest that was driven into the ground and then the intermediary in the middle and the lightest one at the top with an insulator at the very top. In some places like Goose Green there were wooden poles carrying the single wire. On the East, Port San Carlos (KC) didn't want to pay to join the scheme and so weren't part of the system.

Each house had a ring made up of short and long rings. The phones were wooden boxes with a receiver and a handle on the side with which you wound round to ring someone else. So three longs and a short was just that. Three long vigorous turns on the handle followed by a shorter one.

This system was simple and effective although it did have some downsides, which was the lack of privacy. Many people when they heard any rings would pick up and listen. The more people that listened in on a conversation travelling a longish distance the weaker the signal was. Some people didn't even bother going to the phone and just wired their radios into the phone to listen. It wasn't unknown for frustrated users to ask others, in no uncertain terms, to put the phone down so the people trying to communicate could hear one another

4.5 megahertz was the main farm-to-Stanley communications especially from Islands and the West. This was open communication and most people in camp had their radios tuned in to this frequency. I can't remember many houses that didn't have a radio tuned into 4.5 in their kitchen. At the Stanley end there was an operator who passed the messages on to the stores or took telegram messages. If someone died in the community, people would send their sympathies via this very public medium.

In the 1970s these 4.5 transceiver radios were like a black box with a speaker in them and people referred to them as the black box. This apparatus was not that great. Some farms seemed to transmit and receive okay but others had a miserable time. You would hear some people call, call, call to no avail until somebody from another settlement would relay to Stanley that so and so were trying to raise them. It was a worrying situation to everyone as this was the only communication with which to summon help of any kind.

Apart from the mundane stuff there was the doctors' hour in the mornings on every weekday. The problems varied from repeat prescription of Valium, boils on your bum to some serious and dire stuff that I wish I hadn't heard. It was mostly poor old so-and-so must still be depressed. Or 'there's another one on the way at wherever'. Privacy there was not, but many people could diagnose around the breakfast table quicker than the doctor, although admittedly any mistake they made had no come back.

Every farm had a medicine chest that had drugs for most eventualities. The medicine had code names which helped to identify the ones with names that were unpronounceable.

My pick of the traffic was the vets equivalent of doctors' hour. This was also carried out during breakfast. The most appetite-ruining diagnosis and treatment you could imagine. The most sickening that I recall was the treatment for a pig with a prolapse and the description over 4.5 on how to push the arsehole back in with the handle of a wooden spoon. Knowing the vet, he would be quite aware of the timing of his offerings and would enjoy just a smidgen of showmanship.

Sometimes farms would come up on 4.5 and ask another farm to move to 2 megahertz to chat which would have avid listeners scrabbling through the bands to hopefully pick up some juicy titbit. Some people even had two radios so that they wouldn't miss anything.

The black boxes were fairly archaic and they had been around for years and so there was a programme of replacement to a modern transceiver called an AEL in the 1980s. This bit of kit was an all singing and all dancing piece of equipment that had side band, which was meant to give operators some semblance of privacy. Not to be deterred, people found that tuning two radios together you could listen to your favourite channel once again.

Other people had ham receivers with side band, or invested in one, and a full service was soon resumed at those households.

An innovation that came to the Islands, shortly after I did, was the 2 meter set or what people in UK would call a CB (citizens band) or walkie talkie. People put them in their houses and in their Land Rovers and they revolutionised communications in the Falklands. The performance in the Falklands was better than the line of sight that they are meant to work to. Folk began erecting tall masts with beams of many elements to speak to friends and family. The idea with a beam was to point it in the direction of the people that you wanted to speak to. Some places were really good for all-round reception but some, like Dunnose Head, were poor.

The 2 meters had an unpredictable effect on society in camp and were a catalyst that brought in the beginnings of social change. Many managers were called 'mister' and then their first name. I found it novel and interesting but rather a strange way of address in the late 1900s. Anyway, that was the way on most big farms. I saw much of this social etiquette unravel as people spoke to their bosses over the 2 meter sets from their homes, which got some individuals to question this form of address. Most of the older hands still stuck to the formal address, but all the young folk changed over a short time frame. There was at least one farm that hung on to these old ways on the West and probably didn't change until – or even – when it was subdivided, but then everyone that worked there knew that this was expected and this farm didn't seem to struggle to find workers to work for them.

The 2 meter set-up on the vehicle was slightly different in as much as the aerial used was a halo which was a short pipe coming away from the Land Rover with a circle on top. This gave you the best all-round reception as you were driving along or if you were bogged and needed to call for assistance. Before the 2 meters you were on your own on the track and if you got so badly bogged and you couldn't jack yourself out you had to walk for miles for help.

Equally in a convoy of Land Rovers you could chat amongst yourselves or to anyone in range as you travelled along. The traveller could prompt his host to get the kettle on for a nice cup of tea or in the winter a revitalising hot rum to thaw out the weary journeyman.

For people keeping on top of news this was an added bonus and 2-metres could be set on scan to find people talking on other channels to glean some gossip or hear breaking news.

There were times however when the mics have stuck on when the transmit button was stuck after the microphone had moved against something and the comments of the vehicle are plain for all in range to hear. Most conversations were harmless but there have been some real hard-core skinning sessions and inappropriate debates on woman's attributes aired in this way. People try and help out by trying to call and even trying to block conversations out by broadcasting over the top but when the transmit button is pushed in there is no way you can get in touch with the offending 2 meter set and owners.

10. MORE CHARTRES

Green Hill

Green Hill was an outside house at Chartres and it was the next location to be added to my responsibilities. Ron and Marina Anderson had moved there from Dunnose Head. They had three children – Andrew, Sophie and Rupert – and while I was there another child, Stanley, came on the scene. Andrew and Sophie were old enough to be taught. The first few times that I rode there on the school teacher's horse Quane using the schoolies's gear, and once again my backside did some hide softening. Fortunately, Ron was at hand on a couple of occasions to show me the track out and in. I learnt from my mistake at Shag Cove and gave the track's details my 100 per cent attention. Shag Cove was easy in a way because you just followed the coast ridge. Green Hill, to me, was in the middle of some very samey-type countryside.

Bill Luxton, the manager and owner of Chartres, took me out on the very first visit to Green Hill. Managers/owners were like gods in some respects, they were the figureheads of the settlements and some could rule in a very feudal way.

Bill came into the house and we all sat round the table having a cup of tea and a bun. The eldest child Andrew, just couldn't keep his eyes off Bill. He was in awe and totally mesmerised. I don't think there would have been a different reaction if a martian had turned up. Even when Ron spoke to the lad he only broke his stare for a few seconds before he was back gawking at the Chartres Messiah.

Unlike Shag Cove, I did get the hang of the track although I did misjudge Ponies Pass after some heavy rain on one trip. Like a complete plonker I hadn't worked out that it could become too deep to cross safely for a travelling teacher.

Motorbike

During this period, I bought a 650 BSA Thunderbolt from Ron. It was a beast of a machine and very heavy and cumbersome for off-road compared to some of the smaller capacity two stroke trail bikes that were coming to the Falklands.

I had many adventures on this hard-core bike, which aren't all fond memories. One of my first trips on the thing was out to Green Hill. Going out I was getting a feel for the handling and the awesome power it had, but coming back I was getting used to it and beginning to relax. A soft bit came up and I thought I would gun it through and throw up some mud. I just touched the outside of the soft area and gave it some welly and a satisfying arc of mud shot skywards, but the front's less than thrilling action was to sink down up to the handlebars bringing the bike to a sudden full stop. I knew the thing was heavy but I was just about to find out how! I wrestled with the bloody thing for ages before I rocked and half rolled and half pulled it from the mire. It was rare to see other travellers doing camp runs in numbers unless there was a two-nighter which had vehicles converging on the destination from all quarters. There was no one passing to lend a hand and by the time I had been up close and personal with the Thunderbolt in the mud hole, the peat hung from me and I was soaked with muddy water.

There is nothing like this kind of experience to teach you discretion and where and where not to go.

John Hodgkinson

John Hodgkinson, a fellow camp teacher, came to join me at Chartres with the idea that I show him the ropes and then he would cover for me during my mid-tour leave at the end of 1978. He had already had a go at teaching but had encountered a few difficulties. He was six foot four if he was an inch and towered over me, but for all his height and bulk he had very small hands. I don't know why I should remember such an insignificant thing. He also had bright red hair.

John arrived into the Falklands and had everyone warming to him in an instant, by bringing his golf clubs to the Islands and then calling the Falklands a tin pot colony for not having a decent golf course. He then fanned the fires with other indiscretions that were basically insinuations about further inadequacies in the Islands. I know it was his manner which upset some people; people thought he was arrogant. He did not think some of his comments through in my opinion but he was an okay chap as far as I was concerned and I really liked him.

Poor bastard had been recruited from London where he had been working in a sports shop. It is easy for me to comment now but his background suggested to me, with such a contrast between his UK life and what he was going to expect in camp, that he was always going to find it difficult.

I took John up and showed him where I stayed and he was quite insulting about my ex-army bed, the bedside table, the grotty curtains and the general décor. This was before he saw his abode, which wasn't as good.

The chaps in the Chartres cookhouse warmed quickly to this amiable eccentric and didn't hold the golf quip against him. John soon got the hang of buying his quota of booze and wiping it out unceremoniously with the best of them. But he also used to buy a bottle of sweet sherry, which was probably the first to cross the threshold of the Chartres cookhouse (which was allowed in your weekly quota) to drink during the week using incredible will power and planning to last the five week days. The cookhouse gang, particularly the young lads, used to peer through the keyhole, with sheer delight, to watch gentleman John drink his sweet sherry.

John would sit in his bare cookhouse room on a rickety old chair and a small plain table without a picture on the wall, a mat or any other creature comfort and go through a sophisticated ritual of pouring the required measure and then imbibing it, sip by sip, savouring every drop. He could have been staying in the Ritz with his pose and his demeanour. Sadly, he didn't have a copy of the *Financial Times* or the *The Telegraph* to read while he ran the drink over his cultured palate. I'm sure he would have had a brolly in his possession although I never saw it. Perhaps it had been blown inside out on his first day on the Islands.

John's other passion in life was food and he would talk for hours about the meals he had had in some of the best restaurants in London. In fact, he could just talk food and he could eat for England. If the children were distracted and didn't want to knuckle down they would ask about his views on some kind of food and off John would go on another culinary adventure

Deidre Barnes was only really obliged to feed one teacher but she had agreed to feed John as well. We went to supper one night and Deidre had got a feel for John's enormous appetite and had cooked a hill-sized pile of fritters for everyone. We got stuck in but John kept on and on and I was beginning to feel embarrassed at how many John had eaten compared to everyone else. No one batted an eyelid but one would have had to be somewhere else not to notice John's efforts in depriving the other diners – and the hens that fed off the scraps.

We sat around for a few minutes and then made our way back down to the cookhouse. As we were leaving the house John turned to me and said, 'those fritters were lovely, I really wished there were a few more.'

Life, believe it or not, suited John at Chartres and in a short time he had put on some ample condition. I am sure he would have topped the 120 kgs easily.

One weekend Hodgkinson and I decided to go over to see our colleague Rupert Fowkes, a settlement teacher at Hill Cove, on the Thunderbolt. Plenty of power so should carry us there no problem.

So off we trundle, me at the helm and big John on the back. I am not sure what I was in kilos but I was eleven stones and seven ounces in old money. It was incredibly difficult to make the bike go exactly where I wanted it to because of the huge counterweight on the back. It is hard enough on a road when your passenger is a lot heavier than you, but on camp it is very arduous. I thought speed and momentum was the key and so if I wanted to go a certain direction I did it with some throttle. Our progress was not pretty.

Unfortunately/fortunately, I am not sure which, our weekend was cut short just before Teal River House when the fibre glass seat broke leaving the width of a cigarette paper left on the bike to sit on. John remained sitting on the lion's share of the seat on the grass track. We tried to carry on, believe it or not, on the piece of seat that was left but we shot off to one side after not very far, hit a rock and sheared off the gear lever.

Worse was to come when we found that the bottle of vodka that was in the rucksack on John's back, had broken on impact. There was no consolatory drink to drown our sorrows on the walk back to Chartres. Nothing to lift our spirits and to help us appreciate how funny it all was.

In a way this small mishap saved us from some of the track that was less forgiving which was strewn with rocks going over the mountain behind Hill Cove. Having problems that close to base were also a blessing because we didn't put anyone out to a great extent. Breaking down at the other end of a journey would have led to a rescue party to retrieve the bike and the schoolies. One has to make the most of it at times like this and I made do with some low-level abuse to my companion about him being a fat bastard, which had led to the seat being broken along with a ruined weekend.

BSA Thunderbolts weren't really designed to do off-road in the Falklands and the many miles and a number of not so careful owners had taken its toll. It was fairly reliable, although it didn't like water, especially wading. I did have a major breakdown on one occasion when the clutch fell off the shaft. On this occasion I was in a convoy and between the group of bikers we had just enough tools to get the casing off and put the clutch back on the shaft and tighten it so it wouldn't happen again.

The hardest ride I had – remember no roads – was driving to Port Howard during the winter. We got on the clay track and the clay built up on the mudguard and the wheels filled with clay. The riders of the smaller lighter Japanese bikes would flip them on and off the clay track as need be but the Thunderbolt wasn't that flexible, it was an 'all power and no finesse' machine.

A trip to Dunnose Head

While John was with me having a tutorial at Chartres, Robin Montague was showing a new chap, Stan Angel, the ropes at Dunnose Head. We decided to meet up at Gun Hill Shanty, which was quite close to Chartres but on the other side of the water, and it was further from Dunnose Head but still within easy striking distance.

Marshall Barnes was the foreman at Chartres and had four children at the school, and was good enough to take us across to the other side in his boat because it was a flat calm day John sat at the bow reading a copy of *The Times* that Bill Luxton had given us. It was a fantastic caricature of John. I certainly wish I had got a picture of him going across.

I wouldn't say that I was a fast walker but John was very slow and although I tried I just didn't have the patience to dawdle with him so I walked ahead and waited for him. We had a rucksack with all the provisions and we took turns to carry it, with me taking the first leg and John bringing it the second to the shanty.

We were there for a while before the Dunnose Head crew arrived, which gave us time to get the fire revved up and have a couple of beers. We had a memorable weekend. Things reached their zenith after a few drinks, criticising our boss and highlighting his failings – and we felt there were many – including the way our mail would arrive on the plane that we flew to our next place on. In other words, as you were flying to the next destination the mail would be opened at the settlement you just left and your letters would be amongst it. I know it sounds like something rather small to get excited about but mail was a great morale booster and to think that you could have read it if it had been properly directed and now it could be another two weeks or more depending on where your mail was and where you were. If both were on a mainland farm it was possible you might see it within two weeks. If one or both of you were on a small island you might not see it for ages.

It was great to share these common problems and have a bit of a rant.

The next day we were off, back to our respective settlements. Marshall once more obliged us and picked us up in his boat.

11. DUNNOSE HEAD

Community at Dunnose Head

Beats changed again with the Bucklands moving from Shag Cove to Chartres and I moved over to Dunnose Head for a while. I taught Jamie, son of Reg and Margaret Anderson and also Amanda, daughter of Jimmy and Ginny Forster, although Amanda, only in the afternoons because she wasn't old enough to start school full time. Lynne, another daughter, was also there but too young to even feature in the school's activities. Susan Nightingale, daughter of Margaret, returned from Darwin Boarding School which was closed down when the generator shed caught fire.

Dunnose Head was a satellite settlement of Fox Bay East. Richard Cockwell was the main manager of Fox Bay East but Jimmy was in a lesser management position under Richard as the overseer at Dunnose Head. Reg Anderson worked on the farm along with a young lad called Peter Nightingale, who was Margaret's son from her first marriage and he resided in a small cookhouse along with me.

The settlement was very small and had the mere basics, but there was still a dedicated schoolroom of quite a high standard to work in.

We got up to some high jinks at Dunnose Head but although we did have the odd drink the fun wasn't fuelled by excessive drinking as it was at other locations.

There wasn't a community hall and the cookhouse was small compared to most so there wasn't an area to show the films. The overseer's house was the biggest building apart from the shearing shed so the films were shown there. To be able to get a large enough picture projected onto the screen the projector was set up in one room and then projected through a doorway over the heads of the audience and onto the screen hanging on the wall in the next room. It was a novel arrangement but it worked.

Dunnose Head was eventually sold by Packs brothers and split up into three family farms but I often remember the community spirit that this small settlement had.

Jimmy and Ginny went on to own their own farm, which happened to be another part of Packs at Port Howard. Reg and Margaret eventually retired to Stanley and Jamie lives somewhere in the UK. Peter Nightingale got married and bought a farm, which was part of Hill Cove.

Spider crabs

One of our escapades was catching spider crabs in the waters around the settlement. We made pots out of wire mesh and went out in the farm dinghy to set them. We baited the pots and chucked them over the side at different locations. Depending on the weather we would then go out and lift them after a day or two.

We got loads of spider crabs and would bring them back and cook them up and eat the meat out of the legs. It was very tasty too. There wasn't a lot of meat in their legs but there was a lot of satisfaction at being able to win such an exotic product from the sea. In fact, it was Jimmy and I that ate the meat because the others didn't take part in the eating bit. It was good entertaining fun and we went further and further afield to find the best places, although we weren't totally reckless because it was only a little boat.

One crop was harvested and one of the crabs had eggs tucked under its tail. After the meat in the legs I was still peckish so I thought eggs, fish roe, there can't be much difference and ate them.

That night I started to get severe pains in my abdomen and felt very sick and the back of my neck was stiff and felt funny as though there was air trapped under the skin.

In today's Falklands a helicopter would be despatched and you would be bought in to the hospital in Stanley. But then there was little or no chance of the Beaver flying out after dark. It was just a case of sitting it out and hoping upon hope that you woke up the next day, which obviously I did.

The pain was excruciating for four hours, stopping me from sleeping, but as it eased off I did sleep and woke next day feeling a little tired but a lot better. This experience extinguished my desire to mess around in boats, catching and then murdering spider crabs for little more than a spoonful of crabmeat.

Clay

During a Camp Education seminar at Darwin Boarding School we were taught how to win clay from the ground, clean it by sieving it and then dry it to a workable consistency and make pots and ornaments. Our teacher was Rob Rutterford who was on the teaching staff at Darwin Boarding School with his wife Val.

I took this knowledge out on my beat and at Dunnose Head everyone was as keen as mustard and there was 100 per cent participation (unlike the crab murdering and eating). I dug the clay, sieved it through a big garden sieve and dried it by the school fire. It took me forever, especially the sieving and drying, but once done I apportioned a reasonable lump of clay to everyone in the settlement. We made all kinds of things at school and the people of the settlement did likewise in their homes. Someone made a pipe with a long stem with string through it to make it hollow.

The other part of this project was building the kiln, which Jimmy helped me with. We dug a trench and filled it with old wood and then covered it with corrugated iron and then had a drum at the end for the kiln itself. In the top of the kiln was a pipe for the chimney. We then covered the corrugated iron and the kiln with the soil that came out of the trench with the chimney left sticking out. Margaret and Reg decided not to risk their creations in the kiln but the rest of us had faith.

So the great day came and the fire was lit and the fire drew through the kiln and smoke came billowing out of the chimney creating a fearsome heat. It worked to perfection with people feeding the fire with further combustibles.

The heat generated was staggering. You could even feel it through the ground so we banked it down and left the scene.

Although I have got pictures of the work everyone created, many of the items got damaged in the kiln when the chimney melted because no one noticed that it wasn't made of steel or iron. The surviving articles were successfully fired but it didn't alter the knowing smiles that Reg and Margaret gave one another which probably manifested into 'I told you so' in the comfort of their own home.

Home brew

Jimmy wasn't a hardened drinker but he did have a weakness for home-brewed beer. One of my visits coincided with one of these batches maturing and so we had a small celebration. It wasn't disgusting but a commercial company would have struggled to shift it. What it lacked in taste it made up in potency. A couple of bottles of this brew and we were quite merry and too sloshed to think about taking it easy. During the evening Jimmy invited me on the next day's gather, something that I was always keen to do.

So off to the cookhouse I went, weaving like a sailing ship tacking into the wind.

The next day I felt as though a truck had hit me. I felt like that for most of the day. I didn't go gathering in fact I could hardly lift my head from my pillow. Although severely delayed, the gang did go and gather sheep. I could put this down to me being a wimp but I have defended my ego by thinking that over time the residents of Dunnose Head had built up some kind of resistance to Jimmy's brews.

12. ROY COVE

Community at Roy Cove

Roy Cove was built on the side of a small but deep-sided creek and was very picturesque with well-kept gorse hedges and a number of trees. It was one of my favourite settlements. It was small compared to Chartres or San Carlos but had the vibrancy you would find anywhere else in the Islands.

The gorse would have kept the gang in winter work for many weeks keeping it in that tidy manner. The trees must have been planted a number of years ago because they were well grown by Falklands' terms.

The cook was Nelly Betts and her husband was called Sturdee, named after the WW1 admiral that led the British Southern Squadron, which destroyed the German's southern fleet off the Falklands during the Battle of the Falklands on 8 December 1914.

Nelly had a good reputation as a cook because she could provide good wholesome food on a small budget. She made her own jams and pickles and her cakes and biscuits (often called 'hard tack' in cookhouses) and was well thought of island-wide.

Roy Cove was a farm that had invested a lot of money per capita into reseeding large areas of low-quality pastures with improved grasses and then increased stock significantly. Unfortunately, this initiative was short-lived and I am sure there are a number of reasons for this. My explanation is that without fencing they would have been unable to manage these pastures in a way that could have sustained their productivity. Unrestricted grazing would have had all the new grass under too much pressure and limited the long-term potential. Some people felt that the grasses that were planted could have included some finer, more palatable species.

I have been told that the management at the time did want to invest in fencing and also to plant a greater variety of grasses, but I suppose costs would have been that much more, on top of an already expensive scheme. In hindsight perhaps the people who drove this initiative would do it differently but wool is such a fickle product and good prices might have helped to get this work started just as a few years of low wool prices might have finished it.

Roy Cove was synonymous with the Miller family, but by the time I came on the scene they had had a number of different managers.

Joe Newel was at the helm when I did my stint. Trudi his wife and their three daughters Donna, Paula and Cara supported him.

The gang shrank quite rapidly during my time in this area and when families or men moved away they were seldom replaced. Regardless of this fact, there still seemed to be a cohesive unit with a strong sense of togetherness. Among the gang members were a married couple called John and Sue Birmingham. We were to meet again briefly during our time at Fox Bay West where he was the cowman gardener to the manager and his wife, Nigel and Shirley Knight. The Birminghams had moved there after Roy Cove was subdivided. He was also the barman at the club and I was to work together with John a number of years later on two legislative councils.

I didn't really get to know John and Sue at this stage but I did recognise fairly quickly that Sue was very shy and introverted and John wasn't.

Two of the Roy Cove subdivisions were sold to outsiders, which was very controversial but their money helped fund the whole purchase which government couldn't afford at that time.

Davey Duncan

My arrival at Roy Cove was well into my contract and there was an older chap in the cookhouse called Davey Duncan, as well as Brian Hewitt who had found his way there after a misunderstanding at Chartres involving putting some rams out. Willie Ross, his brother Charles and father Colin were also there.

For some reason Davey didn't warm to Brian and Brian wasn't overly fond of Davey and so they would antagonise one another. Brian would say something about Davey being an old bugger and Davey would retaliate with at least he could get the mutton in, which was a huge insult to accuse a shepherd of not being able to do this elementary job.

Davey was a hard old packet who had a glass eye which always went astray when he was drinking and other people would inevitably sit on it. When he popped it back into his eye socket he would put it into his mouth first to lubricate it. When I originally saw him do it I was quite disgusted, but I soon got used to it.

Davey was honest and down to earth and he told me on a number of visits that when he was finished he would shoot himself just like a shepherd does a dog when they are too old to work.

One day I was on another part of my beat when I heard that Davey had shot himself with a twelve bore in his room in the Roy Cove cookhouse. It would have been incredibly quick for Davey but awful for all the others in the settlement who had to clear up the mess.

Life at Roy Cove

Two stories come to mind, one that doesn't involve me but is too hilarious to omit and the other one, which was a great experience.

During my mid-term leave several camp teachers covered various parts of my beat. Stan Angel did Roy Cove during the summer months.

One of the three girls at this time was badly constipated and was taking medicine to help. After a number of days, the medicine didn't seem to be working so the doctor decided to increase the dose.

As this course of treatment was unfolding, Stan, was blissfully ignorant of the issues involved and so taking advantage of a nice summer's day took everyone for a nature walk. At the furthest most point of their ramble the medicine of several days, plus the recent increase, took effect and the poor girl had an accident. It must have been awful for the girl but Stan (the near perfect gentleman) didn't know what to do so wiped the child down with a handful of white grass and threw her undergarment away.

Back at base Stan explained what had happened and how he had had to disregard an item of clothing. In those happy times people had to be thrifty to get by and Stan was told in a good natured fashion that if you threw children's clothes away after every event like this they would end up with very few clothes. With this one of the children was dispatched on a recovery mission and told to swish the offending article in the nearest ditch and bring them home.

Stan left the Islands after a few tours and got married and had children but for a few years after the event I am sure he used to have nightmares about his nature walk at Roy Cove. Most camp teachers were young with little experience of dealing with young children.

Needless to say it wasn't 'Stan' that told me the tale but the mother of the girls. Eventually the story got out for general consumption and Stan's friends ribbed him unmercifully. Everyone in the settlement knew, followed by most of the East and West and they all had a bloody good chuckle at Stan's expense.

The new club at Pebble Island was finished and so a two-nighter was arranged to celebrate the occasion. Usually if a two-nighter was held people would converge on the location using motorbikes, Land Rovers, tractor and trailers and horses from all the other settlements but with Pebble there was a problem. Pebble was an Island. With Pebble you had to accept the expense of a flight or try and cadge a lift on a small motorboat.

Joe, Trudi and the girls were going up in the long wheel base Land Rover with another vehicle to meet the Pebble motorboat at Shallow Bay for a lift across.

Joe, the kind-hearted person that he was, didn't like to turn people away and filled his Land Rover up with others in the settlement that wanted to go. Just Joe's family was a load but with the rest of us it was going to be a very skilled driver indeed to get us along the track without a bogging.

We all left in high spirits talking about what would happen at the do. It wasn't long however before we were bogged. In fact, time and time again down we went and had to be pulled out by the accompanying vehicle. Then disaster struck, we decided not to go through a rutted out gateway but lay the fence over. Unbeknown to Joe there was a broken-off standard in the grass and we got two punctures in one side of the Land Rover.

Only having one spare ourselves we had to rob our accompanying Land Rover for their spare. Up until the 1990s the Falklands was 99 per cent Land Rover so it was no problem, but now neither of the vehicles could afford another puncture.

We ploughed on sinking in and struggling through and sometimes getting bogged.

Back in the 1970s there were a number of different tyres but the two favourites on the West were the small tractor grip tyres with a V-shaped tread which people call track grips (like small versions of a back tractor tyre.) and the Michelins. The Michelins had a blocky tread and were low-pressure tyres that people ran with the minimum of air in and by this method they would spread with the weight of the vehicle and hence be good in the soft.

People swore by their choice of tyres but in my assessment the Michelin was probably better in the soft peaty conditions. The track grips were very good for climbing and getting through mucky clay passes.

We eventually got to the rendezvous with *The Richard*, the motorboat from Pebble Island chugging its way round to its home.

Many of the people that lived on the outer islands had learnt through generations of boat work where all the reefs and channels were. Although there are charts of the islands there were none on display today or any of the other times that I travelled on a small boat in the Falkland Islands. We would seem to be giving a point or little island a rather wide birth only to see the reef below the water showing us all the reason for a particular course.

Two-nighters were always good fun and really a time for all to come together. You book a room with someone you know or if you are like me you book through someone that knows someone. If there is a big crowd many of the houses split their rooms into male and female and you find a space on the floor for your sleeping bag. A two-nighter is usually a time when you hardly get a wink of sleep. Even if you leave the party early there is a good chance someone will find you and turf you out of bed or as the revellers return slamming doors and making a drunken noise.

Like many two-nighters the Pebble one was very lively with lots of drinking and eating and dancing and skylarking. A couple of old wags fell in a puddle on the way up to the hall and gave all and sundry a jolly good laugh as they drained off. Drunken old sods.

One of my strongest memories of this occasion was eating the best tripe and onions ever. To be honest I can't remember eating tripe before coming to the Falklands and it is something I may have refused in the UK. So it is only over time that I have come to realise how good it was. The tripe was in bite-sized pieces in a creamy onion sauce. Those that know tell me that the making of a tripe dish is in the cleaning process. You have to peel every bit of the lining from the paunch carefully and wash it thoroughly. If bits of the lining remain or it has not been washed properly it can have a bitter taste.

The hall was opened to a cacophony of pulling beer can tops that ended in some very sore heads and upset stomachs. And then the visitors had to go home.

The weather was a bit foul and so our departure was delayed and once we did leave we only got as far as Shallow Bay. It was rather late to continue so William (Bones) and Emily Goodwin opened their home to the onward travellers for the night. They had been to the bash as well so we arrived to a cold house without hot water. It wasn't long before the fire was roaring and their many guests were drinking tea and coffee and enjoying hospitality that is hard to imagine anywhere else.

It was still a long run back to Roy Cove with the overloaded Land Rover but eventually we made it and, although a day late, ready to start work. It was funny because although not deliberate I had had an unscheduled day off but unless there were some disgruntled folk ready to inform of your every movement, the Education Department hadn't got a clue what you were doing.

Sadly, I didn't do much travelling around at Roy Cove and this is possibly because there weren't any people in the outside houses and travelling to them didn't take you anywhere else. Dunbar was often occupied but not during my time.

The Pebble Island run was one of many journeys that I made to different functions but it was unique because the final destination was an island. The idea of mainland travel was to get to the venue, if it was a two-nighter, on the Friday night, drink lots of alcohol with your host and then go to the dance.

The quantities of alcohol that were consumed would have the whole concept of 'Health of the Nation' and one or two glasses of wine as an example of the recommended units of alcohol, totally blown out of the water. Even so, this wasn't enough to overcome all the shyness that could be exhibited in the early hours of a dance. Usually men would sit on one side of the room and women on the other and then there was more and more dancing as the evening went on. I often found that once I was relaxed enough to dance I'd lost the ability.

Two-nighters

On Saturday the farm would organise a few events like a darts tournament and sometimes a film. Many would drink the hair of the dog and recover by the second night's dancing. The second night could often be slower to start than the first night but usually people would arrive and shake a leg.

My first two-nighter was an eye opener because it was all country and western music and old fashioned dancing, something that I had not witnessed in the UK. In the UK, country and western to me meant going to towns like Blackburn that had Wild West functions to find out who could draw their replica colt 45 the quickest, or crack a whip without taking someone's, including their own, eyes out.

One of my first two-nighters was at Fox Bay East and Raymond McBeth drove a tractor pulling a trailer with the poor and needy who hadn't got a lift in a Land Rover. It was in the middle of winter and it was bitter and there was a lot of snow about. The driver of the tractor had less comfort than the passengers in the trailer with the tractor being cab-less and he being unable to duck down out of the elements.

Raymond was dressed in his waterproofs and thigh boots and did a very good job of driving us through all the soft camp to our venue at Fox Bay East.

Another time a couple of the youngsters decided that they would walk from Chartres to a two-nighter at Fox Bay. So Ali Marsh, Willie Ross and I set off after being taken over the water in a boat. This walk was 20 miles as the crow flies and a lot more if you take the diversions round tops of hills and other obstacles. They asked me if I would like to go along.

I was young and I thought I was fit. I certainly wasn't as fit as these guys who were working long hours throughout the year on the physical demands of a large farm. We went over the shoulder of Mount Philomel and made a beeline to Fox Bay East and didn't those chaps go up and down dale without slackening their pace. The ground under foot was rarely smooth and most of the time uneven and lumpy or soft and tiring. I had to give it everything to keep up and when we got close to our destination a Land Rovers came past stopping to ask us how we were getting on. I would have quite happily jumped on board but my companions would have none of it and wanted to walk into the settlement.

I had always been fit and active but my life as a travelling teacher had not involved any physical demands at all apart from the odd ride out to an outside house. A lot of this, if I had been proficient, would have kept me fit because I would have trotted most of the way, which makes the rider work a bit. I, of course, dawdled out burning more calories opening the gates than on the actual ride.

Most of the two-nighters were designed for people to socialise with a few drinks, although there were some who didn't overdo the booze.

At some stage on the Sunday people would round up their passengers, if they had any, say their goodbyes and head home through miles of soft ground and sticky ditches and gateways. It was only the seasoned campaigners that could stomach a return journey of a drink at every gate. Most had had enough by the second day and many would nurse a sore head on the return journey.

13. PORT STEPHENS

Life at Port Stephens

Port Stephens was another great place to work, situated at the far south of the West. It did have the feeling in the depths of winter that the southerly winds blowing up from the Antarctic didn't warm up or get deflected by anything before hitting the settlement fair and square.

The cookhouse, although dominated by youngsters, seemed to be run fairly and conscientiously. The building had central heating and the peggy man took his stoking duties seriously which meant that even in the winter it was many degrees warmer than most of the cookhouses that I frequented.

On one of the first days of my stay at Port Stephens I witnessed a horse being tamed in the old style. The people taking part in the taming had this grey horse thrown down and they were mouthing him. This entailed people pulling a leather bit into the horse's mouth until it struggled and that was it, as I understood it. Then the horse was let up with the rider and off they went. The rider on that day was Mel Lloyd and the horse was called Thunder. As I have already mentioned, it was a rough and ready process but there were large shepherd gangs that needed a steady supply of horses and this was how most farms achieved this need. I can still visualise very clearly Mel and Thunder tearing off down the paddock.

Jock and Jose

There was a Scottish gentleman living at Port Stephens, called Jock Fairley who was very much a loner. A lot older than the other members of the cookhouse, he preferred his own company. He spent most of his time, anyway, miles out of the settlement rotavating areas all over Port Stephens' land. He had a big tractor and dragged a caravan behind, when moving from place to place, in which he lived. Most Falklands caravans are a one-roomed box with a peat stove in one corner and bunk beds on the far wall near the door. This was attached to two large runners that were large pieces of timber with iron on the bottom. Like a big sledge with a one-roomed house on it.

Peter Robertson the manager, used to encourage Jock to come to the settlement occasionally with the intention of stopping him becoming completely feral. Even then he would sometimes still live in his caravan rather than the room he had in the bunkhouse.

When he did sleep in his room in the bunkhouse, his room was the first on the left at the top of the stairs.

Jock had decided to take a correspondence course in Spanish and you could hear him in his room repeating after the tutor Spanish phrases on his tape recorder.

A bit like John drinking sherry at Chartres, the young lads were taken by Jock going through his repertoire of Spanish phrases in a strong Scottish accent. At times there would be a marvellous concoction of Spanish, English and 'Jockernese' as Jock struggled to come to terms with his tutorial. At these moments the audience would be in stitches and on the verge of collapse.

Jock would bravely carry on, not just in his room but also when speaking to his colleagues. Again it was a mixture of languages and the others would pick up on this and expand and exaggerate upon the theme so nearly every irresponsible member of Port Stephens was speaking in what was nearly a new language.

Poor old Jock also liked a drink and from time to time he was placed on the black list to stop him from drinking himself to death. After one memorable social, or perhaps not so memorable, Jock, unable to purchase alcohol was found tidying up all the stray tots and half-finished beers, of the night before, to satisfy his unquenchable thirst.

The black list was something that I had never come across before and I was to warm to the concept having seen it in action in the Falklands. It means that someone is put on a list, which is then sent around to all shops and stores, bars and clubs in camp and Stanley. Any person or persons on that list cannot buy or be supplied with alcohol. It is illegal to sell or supply and people have been known to be taken to court for supplying. It is probably only in small societies like the Falklands that it could work and of course people's human rights have been spouted over the last few years which will probably cause the black list's demise. I have seen the positive side of this power and have seen it help not just the people involved but the extended families as well. I am all in favour of people having rights but some people have problems coping with alcohol and in my view need a helping hand not to kill themselves or drink so much they change from caring, considerate individuals into something totally different and make the rest of their family suffer financially and emotionally.

Today it is very difficult for members of the family to put someone on the prohibition order. In the 1970s and 1980s it was possible with reasonable evidence for members of a family or a doctor to put someone on the black list. Nowadays the individual concerned has to think it is a good idea as well, which is sometimes very late or after some incident.

My room was at the far end of the corridor next to a Chilean man who was working at Port Stephens. Jose seemed to be friendly enough when you met him out and about but as the only Chilean I think he was lonely and although he wasn't as old as Jock he was older than the youngsters that were in the majority.

One night Jose had a one-man party and pub brawl in the room next to mine. Shouting and thumping and sounds of stuff getting knocked over and general shock waves reverberated from his room for most of the night. There was such ferocity that I expected a foot, fist or flying object to burst through the wall at any moment.

This one-man destruction derby went on for most of the night with most of us thinking, we should do something, but actually did nothing. Even in hindsight it is difficult to know what we could have done. Trying to intervene may have led to an escalation in violence and have the focus move from inanimate objects to people. It could have become very serious but it is only in hindsight that we know it didn't leave the confines of his room. Calling the police wasn't a possibility and I suppose it would have fallen on Peter Robertson to deal with it if it had spilled over, just as in every isolated farm the responsibility was always with the manager.

The next day someone did ascertain that he was okay and as if by magic the room looked fine so he was either good at repairing damage or it was just noise, but at the time it sounded real enough.

Whatever was troubling him later came to a head when I wasn't there. He totally lost it on one of these sessions and was eventually sent back to Chile.

The swimming pool

Just like many of the other cookhouses, we often looked for something to do in our leisure time to accompany the case of Tennants and bottle of rum. There were water sports and I took the opportunity to dive from the Port Stephen's jetty but it was a bit mediocre, if I was to be honest, compared with Chartres. Even being soused with rum the water was freezing and not many others were swimmers so it was a quick attention-seeking activity.

The best thing with non-swimmers or beginners is to have a safe environment and so we decided to build a swimming pool. Yeh right, and how would you do that without spending a fortune? Well.

For many years farms in the Falklands dipped their sheep because they suffered from ked, a wingless louse fly that is parasitic to sheep, that was devaluing the wool. So when the sheep were gathered in after shearing to be tallied they were put through the dip. These were deep troughs of water and potent chemicals. If a particular sheep was buoyant and wasn't totally submerged there was someone at hand to push them under with a piece of wood. At the far end of the trough there was a gentle slope where the sheep could walk up and out of the dip. They would then muster in a large area where the water and the chemicals would drain off and back into the dip thus saving on water and expensive chemicals.

At Port Stephens this place was a walled area with a cement floor that had an opening at the far end where the sheep came in. We bricked up the hole thus making a complete wall on four sides. We then got the settlement fire pump and pumped the water from the ditch nearby into the enclosed area. Thus was born the swimming pool at Port Stephens.

It was a great project and had us amused for days. Getting permission, finding the materials and building the brick wall in the gap and plastering it. The skilled work was done by Leon Berntsen with the rest of us sitting around in a management capacity.

We couldn't wait to try it out and so once the water pump had filled the pool most of us went for a dip, including Valerie, Leon's wife, who christened the pool by wearing a leopard-print bikini, a garment I thought I would never see in the Falklands.

Stanley International. (Old Family Photo)

Temporary Airstrip blows away in high winds. (Old Family Photo)

Wrecks in the harbour, The Afterglow with the Lady Elizabeth in the background are just two of the wrecks that were on the beaches of Stanley in 1977.

Frans Axel Pettersson with his grandson Tony Pettersson. (Old Family Photo)

Dave Emsley, FIGAS pilot being met at Port Howard.

Camp teacher Mike Pritchard going ashore at Carcass Island with Rob McGill.

Loading passengers and luggage from the beach at Dunnose Head ready to meet the Beaver.

Passengers being loaded onto the Beaver at sea.

Beaver landing at Goose Green, showing the Ilen (blue) and Penelope tied up at the jetty. These boats were used by the FIC to work the many Islands that they owned in and around Lafonia.

Gary McGill takes the horse and cart for a spin with Brian Hewitt in attendance at Chartres.

Quieter times on the Chartres River with Bill Luxton and his son Stephen.

John Hodgkinson reading to his class at Chartres school.

A posed picture for prosperity from l-r travelling teachers Robin Montague, John Hodgkinson and Stan Angel at Gun Hill Shanty.

Keppel Island showing the stone Mission Shearing shed and outbuildings, with the 1950's house in the background, taken from the cemetery.

Sam & Hay Miller at Keppel Island meeting Governor and Mrs Parker, flown in by the Endurance Helicopter.

Gentoo eggs in tea chest

Old telephone

A view of Shag Cove looking over Falkland Sound to the east.

The Shag Cove Troop with wind powered water pump.

A good turn out at the Jetty as the MV Forrest visits Port Howard.

An old John Shaw Press in action. (Old Family Photo)

Amanda Forster with crab pot at Dunnose Head.

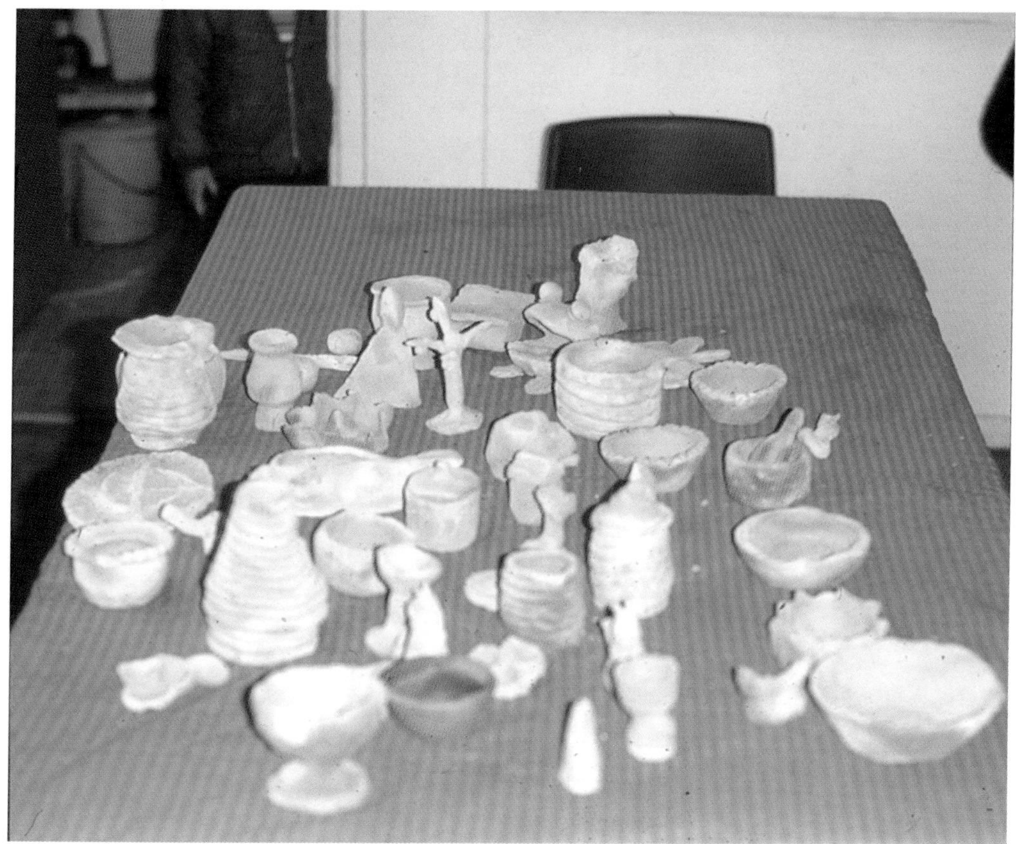

Pottery ready for the kiln at Dunnose Head.

Completing the kiln ready to fire up at Dunnose Head.

Port Stephens with the motor boat just visible in Fegen Inlet, upper right in photo.

Swimming pool under construction at Port Stephens with l-r Harold Dickson, Leon Berntsen, Stephen Jennings and me

Marie Clifton in the tussac at Seal Lion Island

Short-eared Owl in the washing line at Sea Lion Island

Terry Clifton cutting peat on Sea Lion Island. Here he is cutting ½ a yard wide not the normal yard x yard.

The Gulch at Sea Lion Island, where all provisions were hauled up to the cliff top.

Sadly, there were some downsides. The fresh water from the ditch was colder than the sea and after the initial euphoria every one became aware of this fact and there was also no chance of the sun warming this shallow sheltered water because the pump had to run continuously pouring in more cold water to maintain the water level because regrettably the bottom was quite porous.

In that initial stage we all got in and some of us even dived off the walls but it grieves me to say that that was the end of the pool.

Working at Port Stephens

Harold Dickson was also at Port Stephens having moved back from Chartres. His father was the foreman and Valerie was his sister. After drinking at the cookhouse during the weekends we would often end up at Leon and Valerie's and have some huge feeds of chips. There are few people like Leon who are so obliging and he never complained at the amount of potatoes that Harold and I ate. Harold one could understand but I didn't contribute in any way to their household.

I was only sent to Port Stephens to hold the fort because a settlement teacher, Richard Fogerty, had just left and another had been recruited. But I still did a number of visits because it always, then and now, takes forever for new people to be employed and then deployed to the Islands.

There was a sense of community and probably more so at Port Stephens because it was like living on an island. It was so far south and the track was long and arduous from even the next farm, which was Fox Bay West. Anyway there would be table tennis tournaments and other club functions. The store was also one of the best on the West, probably only second to Fox Bay West. Most stores had the basics like booze with flour, sugar, jams and the like. Most stores you went to a counter and the storekeeper would get you what you asked for. At Port Stephens the products were on shelves and you could walk around like a very small supermarket.

I thoroughly enjoyed my time at Port Stephens – there was always something happening, always something to do. One day for instance a chinstrap penguin turned up on the shore and at that time the Robin Woods' book only named a couple of sightings of this penguin. Somebody helpfully caught the penguin and put it in a yard so that people could study it and I could get a picture. It is true that all my shots of this infrequent visitor are by a yard gate and lawn mower. Not exactly the bird's natural habitat.

I taught two children at Port Stephens. One was a young American boy called Eric of about six and Andrew Smith who must have been 14 going on 15 and couldn't wait to leave school and start to work. Eric was an education to me and highlighted the differences that we have in the English language. An example of this was when I got him to read and then discuss the picture as a way of developing his observation skills and he could see a perambulator. I just saw an ordinary mundane pram.

It gave me a simple pleasure to hear him reading *Peter and Jane* with his strongly accented, American English.

Eric's parents were Bahias. There were a number of people of this faith on the Islands at that time. Don was the father and he was the farm mechanic and he was teaching a young local lad (Tony Smith) the trade. The mother was Debbie. They seemed such quiet unassuming people to me.

Eventually the family arrived that was to make my trips to Port Stephens unnecessary. Clive Wilkinson the father was the first to arrive followed by Rosemary, the mother who was to take up the duties of settlement teacher. They brought with them three children to the school. Alistair, Robert and Dorothy.

I found it slightly awkward at first with the three additional children and with their mother teaching but I did my best at trying to show Rosemary what was expected of a settlement/camp teacher.

A trip to Weddell

I had done over a week and my departure was imminent when a trip to Weddell came up. Ted Dickson was going over in the Port Stephens motorboat and Harold, his son, was going as mate and I was also invited to go along. I saw this as a great opportunity for me to visit a place I had only been to before on the Beaver. It was also a great chance for Rosemary to fly solo at the school and then have the chance to ask me about any problems she may have had while I was still there. Once I left any kind of advice would be in the public domain.

The motorboat was in Fagan Inlet to the north of the settlement so on the day of the voyage we travelled over by Land Rover and rowed out in a small wooden dinghy to the boat. I remember Ted pumping out some water that did have me wondering where it had come from but not such a worry that I asked to be taken back to land.

Ted had lived in the Islands all his life and like so many was quite at home in these coastal waters. He was competent but also nervous and always on the lookout for orcas, which I suppose would have been as big as or bigger in some cases than the motorboat. In some respects this extra care was reassuring because if he had thought about killer whales he had obviously calculated the other dangers that we may encounter.

We had certainly picked the right day because there was hardly any wind and it was warm. The sea wasn't at all choppy but it wasn't flat calm either.

It was an uneventful voyage up apart from the scenery, which is pretty special in and around Port Stephens. So we arrived at the Weddell jetty and tied up and Harold and I went to explore the settlement. Ted went about his business with the then manager Bob Ferguson. I have no idea what that business was but it was probably something that they needed and that they had at Port Stephens or as we had made the trip it was possibly the other way round.

Harold and I bumped into Chum Binnie, an elderly chap, who was the cowman gardener at Weddell and was tending what looked like a very productive garden. It was considered to be an easier job than many in camp.

By and by Ted turned up back at the boat and it was time to leave. Bob and Thelma came to the jetty to bid their guests farewell. Thelma decided that Harold and I were mature adults and should have a kiss on the cheek and a gentle embrace, but Harold and I behaving a few years younger than our ages scrabbled to get under the awning at the front of the boat. Two red faces and some excruciatingly embarrassing air kisses later, we were heading back to Port Stephens.

Under the stewardship of Rosemary there had been no problems. I sat in half-heartedly the following day and left the next. It was a sad day leaving Port Stephens. I had enjoyed the adventure, including some amazing wildlife, especially over at the Peaks, where it was in abundance. The views of Indian Village looking over Ten Shilling Bay and the dramatic coast line with the tall sheer cliffs were totally amazing.

14 SEA LION ISLAND

Bird life

Sea Lion Island was one of the most remarkable places that I have ever seen. All this wealth of wildlife within a few minutes walk of the house couldn't be beaten anywhere else in the Islands. Elephant seals and hair seals galore, four types of penguins in large numbers. Every bird that you would see elsewhere, apart from albatross, bred on the Island. Night herons, cob's wren, tussock birds, Johnny rooks (striated caracara), king cormorant, rock shags, southern greater black-backed gulls, dolphin gulls, terns, southern giant petrels – the list goes on. On the ponds there were silvery grebe, chiloe wigeon and the many other types of duck.

In the spring and summer you would hear the continuous braying of the jackass penguins, particularly in the morning and at night, as they stood at the entrance to their burrows. On the first visit I thought I would never sleep through the din because the jackass burrows came right up and around the homestead. The braying of the jackass and the crashing of waves on the shore now always reminds me of Sea Lion Island even if I hear it in other parts of the Islands.

Living on Sea Lion Island

So in we would come and land on the pond and motor over to the west end where there was a little landing stage. The minute I stepped out of the plane and collected my luggage Marie would be filling me in on the happenings since my last visit. Where the bull was or wasn't. If the local ship, *The Monsunen*, had been. If they had had any visitors and she would chat, chat, chat, continuously bringing me up to date. The pond was at the far west and the house was three-quarters of the way down the Island close to the east so by the time we got back to the house I felt fully enlightened on what I had missed in my absence.

When Terry and Doreen bought Sea Lion Island, Terry was still managing Speedwell Island which involved not only looking after the sheep and settlement but working many of the smaller Islands in the Falkland Sound with the schooner *Ilen*, which Terry captained. In his holidays he started to do things on Sea Lion Island. The house was quite small and had two eaves originally, so it looked like two very small houses built beside each other. One of the first jobs Terry did was to put a roof with a single apex on with a chap called Nathaniel who Terry reckoned was a great craftsman who could cut joints to fit just by looking.

Terry was to make many improvements during the time I shared with them. He built a brick chimney, an extension for a kitchen and bathroom.

For me when I arrived it was pioneering stuff although to Terry, Doreen and family it was nothing special. The loo was outside in a small shed large enough for someone to sit and stand in. The loo seat was smooth wooden planking with a hole cut in it and below this was a 5-gallon oil can with the top cut off and a handle attached. This was carried away once it was full.

There wasn't much fresh water and because Sea Lion Island is so flat it is impossible to design a gravity-fed supply. Because of this, all of the house water was caught from the roof and stored in a 500-gallon tank, which stood beside the back door. This could be pumped by hand up to a 45-gallon drum situated just under the eaves of the house above the extension. All the time I was there the water supply was critical. Sea Lion Island had a microclimate of its own and didn't get a fraction of the rain that fell on the mainland. Terry tried many different ideas to win water from close at hand but the efforts were met with disappointment with most water being brackish and limited in use. This situation was solved once a tourist lodge was built many years later and a lot of money was invested in sorting the problem. The water was then pumped from a spring into tanks raised above the level of the buildings.

During the first few visits we would all have a thorough wash prior to going to bed for the night. There was a tin bath on the fence but all the time I lived there it was never used. There is no doubt that this kind of living brought people together but bathing in front of one another would certainly have taken our friendship to another level.

Even when the bathroom was finished one could never have a bath to wallow in up to the overflow, soaking for at least half an hour. Having a bath like that would have been a selfish act most of the time and at some periods would have made everyone short of water for some considerable time.

The tussock bird

Coming from the UK, a small amount of fat would have me gagging or thinking about that pending heart attack, but many Falkland Islanders enjoyed the fat along with the meat. At Sea Lion Island there were a number of big dense tussock plantations, which Terry managed to deliver quality feed to many of his stock. The fat on animals put there from eating tussock had a taste of its own and I found myself tucking into it with relish ignoring the possible downside of such a diet.

In the 1800s a ship brought the blue bottle (blue buzzer) to the Falklands and this fly has been the plague for keeping meat of any kind in the summer months. The wretched things can squeeze through the smallest of gaps too, so that they can deposit their eggs onto one's meat. These eggs in warm conditions soon become maggots and turn all meat into a heaving mass in days.

Not so at Sea Lion Island where they are gobbled up in an instant by the tussock bird who see them as a great culinary delicacy and have a huge appetite for them. Tussock birds thrive on the outer islands that don't have cats but the two don't seem able to live together. These birds are very tame and if you are sitting quietly they will come and sit by you and even on you. At Sea Lion Island they were everywhere in good numbers and so the meat that Terry kept in the shearing shed was guaranteed to be fly free as any brave fly had to fly the tussock bird gauntlet.

These little brown birds would hop into the house for crumbs although there was a negative slant to this because I never came across one that was house trained.

Exploring the island wildlife

I used to go walkabout usually with Marie and Boy, the farm's one and only working dog. We would walk all over viewing the many wonders on display. Marie used to use Boy as a walking aid hanging on to his collar for the entire trip. Boy was an old dog but he never seemed to mind his other job.

Although I enjoyed going for these walks as a gang of three I also liked time on my own to unwind which was difficult on a small one-family location. I got on really well with everyone but we were always in each other's face. There was not much downtime apart from the radio, which consisted of many repeats in the evenings. It hadn't taken me that long travelling to hear too many repeats of *The Clitheroe Kid.* For people that have been blessed by not having heard it, *The Clithero Kid* was a radio show about a supposed child always up to mischief played by a small man. There were some great classics however like *The Goons* and *Around the Horn* that were really good.

I would get up early on most days and wander down to the beach on the north or south side of the Island adjacent to the house, depending on the direction of the wind. On both sides there was a big sand beach covered at certain times of the year by a thousand elephant seals, (end of September/October time). It wasn't just the elephant seal but the business of the whole area with penguins coming in and out, birds scavenging for food on the shore or in front of the sea and many other activities. There was always something to see. On the south side there was a small bay below a dense tussock plantation on the northern perimeter. Elephant seals, whether they are up for breeding or moulting, were always scratching or shuffling grumpily around moving sand and exposing insects which the tussock birds would eat as they flitted among them.

On one particular day I was sitting on the bank on the south side watching seals chasing penguins in the breakers. They would swim in the wave so that they were crystal clear to see from the shore. I was thinking about seals and how graceful and what strong swimmers they are when a Johnny rook (striated caracara), a large bird of prey known for their mischief, grabbed the hat from my head. Because I was thinking about seals I assumed I was being attacked by one so I bolted forward falling and leaping up at least three times to escape from a figment of my imagination.

I was lucky in some respects because Johnny rooks are renowned for stealing stuff including valuable cameras, clothing, and tent pegs. In fact, anything that they can fly off with, and on many occasions never to be seen again, but this bird had got such a great response from me that he dropped my hat as a reward.

The striated caracara is one of the rarest birds of prey in the world with a significant proportion of their total numbers living on the Falkland Islands. Many farmers are less than impressed with this fact, especially the ones that have a stronghold of them on their property. These birds are well known for their vivacious appetite and that includes lambs Again, well before such sophisticated entertainment like video and today's TV, people had to find other stuff to amuse themselves and the Johnny rook was a good candidate to have some fun with.

A favourite pastime was to tie a big rugged alarm clock to an anchor point with something that a Johnny rook couldn't bite through, snap or undo. Then you set the alarm to go off after a few minutes. The whole set-up would be situated by a window for all to see the action. A big shiny thing left unattended was more than these birds could resist and down they would come and take turns at trying to fly off with the clock. They would then fight over it, each trying to pull it from the other. They would be creating a hell of a commotion when the alarm would go off. They would all stop for a few seconds before rolling their heads from side to side in a most comical way as if they were figuring out some unsolvable problem.

These birds were big and substantial. Terry used to have a wind charger for charging 12-volt batteries. It had a single wooden blade like a small plane's propeller on a shaft that drove an alternator. One day during a reasonable amount of wind, a Johnny rook flew into the blade, whether it was curiosity or a misjudgement we will never know, but the propeller was totalled, split along its length. If it had been a gull for instance there would have been a cloud of feathers and not any dip in the charging performance.

I used to like going to see the rockhopper penguins that lived at the west end of the island on the south-facing cliffs. To get there you had to run the gauntlet of the Antarctic skua, a bird with a short, stubby and heavy body with long, wide pointed wings.

The skua, locally called sea hens, would lay two eggs in a small depression in the short grass. At the west end of Sea Lion Island there were hundreds of pairs crammed into a very short area. Each pair would defend their small patch from all comers. Once that egg was laid they defended these territories with plenty of determination, aggression and actual violence. The greater the length of time the egg was incubated and then as the chick grew bigger and the parent investment greater, these birds ratcheted up the 'defence of' in relation to the time and effort they had put in.

As you approached a territory the birds would fly up to gain some height and swoop in, coming within six foot. It was like, 'I would like you to give me your full attention'. If you carried on they would come in lower and if you approached the nest or chick they would come in at chest height. At this stage both parents would be coming in like fighter command. Some people say you shouldn't duck because that makes them come in even lower, which is true to a point but I have seen some individuals with some awesome welts where the birds have hit them, which were caused by that strategy.

Up on Bull Hill there isn't any area where it isn't skua territory and you are continuously leaving one pair's domain and moving into another. I used to hold a fencing baton above my head when I was in that neck of the woods and this would stop them hitting you although not the stick.

For shepherds gathering on horseback in these areas, which mainly occurred on islands, this could be a nightmare. These birds would attack the horses, the dogs and the rider. The horse naturally would get slightly nervous and this would be compounded as the dogs found shelter under the horse's legs.

Back to the rockies. The rockhopper is a feisty little guy, not very big but absolutely fearless. For some reason, probably security, rockhoppers have their rookeries at the top of cliffs and at Sea Lion Island it was at the top of a little less than 100 feet. These small penguins have a precarious path that they use to get to the top and their nests. Once on land they hop with both legs moving as one to get up the cliff face. These birds have been scrabbling up these cliffs for so many years that they have worn a pathway.

The gentoo usually nests off a sand beach or a gently sloping beach. He comes zipping out of the surf and walks up to his colony, and likewise with the kings and jackass although the latter can have a fair journey to their burrow.

I used to sit at the top and just to one side of the rockies' thoroughfare watching their efforts in returning to their nest site. They would congregate in a big group just off the shore preening and splashing around and I presume waiting for their turn to try and get a foothold on their slope. About a dozen at a time would make an attempt. If it was blowing from the south there were times when it was just about impossible to gain a successful landing. I have been there in rough weather when the success rate has been small but even so there was still a steady trickle up to the summit.

Success was all about timing and vigour and also being on the biggest wave out of several. If they came in on a large wave they had to jump onto the rocks at its peak height which was a good start but then on landing they had to hop like hell, especially if the following wave was of any size because if it was there was a good chance that the climbers would be washed back into the sea. On the attempted landing and the initial climb I have seen these penguins bouncing off the rocks sailing through the air like proper birds but seemingly come to no harm and be ready for the next go.

I have sat for hours watching and willing these birds to succeed and return to their mates and their chicks. There is something really engaging about their tenacity, their determination and their difficult lifestyle.

King cormorants are also worth a mention. They are quite big birds, 29 inches from the tip of his beak to the end of the tail. They have bright blue eyes and an orange caruncle at the back of the top beak. They are into heavy industry when it comes to their nests and at the height of this period they are plucking out acres of this short prickly grass to construct their nests. They collect other material as well and at times it is quite comical to see these birds flying back to their nests with a huge amount of material in their beaks. These rookeries, just like those of the non-burrowing penguins, are not exactly an example of best bird manners and etiquette. There is one, season long, squabble with any passing bird and surrounding neighbour.

Terry and Speedwell Island

Terry was a great storyteller and had many tales to tell of running Speedwell Island as the manager and the other islands of that group with *The Ilen*. These islands belonged to the Falkland Island Company.

One of these stories was about a horse that someone had shut in the shearing shed pens on one of the smaller islands. These small pens that have lots of sheep through them in a short amount of time green up really well and produce some good food but not nearly enough to keep a horse going for any length of time. This horse had eaten the area bare and reached out to crop everything down on the other side of the fence as well. The horse had even chewed the wood on the pens.

Terry wondered (probably knew) who could have been cruel enough to shut an animal in in this manner knowing it would starve to death or be desperately hungry before it was found. So he took pity on this horse and let it out and began handling it. It got hand-tame and Terry thought having saved its life and handling it they were building up a rapport and so he eventually geared it up and began to ride it.

Ingratitude reigned with this animal and whatever Terry tried the horse wasn't prepared to repay his debt and didn't want him on his back. Not that it would buck or shy but it would throw itself down every time he went to mount it. Terry was a great exponent of winning a battle of wills so he tried all the tricks he could think of and the suggestions of colt tamers on other farms to try and outwit his adversary.

Nothing succeeded and after time he realised, although never sympathised, at how this animal had become shut in the pens. In a way, it was the horse's loss because there wasn't room for emotion on these farms and every animal had to contribute to the farm in some way.

These were hard times and some may feel brutal but then we are looking at things from a completely new era. People didn't have endless time and energy to perfect kinder ways of breaking horses or training dogs because the rest of their lives were busy with a five-and-a-half-day week and the living jobs.

For many years dogs just ran free around the outside house or settlements. It must have been pretty intimidating on some of the bigger farms with all the dogs running loose. Then it was discovered that dogs passed on hydatid cysts to humans, laws were brought in to eradicate the disease. One of the laws made it illegal for dogs to run loose and all offal had to be disposed of so that dogs couldn't get access to it. The dogs themselves were given a drug called Droncit once every six weeks.

For owners with a lot of dogs that had never been confined it was a huge job to get them into their kennels and cages. They would be okay the first time but once they knew that their liberty was at stake they would have been hard to catch, especially the older animals.

Terry had a large stroppy dog that had many years of doing what it liked outside sheep work and didn't want to be confined in kennels at home on Speedwell Island or on every island where they worked. So Terry wanted this wilful dog to go to his kennel and this dog, in equal measure, didn't want to oblige. When push came to shove the dog sunk his teeth into Terry. Then Terry would be chasing said dog around half the night manhandling him into his kennel without being bitten and after a long day at work, particularly when working the smaller islands, things were wearing a little thin.

Terry had to get the dog to go to its bed but without the struggle. So Terry chained the dog to its kennel and got his stock whip. Of course Terry told a good story but I am sure there were elements of truth in his yarn. Terry said his arm was getting tired and the dog was still refusing to budge and he was just considering changing hands when the dog went into the kennel and Terry was able to shut the door.

Terry reckoned from that day it didn't matter where the dog was or what time of day or night, when he opened the kennel door the dog would arrive so quickly that you would hear it hitting the back of the kennel.

I can't see many people taking this kind of severe action today probably because animal welfare has improved generally and animals see a greater number of visitors on the whole, however I can't imagine people calling in the animal psychiatrist either to deal with their dog 'issues.'

Sedge Island and the Gulch

Sea Lion Island was one of the smallest islands that was farmed full time. There was one smaller island, which was Sedge, which is to the north of Saunders and Carcass off the north coast of the West Falklands. Compared to all other Falklands farms Sea Lion Island had the highest stocking rate, the highest wool per sheep and the best lambing figures and the wethers (castrated male sheep) must have been some of the biggest; ask anyone that had loaded mutton into the sea truck at the Gulch. And yet this level of domestic animals didn't have an adverse affect on the more-than-abundant wildlife.

The Gulch is worth mentioning because it was a natural gap in the cliffs on the north coast of the island. It was not quite as far as the pond that the Beaver landed on but probably three-quarters of the way there. This place was just big enough to receive the sea-truck from the local vessel comfortably. It also had an eight foot or so rock shelf on to which you could load and off load stores. At the inward end there was a wooden slide, which was hinged in the middle so when not in use it could be pulled up out of the way of any destructive wave action. On the slide was a tray attached to a rope that worked off an old capstan, drum-type winch on the front of a vintage Land Rover. All the stores were winched effortlessly up the slide by this method. It was totally low tech, cheap to build, low maintenance and lasted for years with reasonable care.

The fuel was piped ashore to a tank that sat on the shore to the west of the Gulch where there weren't cliffs. Before this drums were off-loaded at the Gulch and pulled up the ramp.

Living on the smaller islands could always be more challenging than on the east or west mainland and it was even harder for more remote Islands like Sea Lion Island and Sedge Island. The coastal vessel would often skip the visit if conditions weren't perfect and being out in the South Atlantic away from the shelter of the main islands they seldom were ideal.

I didn't visit the Gulch on a daily basis but I saw enough of this place to know that it was only the most violent storms that breached the huge barriers of kelp that surrounded this area. It was a natural harbour that could have been utilised far more in mediocre conditions.

Dog versus penguin

I returned after my rounds one day to be informed that Boy had gone to the great sheep farm in the sky to chase sheep and to drag an endless number of children on mini expeditions. Boy's replacement was a bitch with a lot of white and a few dark patches. Because Terry only had one dog it had to be at least good and Terry was lucky enough to get a bitch that could get the job done.

I emphasise again that this dog could work sheep okay but she did have a very bad fault that got worse over time and finally even with her good sheep working attributes Terry had to find her a new home.

The bitch's problem was that she couldn't stand jackass penguins. She would walk or run through a thousand gentoo or rockhoppers in pursuit of her duties but if she saw one jackass the red mist would descend.

No one seemed to know whether it was the way that they went down their holes, a bit rabbit-like, that she couldn't stand but if this happened anywhere near her she would forget the sheep, go down the hole and drag the thing to the surface and kill it. Jackass penguins are no push over and have a hefty and powerful beak, but this dog had its skill honed down to a fine art and as there must have been hundreds of thousands on Sea Lion Island this dog had a lifetime's work eradicating them.

At first the dog would be side-tracked but you knew that after a kill she would be back onside for some more sheep work. As time went on, however, she had to kill more and more before she could settle down for the day's farm work.

It all came to a head when the Cliftons had visitors staying with them and the dog slipped its chain and went off to perfect its murdering technique.

As we all left the house to go and look at the marvellous wildlife the bitch comes over the hill just smothered in blood. Fortunately, these guests were local and aware that these things happen but more and more people were hearing about Sea Lion Island and wanting to visit and who would probably struggle to be so magnanimous.

Many moons before I was born, let alone teaching in the Falklands, a man got so desperate living on Sea Lion Island that he made a raft out of two 45-gallon drums and sailed over to Bull Point seven miles away. The guy must have been very lonely or completely bonkers.

In the house on the west wall or the east wall of my room was a piece of bagging pulled really tight, fastened in place and painted instead of the conventional hardboard. You couldn't tell it wasn't hardboard like the rest of the house unless you were told where it was. The hardboard that the bagging replaced had been used to make a coffin for someone that had gone crazy years ago and killed himself.

Gardens and wildlife

Back to my experiences on the Island takes us to the gardens about 400 yards from the house in a bit of a fold in the landscape. It was pretty special – not like the location at Keppel – because it was on an east-facing slight slope and had a hedge around some of it and in outward appearance it was pretty ordinary. Production wise this garden was pretty phenomenal and produced vegetables of all kinds. The secret to this was Terry carting home the pots that shags build to lay their eggs in, along with a healthy amount of guano. Dug into the garden it was as good as any commercial fertiliser.

Another traveller, Robin Montague, went to New Island, which he said was better than Sea Lion Island, and we used to compare notes. I am sure in the wildlife stakes Sea Lion Island was heads and shoulders in front for accessible wildlife in such a small area although to be fair New Island had far better scenery.

Sadly, in my opinion, Sea Lion Island is no longer farmed but there is a tourist lodge where people pay to come and see the very special wildlife. Some of the staff live in that cosy farmhouse which Terry did so much to make into a comfortable home. Beside the lodge, less than 100 yards away, is an all-weather airstrip constructed by a bulldozer which stripped all the soil off down to the clay and shale.

Revisiting Sea Lion Island

The last time I was on Sea Lion Island was with Toni. I visited with my mother and our long-term family friend Fran. The latter two were visiting so we thought we would accompany them. Toni reluctantly came because her motion sickness makes any flying torture. It was meant to be a short flight but things got changed and the plane ended up flying to another place on the East and then an extra landing on the West before going to Sea Lion Island.

As we flew over Bodie Creek Bridge just a few miles west of Goose Green and twenty-five minutes into the fight, Toni started on her first sick bag and I opened a second in anticipation.

By the time we got to Sea Lion Island, Toni was feeling grim and as we were signing off the flying particulars with the pilot Toni had staggered to the edge of the runway and collapsed.

We all manhandled Toni the few yards to the lodge and were shown our rooms. They were asking Toni if she wanted tea or coffee but Toni, by this time, was past caring and I just told them to leave her and after a few hours we should be able to welcome her back to the living.

It has always been great returning to Sea Lion Island, but the freedom that I enjoyed has vanished along with the fact that I now have to pay along with everyone else.

The wildlife is still very special but the memory of those days with Terry, Doreen, Janet and Marie will always live on as part of that special, fantastic experience.

15. SPEEDWELL ISLAND

Life on Speedwell Island

I did visit one other island at the bottom of the Falkland Sound – Speedwell. I think I made three visits. The Larsen family lived on Speedwell Island. Ronnie and Yvonne with their daughters Josie and Jane. They had another grown-up daughter Betty who lived at North Arm.

I taught Josie who was months away from leaving school. Jane was too young to go to school.

While I was on Speedwell Island a Royal Marine went missing at North Arm. It is all a bit of a mystery even to this day although there are many theories as to what happened. Divers went out from town to search the sea around the North Arm Jetty and members of the North Arm community searched the beaches in the area but nothing was found. It was suggested that there was a bit of a disagreement or even a brawl at the end of an evening in the club.

The thing that I found strange from a far was that the local vessel, *The Forrest*, that transported the marines around the Falklands had left the jetty and was on its way before anyone realised someone was missing. *The Forrest* isn't very big and you would have thought the others would have known straight away that he was missing before they left. Sadly for the mother and families nothing has ever come to light to explain what happened.

Another memorable event was that a big buoy about the size of a motorboat turned up off the back of the Island after a big storm. It obviously had an anchor or something attached to stop it coming ashore but it bobbed about off Speedwell Island for a number of months. It did make me think of some of the single-handed or even any small vessel that sailed in these waters and what would happen if they collided with something like this. Even the two local vessels would not be too big to be badly damaged if they ran into something that size.

Green Patch and Rincon Grande

I spent more time on the West as a travelling teacher but I completed my contract with a flourish on the East with Green Patch and Rincon Grande and I was meant to go to Salvador but ran out of time.

I landed in the Beaver at Green Patch and among the people meeting the plane was a grizzled chap who looked ferocious. His name was Jimmy Sorensen In fact, if I had seen him in a bar anywhere in the world I would have given him a wide berth. It turned out that he was the complete opposite and he was a good-natured, amiable man who was quick to make friends. Back in the 1970s it was only the farm managers, high officials and a handful of others that had a modern Land Rover. Everyone else resurrected the hand-me-downs.

Raymond (Tech) Newman had made a new chassis for Jimmy's Series 1 out of an old square galvanised water tank. Tech had meticulously copied the shapes and measurements from the old chassis, cut them out of this tank and welded them together.

Jimmy Sorensen, asked me to accompany him on his maiden trip from Green Patch to Port Louis. The settlements are fairly close and the track was pretty good so we tanked our way around.

Green Patch had just become the first farm to be bought from an absentee landlord by the Falkland Island Government, subdivided into family-farm sized chunks and sold off to local buyers. The Murrell was sold to Tim Miller and Claude Molkenbuhr. This farm was just outside Stanley but had a hell of a track plus a river crossing to get there. Neil and Glenda Watson got Long Island, Jock and June McPhee got Brookfield, Peter and Maggie Goss got Horse Shoe Bay, Tony and Ailsa Heathman got the Estancia and Terence and Carol Phillips got Mount Kent. Finally looking after the government's interests was Tech, Raymond Newman.

The sale and move hadn't been completed while I was there teaching but there was a lot of excitement in the air from the new farmers who had many new ideas and a lot of enthusiasm and some felt sure that they were going to revolutionise farming.

Last but by no means least I went to Rincon Grande. Rincon was a modest-sized family farm that had, at one time, employed a small gang. There were four houses on the property. Two at Foam Creek, which included a fairly new cookhouse and two at the top settlement, which included the family home of Ron, Diana, Arthur and Andrea Turner. The top settlement was up on a small hill and the Turner's house had a room with glass on three sides that had a panoramic view for miles around.

I lived at the cottage at Foam Creek and was supplied with the basics like tea, coffee, sugar, bread and biscuits and buns and general stores. There was also alcohol. This was as close as you could get to utopia as a travelling teacher. I fended for myself for breakfast and supper and went to lunch with everyone in the middle of the day.

As luck would have it the mushrooms were starting to appear which complemented my lazy culinary ambitions. Breakfast was sorted as I would get up early and leisurely pick enough mushrooms for one or two slices of toast. Brilliant.

Lunch was always entertaining. I would go up to the top settlement with the children and Diana would give me a beer or a gin and tonic and the tots were not miserable and on many an afternoon nor was I.

I probably can't put into words the satisfaction I got from this arrangement.

Compared to some of the places that I had visited, Rincon might have seemed fairly quiet and uninspiring but I didn't feel it that way at all. Combined with all the enthusiasm that permeated from all the new farmers at Green Patch, Rincon was probably the catalyst that had me returning to the Falklands, meeting Toni and ultimately remaining in the Falklands and making my life here.

Diana asked me to come back and work for her, teaching Arthur and Andrea full time and so after an end of tour leave in the UK I packed my bags and headed back to the Islands.

Moving on

When I first arrived in the Islands to work for the Falkland Island Government I had a choice of a two-year contract or three. With a three-year contract you got a mid-tour leave. People on these contracts had to make that decision after six months. The three-year option appealed to me because of the possibility of detouring back to the UK via South America. So with a colleague, Robin Montague, we planned a grand tour of South America and the Caribbean.

Like many things in the 1970s, in the Falklands, something that looks simple turns out to be a complicated issue. I was proposing to do something radical. I wanted to use the money from my flight home to partially fund this epic extravaganza with me making up the difference. I wasn't asking for more money just to be able to use theirs' differently but still using it as intended to get me home although not directly. You would have thought I'd asked to do something immoral or outrageous or was going to spend it on drugs the fuss that was made. It seemed such a waste to just fly home when I was on the doorstep of such interesting countries that I wanted to explore. I couldn't afford to fund it myself either. The job as a travelling teacher was amazing in experience terms but financially it was poorly paid. Even a navvy working on the farms could earn more without too much effort.

Bill Luxton, the part owner and manager of Chartres, was also a councillor. There were children from three families at Chartres that I taught. I would have my meals with each family in turn on each of my visits. As Bill and Pat's son Stephen was at school I would have meals with the Luxtons every three visits that I made to Chartres. I did happen to mention my dilemma to Bill and fortunately he was quite supportive recognising how silly it all was and lobbied on my behalf. With Bill on my side I was allowed to go on mid-tour leave via South America and the Caribbean.

16. SOUTH AMERICAN INTERLUDE

Arriving in Comodoro Rivadavia

A fellow camp teacher, Robin Montague and I had been planning this trip for a while. For Robin this was the end of his contract, for me it was a halfway point.

So travelling with speed in mind, which is light in luggage terms, we left. Not on the ultra-safe F27, but the recent upgrade of the F28 which was a jet, and headed back to Comodoro Rivadavia.

There did seem to be a different atmosphere in Comodoro from eighteen months ago. Young, heavily armed conscripts in ill-fitting uniforms swaggering around with lethal-looking weapons swinging about in the sloppiest and most casual manner one could imagine. As a Brit that isn't used to seeing anyone armed, especially kids in 'macho mode', looking as though they were starring in a Rambo movie, it was alarming to say the least.

God knows if these guns ever went off accidentally. If I were to guess, I would say that they must have done.

There was more than a little tension over three Islands in the Beagle Channel, at the tip of South America Picton, Lennox and Nueva. Argentina and Chile both claimed them and it looked as if Argentina was prepared to use force to settle the issue. They were also having internal problems.

So we spent an evening in Comodoro Rivadavia and had a nice steak supper and a couple of bottles of vino. We spent the night in a very cheap and cheerful establishment before heading off to find the Angel de Giobby coach company's booking office the next morning.

Robin had diligently learnt Spanish through some kind of correspondence course. I, suffering from ignorance, hadn't bothered, thinking I could get through by gesticulating and if all else failed shouting English in a slow, loud and clear manner. For all Robin's work no one seemed to understand a word he was saying which I meanly thought was extremely funny.

So there we were at the front of the queue at the Angel de Giobby booking office with Robin scratching out his Spanish and me thinking it was highly amusing. The queue was getting longer and longer behind us. If we had been able to speak Spanish we might have been able to hear the abuse directed at these English people holding up the proceedings. Before it all turned nasty, an English speaker came out of the masses and told the man behind the desk what we wanted and then told us where to catch the coach. We had taken another step on our South American adventure.

Travelling by coach

Imagine an antiquated vehicle with the windscreen cracked in a number of places and a number of the side widows too. Then think rough and times it by at least five.

So we climbed aboard this dilapidated, geriatric old banger and headed out of Comodoro Rivadavia. It wasn't that far before we were on dirt roads flying along at breakneck speed throwing up a huge cloud of dust behind. These buses stopped for nothing and hardly slowed down as we bombed through the scrubland of Patagonia. Having said that, the buses were constantly stopped by the military and even these drivers would stop when the alternative would have been a hail of bullets.

On the soldiers would come and ask for your documents. We were in fact travelling through the interior of Argentina not only when they were threatening their neighbours but during their internal troubles when tens of thousands of Argentines vanished. Ignorance is bliss because if we had known the full details of these atrocities we would have had many an arse-clenching moment, but although it was disconcerting we treated it as a bit of a joke.

I believe that many of these Argentine conscripts were illiterate. None of them recognised the white card that we, from the Falklands, were supposed to show. At first when the authorities didn't recognise the white card I got out my British passport, which seemed to confuse them even more and they would become quite excitable. I didn't understand the length and breadth of the excitable Argentine demeanour then but now I know a bit more they could just have been saying 'so why didn't you just show me your British passport in the first place? I've just lost ten minutes of *maté* time.' (*Yerba maté* was a popular herbal drink that you make in a gourd and sucked up through a thick metal straw called a *bombilla*.)

So we charged on through the famous Patagonia and saw a few rhea and some skinny cattle but not much more. Health and safety hadn't reached this coach company because outside the military checks it was pedal to the metal regardless of any bad road surface or tight bend.

There were two drivers who took it in turns to drive, but when it was time for a changeover they didn't slow down and pull into a café or even a lay-by. The driver taking over would stroll down from the back and position himself behind the driver. The driver would stand up allowing the new driver to sit in the driving seat. Then with the ultimate goal of not letting the throttle off at all, the driver taking over would slide his foot over as the retiring driver slipped his foot off. The accelerator wasn't allowed to come out of the depression in the floor, made from many years of it being kept firmly down. The chap that had just been relieved would make his way to the back of the bus to drink some *maté* and perhaps later have a doze. The driving time for each driver was about two hours.

The driver change was well practised and clearly commonplace. It didn't matter if we were tearing down a hill or flying around a corner like a speedway bike; if it was time to change, the change happened. The regulars on the bus didn't even have a break in conversation or seem to tense or brace themselves for the pending impact. I say, no one, but two camp teachers from the Falklands who had endured the trials and tribulations of FIGAS were sitting as white as sheets, hanging on for grim death, bracing, sweating and showing every symptom of being terrified.

The broken windows of the bus didn't need any explanation after a few miles on the dirt roads and it wasn't only the coach drivers that were speed merchants with no inclination to slow down. As all manner of vehicles passed one another at breakneck speed stones and debris were thrown up and pebble dashed each other. There was no point replacing the windows until they fell in at the driver's feet.

Poor old Robin had suffered long periods of constipation in the Falklands due to the large meat content of the diet and had to take laxatives on and off for his entire tour in the Islands. A couple of days in the hands of the safety conscious Angel de Diobby staff and the problem was solved.

After our two nights at Esquel we passed into the caring hands of the Don Otto coach operation and although their coaches were newer and more comfortable it was the same approach when it came to driving skills.

From Esquel to Mendoza

The plains of Patagonia seemed pretty samey – dusty, dry and flat, semi-desert plains – but as we approached the Andes the vegetation became lush and rich in diversity.

We stopped at different places on our journey but we eventually made Bariloche, which was very spectacular with amazing views over the Andes. A world-famous skiing resort in the winter but in the middle of the summer the ski lifts sat miles away from any snow. It was very touristy which was a slight surprise.

Mendoza was the end of the line for our coach trip in Argentina. We came into this city and noticed huge drainage ditches beside all the roads. We got out at the depot and caught a taxi to a hotel that we picked out of our South American handbook. The driver must have been an ex-Don Otto bus driver because he was another speed king. In the confines of town he seemed suicidal. He didn't seem to recognise road signs or have a smidgen of road sense. On approaching red traffic lights, he didn't register that this meant stop – although I had witnessed in Buenos Aires that a red light was only advisory.

Anyway, funny old thing, there must have been a green light for road users crossing the other way. Bang!! We ploughed into a large North American car and, surprise, surprise, the driver didn't seem best pleased. Instead of our driver saying 'whoops, I'm having a bad day,' he went on the offensive. As Robin was complaining about his hurt knee the protagonists began to get very emotional which really suggested it was time for us to get uninvolved.

A passer-by, who could speak a bit of English, picked us up and took us to a hotel. He was a local and congratulated us on making such a great choice in holidaying in Mendoza because it never rains here.

It had to have been this bloke's idea of a joke, not only because he picked us up from amongst the debris of a road accident, but that night the heavens opened and it rained torrential rain, thunder and lightning for well over twelve hours. The reason for the ditches alongside the road were suddenly self-explanatory, from being bone dry when we arrived to being raging torrents in danger of overflowing when we left. If anyone or anything were to fall into these ditches while they were full you wouldn't expect to see them or it again.

From Mendoza to Santiago

We caught the Trans-Andean railway from Mendoza to Santiago, although it stopped short of Santiago. It was an amazing trip, winding its way through the mountainsides and passes. A lot of the track on the side of the steepest mountains had fabricated tunnels to protect the track and the rolling stock from rock and snow avalanches.

A road followed the same route. The views were stunning with the train passing Aconcagua, the tallest mountain in the Andes.

I have already mentioned the tension that was building between the Argentines and the Chileans and there were troops of both countries massed on either side of the borders. It was interesting to witness the attitudes of the two opposing armies as we passed through them. The Argentines looked fairly ragbag and undisciplined, wolf-whistling and waving and shouting out comments to the women on the train. Robin's Spanish once again let us down at this point because he could not decipher what they were shouting, but I think we both had a jolly good idea.

The Chileans were far more serious. There wasn't any acknowledgement of the train let alone its contents. Argentina is a bigger country than Chile, but looking at the two armies I know who I'd have my money on.

Robin felt that if it did come to war it would be short-lived, as once the casualties started pouring in the South American psyche would kick in and they would call it a day. This view might have been a sweeping statement but the good thing is that the two countries didn't come to blows. Chile ended up getting the sovereignty of the islands in question, because after the Falklands war Argentina had lost the appetite for battle. Had Argentina won the 1982 war it is clear that they wouldn't have settled so amicably.

We caught a taxi out of Santiago to the airport and slept on the floor until our planes departure the following day.

To Bolivia

Next stop was La Paz in Bolivia where we landed on the highest international airport in the world. We stayed in a hotel in a very steep street in La Paz. Robin suffered slightly from altitude sickness and felt breathless, but I remained unaffected.

The next day we were off towards Lake Titicaca on another South American coach. That night, for whatever reason, I got restless leg and have suffered ever since from this malady. I felt sorry for Robin trying to sleep, with me twitching and moving and never still next to him.

We arrived at Lake Titicaca, the legendary inland sea. As we drove along its shores we saw so many things that we hadn't seen before. It was strange to us but just everyday living for the people who lived there. One thing of special note were the boats made of reeds.

We eventually got off the coach in a small town on the shores of the lake. We had always travelled expecting things to fall into place so we didn't forward book and everything had worked out well up until then. This was where it all went wrong and we trudged around unable to find a room anywhere. We had arrived during a festival week and all the rooms were full.

We were just beginning to think we might have to rough it when a German chap with rather good English and Spanish turned up to make us Brits look second-rate. He suggested that if we were prepared to share a room, some enterprising soul bent on making money would find a spare one. It's not just at football that the Germans show us up, but also our other frailties and annoyingly he was right. This meant we had a roof over our heads and the manager had some extra money in his hand. It was very cramped, without any privacy, but it beat a park bench or the shore of the lake.

The German's name was Gertram, which he told us means raven of the battlefield. I think this name was wasted on him really because he was a podgy middle-aged gent who worked on the German railways. A less battle-like individual is hard to visualise.

In the spirit of European unity and setting aside the fact that Gertram was a smart ass, knew at least three languages and had come up with all the bright ideas, we all went out on the town.

We had an enormous plateful of meat and veg including boiled onions, all washed down with copious amounts of Bolivian wine and a dessert that I have forgotten. What I do remember was the bill. It was a couple of quid. I couldn't eat another thing, I was nicely intoxicated and the cost was minuscule. It must have been the cheapest bought meal of the entire holiday if not my whole life.

Then the most bizarre thing happened. We met up with a high-ranking Bolivian army officer who invited us as tourists to join him at his table. We got talking about where we came from and a number of different things before he delivered the kind of bombshell that few people in Europe would admit to even if they had thought it. He told us that Hitler and the Hitler Youth were admired in Bolivia and how they had thought of forming a youth movement of their own along similar lines.

Poor old Gertram did his best to condemn Hitler but for our part it was rather half-hearted and lacked conviction, but in hindsight it would have been difficult for him to satisfy two Englishmen without offending the host.

By the time we had left the restaurant we had between us probably drunk enough wine to float a small inflatable.

The evening had been so strange that more than once I had to pinch myself to make sure it was real. Robin had also done some thinking about our strange discussions and as the light was switched off slurred out an ill-natured 'Auschwitz!'

We recovered enough the following day to do a touristy excursion to the Island of the Sun on the lake. We scanned every inch of beach and shallow to spot one of the two-foot long gigantic toads that live there.

Totally clueless, we sat as the tour guides told us to be back by a certain time so that we didn't miss our boat back. We were asking each other, 'What time? What did she say?' Help was at hand. Yet another helpful German was able to translate from one language to another without using his native tongue. He told us in North American English, 'The lady says to be back at the boat by two thirty.' God, did I feel inadequate.

To Peru

It wasn't long before we were back on a coach heading for Peru, and eventually Lima, to catch our plane to Venezuela.

Bolivia is a very poor country and there was a large rural population going about their business as we drove by. People leading pigs on pieces of rope, houses made of mud and straw. It all looked rather basic but then in that climate do you really need something elaborate?

The woman of this region wore bowler hats and carried their children on their backs in a kind of sling. They were very proud people and hated having their pictures taken, even if it was with a telephoto lens. They would scowl if a lens were pointed in their general direction. In the markets women would allow you to take pictures for a couple of dollars. Woman would stand around spinning wool from sheep and alpaca's wool with a mushroom-shaped piece of wood that they would spin in their hands. They made many things with this wool, such as hats, jumpers and mats on which were pictures of topical animals and other things. I bought a few souvenirs for members of my family. I got a jumper with lamas on for my father and a drinking hat with pieces that fold down over your ears.

Our coach stopped off at Cusco, Peru, and we stayed there for a few days. I found it a truly incredible place with markets and street vendors all ready to haggle and make that special deal. Or so they say. Haggling is not something I am comfortable with although I have tried when on holiday, it is just a different way of looking at things. I haggled for an armadillo guitar and a set of bolas and a couple more woollen garments for presents.

We went and viewed some of the stonework that the Incas were responsible for. Large stones were made to fit together with precision that beggars belief. How did they manage it if they only had bronze tools?

We went to a place over-looking Cusco where there are some large stones cleverly worked together. The view over Cusco was also distinct, with the sight of clay tiles on every house disappearing into the distance.

We paid to go to a traditional Inca dance show one night. I was enjoying it but a North American redneck got up after a few minutes declaring loudly how he wasn't sitting through this rubbish. He'd obviously been weaned on *Dynasty*, *Dallas* and *Deputy Dog* and other such entertainment. Okay, it did need a little polish, but it wasn't bad enough to deserve that kind of response.

We did a day's run by train from Cusco to Machu Picchu. It was really slow on a single track with a place to pass halfway along. Machu Picchu just has to be seen, but there is also a smaller place higher up which wasn't as sophisticated but raised so many questions – particularly why?

These ruins weren't discovered until early in the 19th century. It is interesting again to notice some of the fine-dressed stonework in parts of the ruin and the more basic construction in others.

I found Peru intriguing and special with a high percentage of indigenous people compared to people of European decent, and some of the rural scenes were very appealing to me.

Lima, however, was a grotty place and the water in such a big city had a dirty musty smell to it. I didn't feel any cleaner after a shower in our hotel. We were careful what we ate and that had stood us in good stead. We had to be careful because Imodium hadn't been invented yet or if it had it hadn't got to the Falklands.

For some reason we went to double check our flights out of Lima. No, we didn't have a flight even though we did have our tickets saying we had seats. So we refused to accept that we didn't have seats and they did their best to persuade us that we hadn't. This went on for hours and we were beginning to get quite worried. Eventually a chap came up to us and said that he would be the pilot of the plane and that he was confirming our flight. I can only assume that they wanted some kind of backhander but we were clueless. Where was Gertram, or some other helpful German, when we really needed one to explain what was going on?

To Venezuela

Our next place to visit was Venezuela. We flew from Peru to Caracas. We did think about going to Colombia but most people we had spoken to had had bad experiences there or knew someone that had, so we gave it a miss.

The hotel we had chosen was not grand but modest and clean and its greatest asset was a bar by a swimming pool. After living in the Falklands where you are dressed up most of the time in warm clothes it seemed strange but nice to be lounging around the pool in our swimming trunks drinking the odd beer.

We must have been scruffy buggers that looked out of place in the hotel environment because some of our fellow guests called the police to have us removed from the hotel pool. Another bizarre experience where at first we didn't have a clue what these police/security people wanted, but eventually the penny dropped that they were trying to heave us out of our legitimate home. We showed them our hotel key, which solved the problem.

To Barbados

From Venezuela we flew up to Barbados for a few days. We flew in on a small but modern turbo prop of about 30–40 passengers via a number of islands. Some of the runways were in challenging locations. My appetite for flying had been shot by then and no one could describe the approaches to some of these island runways as slow, gradual and straight. It was Captain Bob-type, tight banking, flop down and then hard reverse thrust and braking.

We got off in Barbados and were challenged by the immigration officials. Have you got an address where you are staying and how long, where is your flight ticket out? etc. They seemed more worried about people coming into the islands, sleeping and living rough than they were about any contraband.

Anyway, the Barbadian accent is very strong and I stood there like a clown unable to understand my native tongue. I don't know if they thought I was being deliberately obtuse but they began to get slightly irritated. Fortunately, between Robin – who hadn't had a course in Barbadian English – and I we were able to convince them that we did have a place to stay and although our appearance suggested to the contrary, we were not beach bums.

Sadly, I found Barbados slightly disappointing. Even the beaches didn't live up to the worldwide billing. The beaches were vast expanses of golden, white sand but the sea was full of sea urchins, black balls covered with long black spines that were easy to swim into.

It was, however, really the service industry which tarnished the whole experience and can be rationally explained, due to the years of racial discrimination. There was no table service in any of the places we visited and I also felt a huge air of resentment with a sense of 'them' and 'us'. To me, the visit was like the feeling one would have visiting a pub whose landlord despised drink and drinkers.

There were memorable events to lessen the disappointment, such as in one small town there were fake sailing boats that took tourists for trips up and down the coast. We were strapped for that kind of extravagance but were walking by as some vessels were leaving. The people on the boats were throwing coins into the sea and the local youth were diving for this money and trying to get it before it disappeared from view.

We had certainly stocked up on our vitamin D (sunlight) but eventually it was time to move on and off we flew from Barbados and island-hopped to Guadeloupe.

To Guadeloupe and then home

Here we were able, once again, to take on the mantle of ignorant Brits in a French-speaking territory – we were back in our comfort zone.

On Guadeloupe we hired a car and travelled around searching out secluded beaches and interesting sights.

The Caribbean didn't have the rich wealth of culture that the South American countries had but they did have the sea breezes and vast sandy beaches.

After Guadeloupe it was home to the UK after six weeks of travel and experiences.

I think Peru and Bolivia were my favourite places just because of their rich culture, which you didn't have to search for – it was right there in front of you. The vast contrast between me and my life and theirs made it incredibly interesting.

The UK seemed a little mundane as Robin went back to Kent for a few days before heading up to Barrow-in-Furness. Robin had been an easy-going non-bilingual companion on a trip of a lifetime.

I had a little time to hand over my gifts to family and then I tripped out to Crete to see my sister. But it wasn't long before I was heading back to the South Atlantic to resume my adventures as a peripatetic teacher in the Education Department under the leadership of Tom Lamin. More boat and horse rides and a few drunken seminars, the odd two-nighter.

At the end of tour, I did something similar with two other colleagues. Stan Angel and Jonathon Sinclair, the latter who originated from Wick in Scotland. This time we flew up to Rio de Janeiro in Brazil and spent a couple of weeks soaking up the sun and generally enjoying ourselves.

We weren't yobbish by today's standards but we did go slightly over the top in the drinking department. One night we went to a cabaret where you drink as you watch the entertainment. The lead singer was amazing and led a very fine performance. It was memorable live entertainment made even better by meeting the star after the performance as we staggered out to the venue to head for home. We thoroughly overdid the praise, which we sincerely felt that she deserved. I wonder if she remembers the meeting with equal fondness?

Surprising as it may seem, the evening was to become even more memorable on arriving back at the hotel. Stan, the 'Mr Responsible' in a sea of irresponsibility (John and me) had lost the key to our room. None of us, collectively even, had reception-class knowledge of Portuguese. In fact, I doubt if we could have come up with ten Portuguese words and that would be with Pelé and a few other footballers thrown in (and if their surnames counted as separate words).

Off we went to the front desk and found someone who we persuaded to come up to our room where we tried to explain our predicament. I think he told us, without using words like Pelé, that there wasn't a spare key to our room. This went on for at least ten minutes as our befuddled minds tried to unravel what was happening. It was at this point that our so-called Gentleman Stan showed his true colours and explained to the chap in sign language that if he didn't open it he would boot it down.

A bunch of keys appeared quicker than a professional magician could have pulled a rabbit from a hat.

In the clear blue light of the very late next day we realised that the chap had just been manoeuvring for a couple of dollars to reward his efforts and something us three UK oafs should have gladly given. We all felt a little guilty. Stan 'Yobbo' Angel felt slightly worse because he had since found the key in his pocket. It wasn't as if he had lost them, rather he had lost the dexterity of getting his hand into his pocket.

Compared to Rio there was a bit of a shortage of women in the Falklands and this fact made it acceptable, in our minds, to catch up on this deficit over our tours Terribly non-cerebral I know but seriously brilliant when you are blokes in your early twenties and feeling good to be alive.

We ate out a lot and the food was wholesome without being à la carte. I had a really good meal of octopus and boiled veg, including a huge boiled onion on one occasion. The bits of the octopus were so big and the suckers so prominent that it looked like something you stick your soap to in the bath.

Rio did have a full and rich culture that we could only witness with shock in some cases. To live the life of a street person must have been tough as I am sure it is today. Shoeshine boys were everywhere and would hound you for work even when you were sitting having a meal or drinking at a café, shop or bar. On one occasion a shoeshine boy asked Stan if he could shine his shoes, which Stan declined. This young rascal called Stan a capitalist pig in very good English.

I think poor Stan was quite hurt and shocked by this outburst and to be fair quite rightly as he was wearing suede hush puppies that would have been severely devalued by polish.

We did the touristy stuff and went up some of the funny shaped hills on clapped out cable cars that moaned and groaned, shook and swayed in an alarming manner. There is a huge Jesus statue (Christ the Redeemer) at the top of one and we went up there to take pictures. There were some amazing views towards the airport and over the harbour.

We did visit a fantastic market just before we left which sold all sorts of original, unique, articles. I bought myself a nice leather travelling bag, which I used for many years until the zip gave up the ghost. If this had been in Europe or the USA it would have cost a bomb but in this market it was less than £15. Perhaps I could have haggled it down further but to me it was a bargain.

It is a thing with South American drivers that they have to drive flat stick. No wonder they do so well in Formula One. I am sure it is because they are so used to going hell for leather. In fact, I don't think all the talent has been utilised because I would bet on the cab driver that took us back to the airport competing well in Formula One, using his taxi.

We survived to fly back to the UK and dispersed to our various homes after spending a night in Kent with my folks.

17. RINCON GRANDE

Working life

So it was good to get home and catch up but it wasn't long before I was ready to head back down to the Falklands and take up my post at Rincon Grande.

During my time with Camp Education I rarely came into Stanley and probably in the first year not at all. Travelling teachers didn't get the long holidays afforded to their counterparts in Stanley at that time. Teachers on overseas contracts had all the local holidays and then took leave during the UK summer. This meant that a number of teachers had a lot of time off. It wasn't until many years later that contracts changed so that this practice was extinguished. Years later in 2000 and something, camp teachers were awarded the same holidays as other teachers on the islands.

Camp teacher contracts also changed and qualified teachers became the norm. A base was set up in Stanley which travelling teachers could use at any time and when the department called them in for teacher training or for breaks. One-year contracts also came in and many teachers started to arrive from Australia, and particularly New Zealand, bringing with them their distinctive accents.

Increased flexibility also came in as the roads advanced outside Stanley, and eventually some travellers worked driving to different farms from Stanley on the East and bases on the West. Also children were taxied into central locations on the West or Stanley on the East from certain farms.

The Fighting Pigs

Back to the end of my travelling days and the beginning of my time at Rincon Grande I began to come into Stanley a little, more building up to weekly excursions. I used to play rugby and football for Stanley and meet up and socialise with the teaching fraternity that were involved with Camp Education.

So here I was back at Rincon, but this time permanently. Diana and Ron had asked me back to teach their children, Arthur and Andrea, full time. Rincon was in, what people call, the North Camp and lies near the entrance to Salvador Waters, an arm of the sea that cuts deep into the East Falklands. Rincon was made up of two parts, with half being down by the sea called Foam Creek and the other part up on the hill where there were two houses. One of these was the Turner's family home and the other was where I lived on my return. Arthur and Andrea were old enough to go to the hostel in Stanley but their parents had other plans.

The Fighting Pigs, the local band, used to practise in the Town Hall after having a few drinks in the Rose Bar to loosen up. On one particular night Andy Clarke and I went to see fellow camp teacher and lead guitarist Gerard 'Fred' Robson, his brother Raymond on bass and their/our good friend Pete King on the drums with Len McGill doing the vocals. Fred was fair-haired and short and he had a rocker's demeanour with jeans and a loud T-shirt and a cigarette constantly on the go. Raymond was a taller version and had a unique way of playing his guitar while facing his speaker as if he was studying every note that was coming out. Pete was a slim, tall, dark and easy-going guy who was the unchallenged Falklands king of drums at that time. Len was another larger-than-life character that belted out the vocals to the rock numbers that the band played. In the Falklands this type of music was for the rebels with the majority of folk enjoying country music.

Although Andy wasn't playing, he threw in his lot in supporting the band's limbering up process in the Rose Bar. Andy was a large, physically fit bloke with brown hair who came from Birmingham and had a distinct Brummie accent. He came to the Falklands just after me and stayed with Laurie and Mary Goodwin as I did. He taught in a variety of places and ended up teaching full time at Goose Green for a while. He returned to UK in the late 1980s and bought a house in Litchfield. Unlike many camp teachers of that time he was qualified.

Nearing the end of the evening Andy disappeared back to his current lodgings. There was usually a certain care within the group and this night something made me go and check that my inebriated friend had made it home. He was staying at the Police Cottages just over the road from the Town Hall. Looking over the gate there was Andy, lying on the path, as if he was in the middle of a star jump. I had also been supporting The Fighting Pigs' limbering up process in the Rose Bar and so opening the gate wasn't that straight forward and I ended up breaking the top of the gate off before I realised that it opened the other way.

This setback wasn't going to put me off my 'goodwill to all men' and all that and so I got hold of Andy and peeled him off the frosty ground and guided him along the path to the back door and in. I had a rummage under the sink and found a bucket and things seemed to be going well. I manoeuvred Andy through the door and into the hall as quietly as I could and headed north in the direction of his room. As we negotiated the turn a large red-faced man in his underpants came down the stairs. I made my excuses and legged it, leaving Andy to his host.

This was the first time I had met Tony Pettersson the man who was to become my father-in-law some years later.

Andy Clarke

Andy's reign at the Petterssons' was a long and memorable one with some incidents that can't be recorded. One that can, was another occasion when his friends escorted the none-to-steady Andy back to his abode. This time there was a group who negotiated the front gate without incident and got him into his room downstairs at the front of the house. Evidently Tony was getting used to Andy lodging with his family, because he didn't make an appearance this night. In hindsight perhaps he should have because after depositing Andy the door was shut on his room.

Next day there was a trail of blood leading from his bedroom to the kitchen. Andy had got up sometime during the night and felt a little peckish and decided to make himself a sandwich. We all thought, and Andy did too, that he had cut himself with the bread knife in his lesser state. Wrong. Andy had in fact struggled to find his way out of the room and while groping around in the dark had managed to fall putting his hands through one of the windows.

Working on the farm

I was to eventually take lodgings at this understanding household. The Police Cottages were a significant row of stone houses, one of which was the home of the Pettersson family for a number of years before they bought their own property from Roger and Norma Edwards on Davies Street.

This purchase was around 1987 when Toni was pregnant with Caris and so many years in the future.

In 1980 I moved my worldly possessions to the North Camp and lived a life of Riley at Rincon Grande in many respects. No Beaver or Islander every two weeks. No living out of a suitcase here, there and everywhere. Don't misunderstand me, I loved being a travelling teacher most of the time, but after three years this was a nice change.

I suppose I was a private teacher but I was also allowed to work on the farm, which was icing on the cake for me. I decided that I wouldn't mind having a go at cutting the settlement's peat. There were only three functioning houses so it added up to around 600 yards.

I didn't know how to do it but I was keen and I had a spade. The idea is something like this. A cubic yard is 64 sods of peat of 9-inch squares in four ritts of 16 sods. So there were quite a few sods to cut.

The best cutters are the ones that think about minimising the energy expended to maximise the work done. I learnt that placing as many as I could reach away from the pyramid helped me, but there are numerous different ways and opinion is mixed on how far behind you your building and spreading should be. I think it is whatever is comfortable for each cutter but there is thoughtful debate on the issue.

The first problem that I encountered was that some athletic individual had planned to cut the peat and had long-ritted and cross-ritted the banks. Work done for you one would think but the cross-ritting was three ritts to a yard making the sods 9 x 12 at their smallest which is okay if you are King Kong or the Terminator but not if you are me.

The second issue is that I had gone to the peat bog with a good peat cutter, Kacks Browning. He bombed out 25 yards in ragtime. He was so clean that one would think he had been cooking or undertaking some domestic chore. The peat he had cut sat neatly on the bank well spread, not one sod on another, and the 3, 2, 1 looked as if it had been placed by hand. 3, 2 and 1 was where the cutter stacked peat on the edge of the bank, reducing the number of sods you had to spread. So three sods would be put out first, then two on top of the three and then one sitting on top of the two. The sods on the outside, as you were cutting, were the lightest and so needed less energy to roll to the outside of your spread. The ones on the inside went into the 3, 2, 1.

I, on the other hand, was smothered in peat; my few yards looked pitiful in quantity and looked a jumble with some sods on top of others. In comparison my efforts were pathetic.

Fortunately, Kacks was at hand to help and he took me down to the shearing shed to a grinder for sharpening shearing gear. He gave my spade a severe working over, putting an edge on the front and both sides and a shine on the blade. He showed me how to tape up the handle carefully with insulating tape over where the shaft and blade met and where they were fastened by a pin, to save your hands unnecessary punishment.

I never got as proficient as Kacks, because I always got smothered even after I had cut thousands of yards, but I did become able to do the job reasonably well. Kacks's generosity helped me no end and although I couldn't undo the marking done by Harry Rozee I had a spade that had been transformed from a blunt awkward instrument to an implement of work. The effort of pushing it into the peat had drastically reduced making the job that much easier.

I carried on cutting the peat at Rincon, which was my first serious peat-cutting effort.

Kacks Browning

I didn't live down at Foam Creek after I became full time. I lived in the cottage just below the family home. What a view from up there overlooking the majority of Salvador Waters and from my kitchen window you could see Salvador farm across the water. I looked over there at these near neighbours for two years but didn't visit the settlement until well after the war.

Kacks was a handy man to have about the place and he did a lot of work tightening fences and making things look better around the settlements. Kacks went to town for a holiday at some stage and then got marooned in Stanley and so Diana asked me if I would bring him back on my bike. It sounded a reasonable request and so I sought out Kacks and we made a time to leave Stanley. Kacks had made the best of his time in Stanley and had obviously celebrated to excess. He arrived a little unsteady on his feet so I handed him my rucksack and we left for Rincon.

It wasn't that far before I realised that Kacks was far from sober and he was swaying about in an alarming manner on the back. Fortunately, I was a little heavier than him so I was able to keep going, but on a number of occasions I had to reach behind me to grab my sloshed friend and push him up into the vertical. I did think that the rush of cool air, as we sped along, would revive him but I was sadly disappointed. In fact, he got worse and I began to suspect that his opinion of my driving was so low that he had fortified himself for the journey, moments before my arrival.

We managed to get up and through the Two Sister's gate and head towards the Corner Pass in the Murrell River before anything untoward happened. But then Kacks started to fall sideways off the bike and driving on the soft ground I was unable to reach behind and hold him on. Another feature of Kacks's inebriation was that although his body seemed to have lost all powers of control this power seemed to have congregated in his hands which hung on to me with a vice-like grip. So when Kacks went off I usually went with him. It was becoming a bit of a nightmare and I was a little cheesed off when we broke the front brake lever and twisted the handle bars and were still far from our final destination. Kacks didn't seem to be enjoying the trip either and would spend longer and longer lying on the track and it was taking more and more of an effort to firstly wake him up and then secondly get him to sit back on the bike and resume our journey. At the top of Long Island Mountain, I had had enough and I think Kacks had too because try as I might I could not wake him up and he just lay in the grass as peacefully as if he was in bed.

I got my hand-held 2 meter radio out and called for some assistance, detected a little reticence in the voices of the rescuers coming to my aid, but I didn't say how hard I had worked to get my passenger that far. So Ron set sail from Rincon in the Land Rover and came to the top of Long Island Mountain for their man. Kacks, refreshed from a few hours sleep, was able to greet the arrival of the Land Rover with renewed vigour and virtually jumped up and bolted to the passenger door.

Gathering

Gathering was one of my favourite jobs. We would leave the farm on horseback, the dogs milling round and everyone shouting as we headed out. Diana would ride a brown horse called Big Colt and for a Falkland Island animal he was tall. Arthur would ride his grey mare Carmen, and Andrea, her chestnut mare called Rio. I can't remember what Ron used to ride but I rode a collection of different horses.

The first gather I went on I rode this broad, black horse that belonged to Jim Lellman, a schoolteacher in Stanley. So off we all went eventually taking up position in the area that we were gathering. I had to wait at a certain position and when the sheep came together chase them down towards the other gatherers.

Many town horses were used for riding around in groups and this horse was no exception. So once the other horses left us and we took up our position it got slightly agitated. He did a little rear and tried and turned first one way and then the other but I had had three years of honing my riding skills as a camp teacher so I showed him that we had to go my way. I hadn't had to ride a really bad bucking horse but I knew I could probably sit a couple of decent efforts. Anyway this horse was so wide it was like riding a double bed and being large his movements were slow and ponderous.

Fat he might have been but he was also a tactician and must have worked it out that rearing and shying was going to involve effort for little reward and so he then moved into rearing in earnest, which was quite a feat for a horse of that size. I just shifted my weight as high as I could to make it even harder for him. He then moved on to falling sideways as he reared up. I rode a few of these and then thought 'sod this' I don't fancy mistiming the dismount and getting flattened out like a human pancake.

He was determined to return to his friends. Once I dismounted he continued to annoy. He carried on rearing up and came down towards me. And then he rubbed his head on me. Not many horses are like this but it took the edge of what would have been a great day out.

Once the sheep were together and we were riding close to one another he was fine. Although I found his behaviour more than a little vexing, in the horse's defence, he had probably always known riding where everyone was together. He had the seaside donkey mentality.

Jim's horses also had another bad habit, which was brought on by his riding style. When Jim was riding and his horse tripped or stumbled he would give it a crack with his whip to remind it to pick its feet up. I have known other riders who would do the same. My experience was that far from stopping a horse tripping it made them take a huge leap ahead if they did stumble in anticipation of the customary whack. For riders that weren't Jim and therefore not ready for this leap, the sensation of having all the joints in your body taking up the slack after every stumble got more than a little tedious, especially on a long ride. True enough, if you were a regular rider of Jim's animals you could never completely relax.

I can't remember complaining, although I would have certainly talked about the experience, but after this gather I was promoted to riding Molly. She was brown, tame, and a good camp horse. By that I mean that she wasn't pulling all the time to head for home the minute you left the stable and she was very willing and comfortable to ride. She did have a negative feature however and that was that whoever had mouthed her hadn't made the best of jobs. In fact, there were times I am sure where it would have made little difference whether the bit was in her mouth or under her tail.

Motorbike

As part of my package at Rincon I was given a small motorbike, which I used to go down the track and visit Green Patch and Stanley. It was a two-stroke trail 125 Suzuki, small but a game little machine.

At this time there weren't any roads outside Stanley. Even some of them inside, like Callaghan Road, were unsurfaced. The trip to Rincon from town or vice versa was many miles of dirt tracking along a myriad of different tracks made by Land Rovers, bikes and tractors over the years heading in the general direction of the next settlement through streams, along beaches and rotavated tracks if you were lucky. It was straightforward when the tide was out but when it was in from Long Island to Rincon it was challenging going up in the camp to find a little-used pass. On a bike it was still relatively easy.

Long Island Mountain was a place that was severely cut up across the many possibilities used by people climbing to the summit. In the summer it wasn't really an issue for a driver with modest experience, but in the winter it was a case of zigzagging and finding some vegetation to get a grip on. As long as you could maintain your momentum you had a good chance of progressing. There were a few drivers that used to make this kind of travelling look easy, but not many.

Reaching the top gave one a feeling of satisfaction but it was only a part of a much bigger journey. Soon after the top you had to ford Turners Stream, which was okay most of the time but would become impassable after rain. Then there was some serious ploughing as you sank in crossing the peat as you made your way to the Corner Pass in the Murrell River. Again the pass was fine most of the time but would become too deep after rain. When it was too deep you could then backtrack and head inland to find a bridge over the Shanty Stream and then head back in the direction of Stanley. This bridge had been damaged where some character had driven his tractor and trailer across the bridge designed for much lighter fare, like sheep, horses and maybe Land Rovers. There was now a big gap from the bank to the bridge. If you jumped your bike onto the bridge with too much vigour there was a good chance that on landing on the slippery wooden decking you would go flying. Too little and the front wheel would gain the bridge but the back would fall down into the gap. I used this bridge only when I was desperate.

During my time at Rincon I began to see Toni, so I drove to town most weekends whatever the weather. I knew that track like the back of my hand. One foggy night I was in town and someone was lost on the track to Green Patch. I listened to what they had to say on the 2 meter and deduced that they had somehow gone through the Corner Pass twice and were heading back to town. They argued that they hadn't gone back through the Murrell River and that they were up by Turners Stream at the back of Long Island. It was difficult to say because there are no landmarks of any significance. The odd fence, peat bank or gateway was all one had to go on, however it did turn out that they had turned 360 degrees, crossed the river twice and were now following the track back to Stanley.

On one epic trip in the middle of winter it was so cold that the ice built up between the spokes until I had solid wheels on the bike and where spray from any water stuck to the bike like small boiled sweets.

Another trip to remember was when the marines had lost a missile in the Moody Brook area. Blissfully unaware of this, I came blasting down the very area that it was lost in. The chances of me hitting it were rather remote but there was still a chance.

Toni and I did many miles on bikes in and out of town and exploring the north coast from Rincon down to Volunteer Point. It was a place teeming with wildlife – penguins, shags, ducks, geese, and every small cove had a harem of elephant seals. Today there are not many elephant seals hauling up to breed there.

Even sheep were entertaining in some respects. During lambing when we were travelling through the camps we would occasionally surprise a ewe whose lamb would be lying in the grass bogs. Sometimes the ewe went one way and the young lamb just focused on the bike thinking it was its mother. The lambs could really run when they thought they were being left behind so you had to go twice as quick as them to stop them chasing you and not lead them miles away from their mothers.

Another thing is that some ewes get cast when they are having their lamb and can't get up and so we did a lot of shepherds' work on our travels. It is more of a skilled job than it sounds because if the ewe hasn't been down for long, as you get her to her feet, she does a Marian Jones and you are left with the lamb. If she has been down for a day or so she needs a bit of physio before she is able to move off. With the former, as you are pulling the sheep to its feet you are running hard in the opposite direction hoping the lamb has the mental capacity to recognise that its mother is the four-legged woolly thing running in the opposite direction to the two-legged multicoloured thing.

At certain times of the year the Falklands were good to live off the land and sometimes we would drive back to town with goslings hanging from the handlebars. Add to that a pillion with a big rucksack full of spare clothes etc.

One trip, when coming back fully laden, the front wheel of the bike kept lifting regardless of how I tried to put my weight over the handlebars and eventually up and over we went. Luckily we landed on a soft patch kicking the bike away as we fell. My driving ability was criticised at the time but it wasn't many days before it became a great memory.

The Falklands weather is renowned for changing many times each day and certainly regularly by the day, so that one day is foul beyond belief and yet the very next day can be beautiful. On one of those foul days we put on all the extra jumpers, thick socks, waterproofs and thigh boots. Returning two days later there isn't a cloud in the sky; it is flat calm and warm. We stuffed all the gear in the rucksack only for Toni to fall and get cast on her back while going to open a gate.

I hope I added something to the society when I lived at Rincon. I picked up the mail each time I came from town. On one occasion there were a number of magazines, and I headed for Green Patch and Terence and Carol Phillips. I shot through Turners Stream but hit some softer stuff than normal and the bike slowed so quickly that the momentum of the magazines flipped me over the handlebars onto my back. I hit the ground with a good wallop and winded myself and had to lie there for a few minutes before I carried on.

People had tried to improve the tracks, especially making access from Green Patch to Long Island a little easier. Over some of the little brooks/ditches farms had put in bridges. These are really a couple of sturdy pieces of wood for bearers and planking. There was one of these a few miles out of Green Patch. I was running a little late and so I was picking them up a bit when I saw a vehicle coming in the other direction. We closed on each other and came together just before the aforementioned bridge, with me being a little closer than Raymond and Marlene Newman and family. There's nothing like a bit of showing off, especially on a motorbike, so I shot down towards the bridge and gave it a big handful as I hit the bridge.

With a big roar and a quick 360 degrees the bike and I shot into the ditch. The wet wooden planking was just like ice and needed care and respect when traversing. It wasn't the result I was looking for. I didn't hear any laughter as Raymond pulled the bike off and pulled me out of the ditch. It was only my pride once more that was badly dented.

I had bought myself a XL 250 Honda for £600 from Ben Berntsen. It was a good handling machine but you had to keep it wound open to get the best out of it. The most popular bikes of the time were the SP 400 Suzuki's although there were a number of different lightweight Japanese 2 strokes.

Following a track was an art form made all the better if you were on it regularly. My idea was to follow the track but keep off it if I could. When a section got cut up you would avoid it blazing off to one side or the other. A lot of decisions were made on the spur of the moment.

Bozo, my dog, was born in this period. He was the result of a Huntaway dog and a Collie mix mother. Toni and I took him out to Rincon in the top compartment of the rucksack. We were whistling along when I decided to cut out a bit of rough stuff and go to one side. It happened to be a wrong move because the edge of a natural peat bank loomed up. I had two choices one to try and stop before the four-foot drop – no chance! Or accelerate and try to jump it, two up, keeping the front wheel up to stop us cartwheeling to a painful conclusion. We jumped and landed with a heck of a smack. Bozo gave out a howl of pain or surprise. Toni had slid back onto the mudguard on impact. No bones broken and the bike frame was still in one piece.

The bigger community

Carol and Terence's was like a second home at Green Patch and I always called in with mail on my way back to Rincon. Carol would make me breakfast. I didn't only deliver the mail but I also got down there helping out with different jobs at times. It was a privileged position for me to be a small part in witnessing the start of the sub-division process.

The biggest gather I ever did was helping Carol and Terence gather Mount Kent. It was a long and eventful day starting off with Toni and myself and Marvin Clarke riding out from Stanley and starting the gather by Wall Mountain. As we came from one direction others started from other points and we gathered the sheep north.

Toni rode her pony Bluey, and I rode a small mare called Silver Blaze. Silver, although much smaller, was a bit like Jim's big black mare that I rode at Rincon and liked to be ridden in the company of other horses. She also did a small breach and a half-hearted rear but once we moved off she got over it and never looked back. After a while she was as good as gold. She was a good mare to ride with a comfortable gait. She was also an able animal in the soft. The point of comfort was a bonus if you were sitting on an animal all day and being good in the soft is always an advantage riding in the Falklands.

No one knew about the depleted ozone then and everyone's exposed skin just took whatever it had to. At the end of the day there were some very red faces and unbelievably Toni's face was quite swollen. Although people have worked outdoors since the beginning of time and just went red and brown. Today not everyone, but many people, take precautions to protect their skin.

I thoroughly enjoyed my time at Rincon, which was sadly and inconsiderately brought to a premature end once the Argentines invaded this pleasant land.

Shooting

The Pettersson family were big in full bore rifle shooting and both Derek, Toni's brother, and Toni would accompany Tony up to the range from an early age and participate at the first opportunity. They were all cracking shots. So while we were courting Toni invited me up to the range, which was then to the north of Sapper Hill. I didn't see myself as a Davy Crockett but I thought I was proficient.

So everyone took their turn and eventually it was my go. There was more than one person shooting at any one time but each shooter had his own target. I let drive and after I had let go a few shots some people started laughing. The folk up at the butts wanted to know who was shooting on number two target because they were hitting the ground in front of the target and showering them with soil. From that time on I left the full bore to the Petterssons.

Every year to raise funds for the club, members would organise the Rifle Club supper. It was always a very local bash with traditional music and a bloody good feed. A bar was also there to raise funds followed by the prize-giving where the top shots won their cups and medals. Once it was over they would fill these cups with booze and go around the tables offering people a slurp. If the evening at the bar wasn't enough the cups would definitely see you off. Probably just the alcohol in the cups would be enough to have one comatose.

These dos have always been very well attended but sadly the participation has reduced over the last few years. There have been some memorable evenings. Tickets are given out to members who sell them to their friends. We always try and invite people and we always make a great evening of it.

We had got into a group of about a dozen that went travelling and camping at Christmas and some winter activities like a weekend away duck shooting each year.

Derek made a number of friends from work, and used to bring them out to Sussex Farm, our home, and we got to meet a colleague and his wife and they were special guests attached to our group.

The Rifle Club event came along and these new friends were invited to join us for the Rifle Club supper. It is true to say that this lady scrubbed up quite well and being not only new to our group, but also new to the islands, she and her husband were ignorant of the dances that we did. There wasn't a lack of willing partners to show them all the different dances and steps.

A few hard-core revellers get back to Derek P's house to finish off the evening and I suggested to Ted that he couldn't have got any closer to the lovely Linda if he had tried. I accused him of having her powder on his cheeks from a close encounter and scrutiny whilst dancing. It was all said in bad taste after the excesses of another successful Rifle Club supper.

Our next outing as a group was teal duck shooting where we would drive out to a place called Egg Harbour. There was a large house and it was close to all the ponds and creeks, which had teal ducks.

We arrived on Friday night and got the fire going. We had a few hot rums to compensate for the cold and then all sat round in the kitchen chatting, eating and having a few more drinks.

Late on in the evening, when the amount of booze had vanquished shyness, Ted believed this was the opportune moment to apologise to Linda for inappropriate behaviour during the Rifle Club supper. He came out with a sincere apology and excuse for his indiscretion. Of course, Linda doesn't know what the hell he is on about and so asks Ted why he thinks he behaved so badly. Instead of coming up with some kind of excuse about memory loss, he laid the blame for this misinformation at the feet of the perpetrator.

Linda then asked why I would want to make up stuff about Ted, which was slightly difficult to explain.

The Rifle Club has continued to do really well on the international arena winning prizes at Bisley on a regular basis. Although it is one of the oldest clubs and does remarkably well in competitions overseas the membership has become quite small.

Seminars

During my time working as a teacher on the Islands we had a number of seminars. The best ones by far were the ones run in camp where there was awesome camaraderie with fellow Darwin Boarding School, settlement and travelling teachers.

It was a great opportunity to relax and socialise – yes we drank too much – but we also worked hard and were able to interrelate on our many challenges. Most of the time teachers would be visiting a self-contained community where there wasn't the opportunity to complain about the support you were getting from the Education Department, or controlling a difficult child, or perhaps difficult accommodation. This was one of the few times that you met your colleagues and could compare notes and glean different ideas.

One of these seminars was held at Darwin Boarding School, which was a purpose-built boarding school for camp children. We did a lot of training on teaching methods and it was at this venue that we were taught how to win clay from the ground all the way to building a kiln and firing your pots etc. Rob Rutterford was our instructor and I was able to use this work on my rounds. Rob and Val were two teachers that taught at Darwin Boarding School. Val gave birth to twins before the conflict but unfortunately they didn't come back after the war in 1982. These seminars were run over five days but seemed to pass so quickly.

At the end of this particular seminar we all returned to our settlements or beats apart from the staff of Darwin Boarding School that remained. Andy, a travelling teacher, also remained behind but I can't remember why although he was probably filling in for some one.

Anyway, one night the fire alarm went off at Darwin Boarding School and the rest of the staff joined the teacher on duty as the building was evacuated and the source of the fire located. The smoke got thicker and thicker as they converged on the fire's origin. Eventually they tracked the fire down to a single room and to a chair with smoke billowing out of it with Andy sitting there sleeping, oblivious to the situation confronting him and the whole school.

Funny to relate but very serious at the time because like most buildings in the Falklands it was made with over 90 per cent of wood and so was a natural fire hazard. Andy had fallen asleep with a cigarette that had set fire to the chair, although fortunately the chair had only smouldered and created dense smoke – not enough to asphyxiate Andy or anyone in the building.

Another seminar of significance was the one prior to 1982. I didn't really enjoy the seminars that were run in Stanley. I might be paranoid but I always got the feeling that town teachers thought working in camp was a doddle, although I thought most of them – not all – would have struggled to cope.

18. DIVING FOR TREASURE

Looking for the Coquimbana

Dave Eynon and I had been diving for a wee while doing different things ever since he had offered me a third partnership in looking for ships and their cargos in Falklands' waters. I agreed to work full time with Dave

Before the Panama Canal all ships that wanted to access the west side of the Americas had to go round Cape Horn at the bottom of South America. Cape Horn was a treacherous region for ships with storm force winds and mountainous seas. Many vessels of that time got a severe beating, losing their rigging or becoming demasted. With the prevailing winds and currents, a lot of these crippled ships were blown or limped back to the Falklands for help and possible repair. Some just sank or came ashore on the Islands. Other ships just came to grief around the coast as they sailed in these waters.

Dave, like me, had been a travelling teacher. He had met a local girl but had left to study to be an engineer. Now he was back hoping that he could make a living by finding and salvaging valuable cargoes from the many ships that had floundered around the Islands. He and Carol had two children, Leeann and Christopher.

As usual it was not straightforward because Toni and I had already agreed to go and work for my sister in Crete and try and see some of the rest of the world at the same time. Toni had taken a lot of persuading – sun, sea and carefree life, and I played down the negative sides. I also showed her slides of the Mediterranean lifestyle and diet. After many months of indoctrination, I finally persuaded Toni it was the right thing to do, so in preparation to leave she resigned from her job as Secretary at the Agricultural Department.

I now had to persuade Toni to give up a joint dream and indulge me in my own passion. Toni struck a deal: if I came, cap in hand, with her to ask for her job back she would give up all her dreams of travel and sun and let me muck about in the South Atlantic. So off we went to the Agricultural Department where I dutifully grovelled for Toni's job, which they were happy to give back to her.

I had completed a six-week commercial diving course in the 1970s, and so I did have a strong foundation of all number of things, but ultimately I had a sense of adventure that drove me into this kind of enterprise.

We did some dives around Stanley on some wreck sites that were remarkably boring, and then other similar dives. Dave had planned to find other valuable wrecks and the first of these big ones was the wreck of the Coquimbana. This ship had floundered on the

Tyssen Patch, a reef that is southwest of Great Island in the Falkland Sound between East and West Islands. So we carted inflatable, diving kit, fuel and other essentials by Land Rover to Wreck House, an outside shepherd's house on North Arm farm's ground, which is opposite Great Island, and shipped everything over using the inflatable.

You have to bear in mind, once again, that apart from a short road from Stanley to Pony's Pass, a distance of a few miles, the rest of the way was pretty varied with some difficult terrain. Around Bluff Cove and Fitzroy, where you picked your track from hundreds (and I use the term 'track' very loosely), it ranged from rutted out areas to lightly used pieces that were hard to follow. It was usually the passes or wooden bridges that forced you into a bottleneck where you could not avoid cut up ground and the chances of getting stuck.

There was a clay track from the south side of Fitzroy Ridge that went all the way to North Arm, with some large gaps here and there and it also went west towards San Carlos from the Puzzle Gates outside Goose Green, although it petered out on the south side of Sussex Mountains.

To think of an endless, smooth, fast clay track would be misleading, because even in the summer, when it was at its best, there were pieces that had been so badly rutted out that they were impassable with a Land Rover, with the vehicle's wheels sinking down into the ruts and the axles, chassis and body work getting hung up on the piece in the middle. You would drive along coming off the clay track to go around these wallows. Many of the worse areas, where travellers had had their issues, would be marked with broken rope where fellow travellers had had to pull one another out.

Once you got to North Arm there were very lightly marked tracks going to places like outside houses or lamb marking pens and one of this type of track went to the Wreck House. Neither Dave, Carol nor I had ever been in this area, and North Arm and all of Lafonia are relatively flat and featureless which makes it extremely difficult to navigate.

So we got everything to the Island where there was a one and three-quarter house with an upstairs. There was also a shearing shed and pens. Of course in any self-contained house there is everything that needs to be done to support living, like chopping wood because there was no peat, and cooking and sorting water.

I wasn't really ready for this enterprise, apart from in spirit. I did not have any diving gear; it was all Dave's. Dave had a dry suit and let me borrow his wetsuit. As any diver will tell you regardless of the thickness of the neoprene the tighter the wet suit the better as it insulates the body from the sea, warming the water that gets between the suit and you. Factor into this equation that Dave is a good four to five inches taller than me, and he was also heavier by a large margin. So when I got into the water, plenty of cold seawater got between the neoprene and me and was constantly replenished as it sloshed in and out, especially along my back.

We had rehearsed the methodology of the search and so we waited for a reasonable day and were off. We left the small bay at Great Island, went north around the top of the Island and headed to the top of the Tyssen Patch. Because the weather is very unpredictable, many times we would leave in ideal conditions only to head home with the wind getting up and the waves growing by the minute and the conditions in the boat getting worse in equal measure.

On that first dive we swam gently along, six to eight feet apart, looking for the copper wreck that could be worth as much as £80,000 if we found it. It was not really the money that motivated me, but the adventure, however the one-third share of £80,000 would have been over £26,000.

The first dive was not too bad, because the adrenalin had kicked in and it was so exciting swimming in the South Atlantic. However, more rational thought might have frightened us out of the adventure:

a) there were no emergency services apart from two local vessels. One which was mostly in Stanley and *the Mounsunen*, which could be anywhere supplying the camp with provisions and collecting wool for Stanley for onward shipping to the UK.

b) the Beaver might have been able to help us if it wasn't rough, and

c) there wasn't a recompression chamber anywhere on the Islands, although swimming along the Tyssen Patch wasn't very deep. It was life on the edge.

I was very cold when I came out of the water and I had used my air quicker than Dave, because I was so cold. My teeth chattered and I could not speak coherently, but although we had not found anything we were excited about the prospects of finding our wreck. Each time we finished a dive, we left a buoy to mark the start of the next dive.

There were many days when it was too rough to attempt to dive so we burnt more wood and then had to find and chop more. We also had a lot of each other's company. I was a little bit of an imposter in as much as Dave, Carol, Leeann and Christopher were one family but I didn't feel at odds with all my training as a camp teacher living with different people island-wide. We did have the odd break where we went back to Stanley and recharged our enthusiasm and on one of these breaks I brought Toni back out.

So that was the routine. Out, lob in, swim until my air ran out, back into the boat, drop a buoy and back to base. After about five of these Dave was getting impatient and felt that we weren't covering enough ground. He came up with a plan to have the inflatable pull us through the water on ropes. The ropes were duly measured and cut and then, thank god we had a practice run in the shallows of the bay in front of the house. This trial was a complete disaster with our combined weight underwater too much for the inflatable, which made it impossible to stay on any planned course. Equally, underwater the force of water made it extremely difficult to do anything apart from hang on.

Dave wasn't one to give up easily and gave instructions to Carol to pull us using more power, thinking this might help. In one of these trials Dave seemed to have rapped his hand around the towline and couldn't let go and looked to be in trouble but Carol soon stopped as our combined weight pulled the boat into the kelp which was just as well. Dave leapt up in the water not very pleased with events but it was just momentary frustration. Regardless of our determination it was clear that it wasn't going to work.

In the trial the force of water had ripped my snorkel from the strap of my mask and

Dave encouraged me to go and scour the beaches. So off Toni and I went to search for the snorkel. We were strolling along chatting and looking down when we heard a cough. Before I could say sea lions, they had charged into the sea. I looked round to see where Toni was but all I saw were the bottom of her trainers as she was legging it in the other direction.

While Toni was out we did a number of dives on the patch. Dave always took his camera and often took shots of different things but on one particular day he discovered that the rubber strap was perished and so left it behind.

In we went at the buoy and began our swim along the outside edge of the reef. As we swam along I saw an enormous sea lion on my right side towards the open sea accompanied by half a dozen clapmatches (female seals). We carried on swimming but I swam inside the outside curtain of kelp keeping a thick amount between the seal and me. The sea lion was the leader and just swam parallel with us for about a minute and then swam straight though the kelp and came boldly up to me cocking his large head from one side to another in an inquisitive manner as if he couldn't believe what he was seeing. He then moved in and I felt his nose on my mask and then he backed off again rolling his head from one side to the other. He then approached Dave who made a big shout and waved his arms. The lion rolled his head once more, looking at Dave in this disbelieving manner, and swam off with his harem in pursuit. At that time I think if Dave had had a camera when the lion put his nose on my mask it would have graced the front page of the *National Geographic*. We carried on and finished the dive and came back for a cuppa and tales of what could have been.

At no time was I scared. At that moment I was pretty fatalistic I just thought this 600 -pound beast was in its element and there wasn't a lot I could do even if I had wanted to. I thought that the kelp would provide a slight barrier but it didn't.

A few days later we had a less appealing encounter with a clapmatch.

We lobbed in as usual and started heading southwest along the reef. I was on the outside and Dave on the inside looking and looking as the cold water sloshed along my back as we finned along. Out of the corner of my eye I saw something symmetrical and unnatural and I motioned to Dave to look. As I did, I looked southeast-ish. I saw the meagre remains of the ship and a few stunted ribs attached to the keel. Stone ballast was evident, which was a surprise for a ship that was meant to be carrying so much copper, and amongst this were a few copper ingots. As for the round thing that had first caught my eye it was the metal tube that the anchor chain goes through to protect the wood on a wooden ship.

We had found the wreck after weeks of looking and there is nothing like the feeling of success. However, we didn't have time to celebrate as events took our minds from fully focusing on what we had achieved.

As we are examining the wreck, a clapmatch came swimming in at speed and straight at us, showing her teeth like a savage dog, making her eyes big and blowing air out of her nose. It was definitely an attack. It wasn't a curiosity encounter. She had come from nowhere as far as I was concerned I certainly hadn't seen her studying us from afar.

I took out my divers' knife and tried to get the light to hit the stainless steel blade and make it obvious. As a weapon it was limited but it was better than nothing. I thought it might stop her if she actually got hold of one of us and wouldn't let go. She came darting in again, singling out Dave who stepped back and fell, momentarily getting tangled among some stringy kelp. Dave who was usually so calm grabbed me and I thought 'fuck me' I am going to drown and die. Just as quickly, Dave signalled back to back and up to the boat.

Usually we would go up and hand up the weight belts, the bottles, mask and snorkels and then having reduced the weight, up and in. This day it was up and straight in. I can't remember being cold and speechless for a change.

The ladies in the boat had also been under attack and the clapmatch had hit the boat a number of times. It was at these moments when we did stop and think of the safety aspects and how would we get help if this seal, with its personality issues, had bitten one of us or sunk its teeth into the tubes of the inflatable. Toni for one could not swim. We had had enough excitement for one day and returned to Great Island, to congratulate ourselves on getting home unscathed.

We went back the next day to recover an ingot. We were hoping the seal with an attitude wouldn't be there but once again she appeared from nowhere the instant we lobbed in. She still wasn't in the best of trim. We were sort of ready this time and the plan was for Dave to make a lifting basket out of some rope as I kept the seal occupied with a state-of-the-art defensive weapon in the guise of a fencing batten. The seal did come charging in but although we had nothing more than a flimsy piece of wood she didn't press as hard as she had done the day before

Once back in the boat we heaved the ingot to the surface and into the boat. Dave then took a fix on a number of points on East and West Falklands so that we could return at any time to lift the rest of the ingots. Pity they hadn't got GPSs on the market in those days.

It was a fun time but over thirty years later we haven't been back to recover the few remaining ingots. In fact, documentation has been found that shows that the ingots were salvaged many, many, years ago. In less than twenty feet of water it would have been relatively easy; weather dependent. What still confuses me is why a ship supposedly carrying all this copper would carry ballast, which was clear to see sitting in and around the remains of the keel.

Looking for *Luige* Grey and hunting sheep

We did a run down to Ruggles Island on one of the better days to look for the *Luige Grey,* a ship that had come to grief off the bottom end of Ruggles while carrying a cargo of marble statues. We dived from shore into some of the thickest tree kelp I have ever seen, let alone dived in. You couldn't swim through a lot of it. An amazing spectacle but we found it difficult to find the main part of the wreck and because our time was very limited we didn't. Going home in the inflatable the wind started to get up and Dave handed me the tiller. I tried to maintain a fast speed keeping on the back of the waves. It was getting more than a little choppy as we pulled into the shelter of the Great Island bay.

Jimmy Miller had kept us in meat for most of our stay at Great Island but he was off gathering and driving sheep for North Arm farm and so was unable to help us on one occasion. There happened to be five sheep on Great Island and we thought we should be able to outwit a mere sheep. We would wear them down, catch and sort. No problem.

I'm not kidding you, the bloody things must have been training for the Olympics in long-distance endurance running. We chased those bastards up hill and down dale but it wasn't the sheep that got knackered. So the Great Island hunters went back home empty handed.

We did have a .22 rifle but you needed some sharp shooter to hit one of those woolly athletes, as the closest we got was about 400 yards.

I'm not sure whether the sheep took pity on us or they just became complacent with our pathetic attempts to catch them, but on about the third day of trying, when we were on the verge of thinking a drive up to North Arm would be easier, we got to within 300 yards of them as they ran past on the coast line. I took careful aim with the .22 and shot at one of them three times.

The sheep disappeared over the bank and onto the beach as everyone in the party gave me disparaging looks suggesting that any one of them could have done better. I wished someone else had taken the responsibility so that I could have dished out some scornful looks.

We were all feeling a bit low when someone spotted the sheep in four-minute mile pace coming back from the beach onto the camp. We also noticed one of their number missing. We ran down to the beach like an Apache war party whooping and carrying on and there before us was the king of ignorant sheep making for the sea. I knew that once he was swimming we would lose him. I was a lot smaller than Dave and I could run a lot quicker and I dashed down across the beach and into the shallows as the sheep was just becoming buoyant and beginning a spirited doggie paddle.

Although he was wounded he had a never-say-die attitude and kicked and struggled until I was absolutely saturated. I did feel a little remorse at how we had caught him but I was now wet and cold and slightly annoyed at this inconvenience so it helped me get over this sorrow and dispatch him.

The hunt had been an ordeal but the skinning and gutting procedure defies belief, looking back. I would now suggest it verged on the inedible but we had succeeded in winning our food which gave us immense primitive satisfaction. True to the bitter end, this sheep provided some tough, rubbery meat, in all its forms, which we ate basically because there was nothing else.

Looking for *Craige Lee*

At the end of our quest we decided to go down to Bull Point to see the old lighthouse and the wreck of the *Craige Lee* that was washed up on the shore years ago.

We were sitting in one of the bays watching the rollers coming in and just feeling and enjoying the power of the sea when a pod of killer whales came in and swam around for a few minutes. I couldn't help but feel incredibly vulnerable for a while just by thinking about what we would have done if these animals had turned up on the Tyssen Patch when we were out there. Not only would we as divers have been terribly exposed but the inflatable would have been dwarfed alongside these creatures. I have read that an orca wouldn't eat a human but I am not totally convinced. I wouldn't be part of a study to prove the point just in case I became a neoprene snack.

There were dangers but they were minimised by Dave's meticulous planning and his maintenance and care of equipment regime. Regardless of how tired we were we would always carry the outboard to the fresh water drum and run and wash it in fresh water along with our diving equipment. The spare engine was tried and tested before and after every dive.

There were the ordinary times when we put air into the bottles after every dive just in case the next day was fine and checking the diving gear for perished rubber or damaged gear that might put our lives at risk.

Today, if we go, there are emergency services like a search and rescue helicopter that could be with you within an hour with a doctor and be able to whisk you off to a recompression chamber.

Billy Rocks

Dave Eynon and I had been planning a dive on the Billy Rock for ages and were waiting for the right weather. The Billy Rocks are a treacherous reef that had claimed a number of vessels in the 1800s and early 1900s as they approached Stanley and Port William. A couple of days before the invasion it was flat calm, and even though I was meant to be attending a Camp Education seminar in Stanley, I was shockingly hungover and I decided to go diving instead. Yes, I know, not the right attitude on a number of fronts, but there had not been a decent day for weeks and here it was and I did not want to let Dave down. Probably the greatest and most selfish reason was that I had been looking forward to a dive on the Billy Rocks for ages and here was my opportunity.

We zipped out to the Billy Rocks in Dave's inflatable and lobbed in and down we went. I remember shags looking as if they had propellers instead of back legs and an amusing octopus but it was not long before I had scoffed my air and had to go to the surface. I came to the top and had a good chuck. The whole thing had been a bad idea. Very bad, but missing one day of the seminar however was the one plus.

Beginnings of war

Although I worked privately for the Turners at Rincon it was in their interest and the Education Department's that we had a working relationship, which gave me access to resources and training.

Back at the seminar, questions were asked about attendance. I was straight up. I went diving rather than being told more stuff from some patronising geek who had absolutely no idea about Camp Education.

The Camp Education Supervisor was not amused and so put me on the last day of flying back to Rincon. For this reason and this reason alone I was in Stanley when the invasion by the Argentines unfolded.

The war changed a lot of things and Dave and I eventually went our separate ways. Dave went into the fishing business and diving services and I went into farming. In the last year or so Dave has retired from his working activities and has talked about returning to the Tyssen Patch to recover the rest of the copper. Of course I would jump at the chance to go back to complete the job but to me it was always about the adventure and the challenge of overcoming the obstacles that confronted us.

19. WAR DIARY 1982

There had always been tension between the Argentinians and the Falkland Islands ever since I arrived in 1977. It was shown in little things, such as the mail being withheld, as at that time all airmail came through Argentina. Veiled threats from the government of Argentina were also commonplace, but I suppose we just thought it was sabre rattling.

The Argentinians couldn't make their minds up on the best way to take over the Islands. One moment they would invite Islanders over on a hearts and minds tour of their country, showering them with gifts, and the next they were stating clearly that they wouldn't wait forever for the Island population to want to become Argentinians.

It all became quite serious when Argentinian scrap metal workers went to the British island of South Georgia and ignored the landing protocol. The next report was of the Argentinian flag flying and military personnel observed on the Island.

This wasn't the first time the Argentinians had occupied a British Island in this area, as an Argentinian had been on Southern Thule, one of the Falkland Dependencies off the Antarctic Peninsula, for a few years, talking to radio operators worldwide.

However, the events in South Georgia started to feel like a little more than the usual Argentinian belligerence. Even so, I can't remember anyone saying that the Argentinians would invade us next.

On the evening of 1 April 1982 I was staying in Port Stanley with my girlfriend's family, the Petterssons. We all realised there was something pretty serious happening, because the Islander aircraft landed on the racecourse, in Stanley – rather than the airport, which is on the outskirts of the town – and the radio station announced that the Governor was to address us all and it was very important.

Eventually, Governor Rex Hunt came on the radio and told us that the Argentinian Navy was at sea and heading in our direction. If they maintained their present speed, they'd be off Cape Pembroke at dawn. He then mobilised the Falkland Island Defence Force telling them to present themselves at the Drill Hall. He went on to say that the broadcasting station would stay on air all night, keeping us up-to-date with the latest events.

My girlfriend Toni's brother and father started kitting up and left to do battle with the Argies. Toni, and her mother, Heather, hardly seemed concerned, so it all felt rather detached and distant. It was as though it couldn't be happening. We just sat there, in silence, looking at each other in a kind of limbo.

To add to the feeling of 'it can't be happening', our gallant soldiers returned to make some sandwiches and to fill a flask with coffee.

We stayed where we were, glued to the radio, listening to the updates that were broadcast every hour. The Governor had a direct line to the studio and came on to speak to us a number of times. At one time, he told us that President Regan had spoken to Galtieri, President of Argentina, and asked for restraint.

My feeling was that the Argentine action was probably just a show of strength to frighten us into further negotiation towards becoming a part of Argentina.

At about 3.20am on 2 April, the Governor addressed us once more, and told us that several Argentinian vessels had been seen off the Cape Pembroke Lighthouse, and a vessel had been seen coming through the Narrows into the inner harbour of Port Stanley. He therefore had no choice, but to announce a state of emergency.

The Pettersson household, minus the men folk, got up on mass, dressed hurriedly and congregated in the main bedroom, which looked down the front road past the Police Station. You could also see the public jetty, and in the far distance, the hill in front of the airport.

The first shots we heard came at about 6.15am. Royal Marines roared up below the house on a motorbike, in a Land Rover and some running on foot. They set up a machine gun post in the T-junction below our window, less than 50 metres away, as we looked east along Ross Road.

We could hear them clearly shouting at each other. One marine was shouting over his radio to others, 'What the f*** do you think you're playing at? Just remind your men we wear the same f*ing cap badges as you do. Stop firing at us.' Another fellow could be heard shouting, 'What the hell are you fighting for? We might as well give up.'

There was a bit of a lull. Marg Morrison, from next door came around before it got too hot, because she was alone in her house. Heather, Toni's mum, appeared to be magnificently cool, but Toni's stomach was upset and she kept rushing to the loo.

Heavy firing started from the south. I thought maybe the radio station had been taken, but it kept broadcasting and the Governor came on to say that the situation was critical and that Government House was under siege from about 200 Argentinians. He went on to say that the enemy was deliberately disabling vehicles and not targeting people.

We went back upstairs to the window. There was more shouting from all directions. Falkland Island Defence Force members could still be seen behind the Telephone Exchange, opposite the Police Station on the front road and the police, including reservists, were in the road in front of the station.

As it got lighter we could see a great amount of activity in the area of the airport. Large armoured personnel carriers and lots of infantry were on Canopus Hill, on the town side of the airport, named after the First World War battleship which fired the first shot at the German Southern Squadron. Argentinian helicopters could also be seen sweeping north to south from the airport and we could only speculate that they were ferrying more troops forward or maybe harrying British Royal Marines who might be withdrawing from the area, which was now swarming with the enemy.

It became obvious that the Argentinian forces had come ashore in several places to converge on the town. Troops landed on the coast to the south of town and split into two groups, advancing specifically on Government House and Moody Brook Barracks simultaneously.

It was clear to us, from the number of Argentinians coming over Canopus Hill, that there must have been a major landing in the Pembroke Peninsular, probably Yorke Bay, which was a large flat sand beach, ideal for amphibious vehicles and landing craft to come ashore.

The weather was perfect, with a yellow sky and a few black clouds. It reminded me of pastel picture washes we once did at school and then flicked Indian ink on to the paper to make it interesting.

Because it was flat calm, you could hear the throaty roar of the landing craft and the small arms fire pin-pointed troop movement as the Argentinians closed on the town.

Head of the broadcasting station, FIBS, Patrick Watts, continued a running commentary assisted by the Governor's rapidly decreasing bulletins from Government House, and people in the local community who were phoning in with sightings and experiences.

The assault on Government House came to a halt after three Argentinians had been shot as they tried to winkle Rex Hunt out.

Tom Davies, an expatriate working for the Grassland Trials Unit, reported over the phone, via the broadcasting station, that his house, situated at the east end of town, had been hit by a mortar bomb or shell. It now had a big hole in the roof and a large crater in the garden. The walls of the house were wafer thin and it was peppered with shrapnel. The Davies Family were some of the luckiest people that day.

Heavy bangs, which shook the town, were going off every few minutes accompanied by automatic fire. Some were a deep-sounding thud, thud, thud while there was rapid high-pitched fire from others.

Falkland Islander Marvin Clark came on the radio and gave us a welcome respite from the depressing one-sided action, to tell the listeners that an Argentinian Army armoured vehicle was stuck in the peat behind town. Other reports came in adding sightings of action in and around the town.

The Argentinians then broadcast over the Falkland Island Radio Station frequency. While no one could understand the words, it was clear enough that they were calling us to surrender.

The Governor came on the radio and said he 'wasn't surrendering to any bloody Argy!'

Comodoro Gilobert, who worked for LADE, the Argentine Airforce, which provided the air link to the Islands and who said he was only in the Islands by chance, then played his cards. I felt he had been planted there on purpose. He must have thought we were all very naïve. The Governor, however, accepted his word and he became the chief negotiator.

Dick Baker, Chief Secretary of the Civil Service, appeared with a white flag tied to his umbrella – a very British gesture if not rather pompous – with Comodoro Gilobert, walking calmly from west to east from Government House. They stood in the front road for a while, just east of the Town Hall. After a few minutes they entered the Police Station. Shortly after, they reappeared and stood in the road once more.

Rex Hunt then asked Patrick to broadcast a message to the invaders agreeing to meet a delegation outside the Catholic Church, not that far from where Dick Baker and our new chief negotiator were standing.

It wasn't long before an Argentinian admiral escorted by two other servicemen arrived, marching up the front road from the direction of the public jetty. The two groups met in the middle of Ross Road, turned and walked to the west in the direction of Government House.

Shooting was still going on spasmodically in several locations around town as the Governor came on the radio once more, to say that there was now a truce. This didn't stop a large, tracked, amphibian, armoured, personnel carrier advancing up the front road and looking very menacing outside the Police Station, which seemed to be the focal point of most of the morning's drama. Ten Argentinian infantrymen accompanied it.

Hercules transport planes had already arrived and were starting to land at the airport and a couple of large helicopters were also milling around in that area. More big, armoured vehicles could also be seen plainly on the hill west of the airport.

I think we islanders were all frightened, but this didn't quell our curiosity. Occasionally, during the morning, it felt as if a frozen hand was delving through my intestines, especially after the houses were hit on the east side of town and I wondered, at first, if the Argentinians intended to flatten Stanley.

The Governor had no choice but to surrender to the overwhelming odds of the Argentinian forces, but he did so with style, telling the Argentinians that they were not welcome on British sovereign territory.

Patrick's radio broadcasts had been going non-stop from when he first knew the Argentinians were on the way. He stopped when someone stuck a gun in his back. He still heroically refused to do their bidding until they removed it. He was criticised by some for saying that he was glad it was over, but I don't believe he welcomed the Argies, but meant it in a humanitarian way, with relief that the fighting was over.

Technically we weren't allowed outside, but most people got their pets in and fed their various domestic animals.

Over the next few days the broadcasting station, under new management, began to deliver edicts. Stanley radio became LR A60. Our local announcers were still able to stamp their own identity on their unwanted overseers. Dave Emsley managed to tell us of the Argies bumming cigarettes from him during one of his stints behind the mic. Dave and Patrick Watts managed to console local listeners by saying 'LR A60 the Falkland Radio'. The new editorial jackboot removed the reference to Falkland Radio, but that didn't stop another rebel, Mike Smallwood, saying 'This is Argentinian-occupied Stanley'. These small things were great morale boosters.

On the first day of occupation the Argentinians who worked for YPF (fuel) and LADE (the external air service), other Argentinians, and even one or two locals with Argentinian connections, appeared with big smiles and drove round with the jubilant invaders. A few loyal and intrepid souls went out to see what was happening.

The Argentinian army didn't cause that much damage to town, apart from the huge vehicles that damaged the roads. The worst affected areas, due to the fighting, were at the east end of town and due to exceptional luck, no one was killed. A house which was evacuated, thanks to the early warning, was demolished.

The Royal Marines were captured and forced to strip, but six got away. A truckload of the prisoners roared down the front road in front of the house. They jeered at the Argies and shouted to locals that they'd be back with the thumbs-up sign.

Huge Argy flags appeared on the flag staffs or anything resembling one. An enormous flag adorned the pole outside the Secretariat, the building that until then looked after civil administration. The flag was about twice the size of a double bedsheet. It clung to the pole, where, on several occasions, a young soldier was enveloped by this vast monstrosity. Eventually the pole broke which then had the Argies searching for a more modest flag.

The flag had a lot of abuse hurled at it from the town's folk who didn't like this loud display. For a few days, the Argies, especially the younger ones, strutted around looking for recognition from the populous. Everyone just ignored them. There wasn't any open hostility, just a kind of quiet tolerance.

The assault troops with their huge armoured vehicles didn't stay very long. They were soon replaced by the regular army. However, the effects of such large machines were with us for years. Water started gushing out of ruptured water mains and the pavements were crushed. I noticed one or two of these vehicles had rows of pockmarks where British guns had found their mark. As they roared off, our house shook. Next they were seen motoring up the harbour and into a vessel with an open and shut front.

The army which then arrived was different from the initial assault force. The majority looked very young; some appeared to stagger under their loads.

They would enter town from the direction of the airport singing patriotic songs, cheerful and confident. I think they thought they were liberating us. It must have been a body blow for these youngsters to be totally ignored. By the time they got to the west end of town, the true character of the troops' make-up was crystal clear. Sour-faced officers would bellow in a nasty, insulting manner at the men – and were rarely carrying their own gear. Instead, they bullied the scrawniest troops to carry their packs. The ordinary soldier looked genuinely brow-beaten and dejected.

At first, I saw the soldiers happily posing for pictures, taken by locals, not understanding they weren't pictures of liberating troops, but pictures to show future generations of Islanders the invading Argentinians. Cameras were soon a dirty word with the Argy authorities and they began random stopchecks looking for them.

One prominent building was searched and a label was left saying 'You have the right to freedom'. The occupants were told not to remove this sticker or they would be liable for yet another search. What did the Argies think they were doing?

Journalists from Argentina arrived. Many locals told them exactly what they thought,

MESSAGE OF THE MILITARY GOVERNOR OF THE NATIONAL TERRITORY OF THE MALVINAS AND SOUTH ATLANTIC ISLANDS.

TO ALL INHABITANTS OF THE NATIONAL TERRITORY OF THE MALVINAS ISLANDS, GEORGIAS AND SOUTH SANDWICH.

- THE ARGENTINE REPUBLIC HAS RETURNED TO THESE ISLANDS ON THE SOVEREIGNTY OF WHICH HAS UNDENIABLE TITLES, AFTER 150 YEARS OF USELESS CLAIMS TO THE UNITED KINGDOM, WHICH OCCUPIED THEM BY FORCE IN 1833.

- FURTHERMORE, WE HAVE HAD DISCUSSIONS FOR 15 YEARS WITH THE BRITISH GOVERNMENT TO REESTABLISH THAT SOVEREIGNTY, WITHOUT ACHIEVING ANY PROGRESS, NOTWITHSTANDING THE REPEATED RESOLUTIONS ISSUED BY THE GENERAL ASSEMBLY OF THE UNITED NATIONS ON THIS SUBJECT. THE ONLY PROGRESS MADE CONSISTED IN ACTIONS INTENDED TO IMPROVE OUR LINKS WITH THE ISLANDS, TO PROVIDE A MINIMUM KNOWLEDGE ABOUT OUR COUNTRY AND CONTRIBUTE TO IMPROVE THE STANDARD OR LIVING OF THEIR INHABITANTS, EVEN AT A HIGH COST FOR US, IN ACTS OF GOOD WILL OFTEN NOT APPRECIATED.

- WE HAD NO OTHER WAY THAN THE OCCUPATION TO ACHIEVE THE DEFINITIVE INTEGRATION OF THE NATIONAL TERRITORY WAVING OUR FLAG AGAIN OVER THE MALVINAS THAT BELONGED TO US SINCE 1810, DATE OF OUR INDEPENDENCE AND AS TERRITORIAL HEIRS OF SPAIN, WHOSE POSSESSION OF THESE LANDS WAS EFFECTIVE AND UNDISPUTABLE.

- I AM DEEPLY SORRY THAT THIS FACT HAS TAKEN PLACE IN THIS WAY, IN SUCH CIRCUMSTANCES THAT HAD TO BE VIOLENT INSTEAD OF BEING PACIFIC DUE TO THE OBSTINACY AND STUBBORNESS OF THE COLONIAL GOVERNMENT, WITH A SAD TOLL OF CASUALTIES ON OUR SIDE. THIS COVERS WITH GRIEF AND SORROW A DAY WHICH WE COULD HAVE WISHED TO BE ONE OF CALM AND SHARED JOY. BUT THIS WILL NOT CHANGE OUR SPIRIT AND ATTITUDE.

- THEREFORE, I WISH TO STATE VERY CLEARLY TO YOU THAT WE HAVE NOT COME HERE AS CONQUERORS TO TAKE POSSESSION OF YOUR PROPERTY OR TO CONSIDER YOU OUR PRISONERS OR VASSALS.

- ON THE CONTRARY, I REAFFIRM IN THIS ACT THAT, AS IT HAS BEEN POINTED OUT PERMANENTLY DURING THE DISCUSSIONS HELD SINCE 1967, WE WISH TO RESPECT IN EVERY POSSIBLE WAY THE PRESENT STYLE OF LIFE OF THE

INHABITANTS OF THE ISLANDS, TO MAKE THE STRONGEST EFFORT TO MAINTAIN THEIR PRESENT LEVEL OF ECONOMIC ACTIVITY AND PERSONAL WELFARE, RESPECTING PRIVATE PROPERTY AND THE BASIC FREEDOMS AND RIGHTS OF ALL. WE ALSO WISH TO PERFORM A STEADY ACTION TO FULLY ACHIEVE THE "MALVINAS PROGRAM" WHICH IS BEING CARRIED OUT, AND STUDY OTHER TENDING TO PROPEL THE RATIONAL EXPLOITATION OF THE NATURAL RESOURCES OF THE ISLANDS AND THEIR AREA OF INFLUENCE, SO IN THIS WAY PROVIDE BETTER POSSIBILITIES AND PROGRESS FOR THEIR INHABITANTS.

- WE WISH, AS SOON AS POSSIBLE, TO WORK TOGETHER, IN COOPERATION, WITH ALL MEN AND WOMEN OF THIS LAND WHO WISH TO COME TO US WITH IDEAS, DISCUSS MEASURES IN BENEFIT OF THE COMMUNITY OR CRITICIZE WHAT COULD BE WRONG. IN THIS SENSE YOU WILL ALWAYS BE WELCOME, WITH AN OPEN SPIRIT, EITHER BY ME OR BY MY ASSISTANTS.

- IT SHOULD BE CLEAR THAT AS FROM TODAY ON, WE CONSIDER YOU ALL INHABITANTS OF THE ARGENTINE REPUBLIC, WITH THE FULL RIGHTS ESTABLISHED BY ITS CONSTITUTION, LISTED IN ITS ARTICLE 14, SUCH AS, TO WORK AND TO PERFORM ANY LAWFUL INDUSTRY, TO NAVIGATE AND TO TRADE, TO PETITION THE AUTHORITIES, TO ENTER, TO STAY, TO TRAVEL AND TO LEAVE THE ARGENTINE TERRITORY, TO DISSEMINATE THEIR IDEAS THROUGH THE PRESS WITHOUT PREVIOUS CENSORSHIP, TO USE AND TO DISPOSE OF THEIR PROPERTY, TO ASSOCIATE WITH USEFUL PURPOSES, TO PROFESS FREELY THEIR WORSHIP, TO TEACH AND TO LEARN.

- YOU CAN SEE THAT THE ARGENTINE CONSTITUTION, SANCTIONED IN 1853, ESTABLISHES THE RIGHTS, FREEDOMS AND PRIVILEGES OF CITIZENS WHICH ARE SIMILAR TO THOSE THE BRITISH SUBJECTS ARE ACCUSTOMED TO ENJOY. ALTHOUGH SOME OF THESE RIGHTS HAVE BEEN SUSPENDED ON THE MAINLAND DUE TO THE ANTI-TERRORIST STRUGGLE, WE HOPE THAT HERE THEY WILL BE ABSOLUTELY IN FORCE.

- I KNOW THAT YOU MUST HAVE SERIOUS DOUBTS AND PREJUICE TOWARDS OUR PRESENCE HERE AND YOUR FUTURE LIFE AS INHABITANTS OF THE ARGENTINE REPUBLIC. ANYONE WHO WISHES CAN TAKE STEPS TO BECOME FULL CITIZENS, AS MANY ALIENS, INCLUDING BRITISH SUBJECTS, HAVE BECOME SINCE MANY YEARS AGO.

- WE HOPE THAT FUTURE ACTS WILL ALLOW US TO CLARIFY THOSE DOUBTS AND OPEN A VENTUROUS PERIOD OF WORK AND PROGRESS TOGETHER.

- THEREFORE, I ASK FOR THE PROTECTION OF GOD AND I HOPE TO COUNT WITH THE COOPERATION AND GOOD WILL OF EVERYBODY, PUTTING AT THE SERVICE OF THIS ENTERPRISE, ALL MY WILL, MY STRENGTH OF SPIRIT AND UNDERSTANDING. AT THE SAME TIME I ENGAGE MYSELF, MY WORD AS GENERAL OF THE ARGENTINE ARMY TO YOU.

but the journalists would say things like 'This is also our home' and other such crap. They took pictures and interviewed soldiers. All of these interviews were set pieces. The soldiers that were picked walked up the road, then the reporter would pretend it was a random interview. Argies also started taking pictures of each other outside the more important buildings.

It was announced that telegrams could be sent, so off I trudged to tell everyone at home that I was fine. Fortunately, I was one of the first and didn't have to queue. An Argy soldier stopped Toni and I. He told us that we weren't allowed in. Toni speaks a little Spanish, but we ignored him, and pushed forward with a curt 'Telegrams!'

Later, we had to return to send telegrams for others and by then, there was a long queue outside. Telegram pads and pens were on the doorstep outside and we wrote while we waited our turn.

Four Argentinian Mirage jets flew over in a rather shoddy fashion. One plane looked as if it was trying to do a barrel roll. The plane rolled over on its side nearly halfway then spun back. Everyone outside the Cable and Wireless office roared with laughter and made derisory remarks to the utter dismay of the onlooking Argies. We didn't know then how brave the pilots were and how they would come to attack the Task Force time and time again, with these pilots taking some heavy casualties.

Transport planes came into Stanley Airport hours after they had taken the Islands over. The Argy Hercules was the main workhorse. On a few occasions two Pucará aircraft flying at each wingtip in formation would accompany the Hercules. It was a poor military display as far as we were concerned.

All the Islanders commented on the tender age of the Argy soldiers. It was also quite obvious that the ordinary private was pathetically thin and frail. Within a few days we learned that a few soldiers had started to beg for food.

There were a few very brave people in Stanley who helped people considerably, endangering themselves by deliberately opposing Argentina. These people issued, renewed and got in order passports and papers for people wishing to leave. I had no intention of leaving the Falklands, but I didn't want problems if they started sending expatriates back to Britain.

I was one of the people seeking aid. My passport was out-of-date by nearly a year. The passport however had some current visas. Life in Stanley had never stretched to a photographic booth. Passport photographs were done by photographic enthusiasts such as the Senior School Photography Club. Sadly, these facilities were not available at this time.

We were forced to improvise. Toni's brother took pictures of me standing against the only available light-coloured background – the sitting room door – with his Instamatic. A crafty snip here and there with scissors soon got the required size and shape. If you looked carefully at the picture you can make out the panels and other features of the door.

The end result, backdated with an authentic stamp, was a combination of old and new passports, lashed together with a blue ribbon and a red seal on its ties. Once my passport was valid, I had many options open to me. I could move about within the Islands and be able to identify myself.

After a few days of occupation, Britain admitted that the Argentinians had invaded the Falklands. We had been dismayed to listen to the BBC for more than 24 hours saying they couldn't confirm the Argentinians had invaded.

However, when a positive reaction came, it arrived with a roar. There was to be a task force led by the Hermes and Invincible and a requisitioned merchant armada. Britain was prepared to come and fight. Everybody living in the Falklands knew the Argentinian attitude – they wouldn't leave the Islands whatever was said. This meant one thing to me – a fight in Stanley – and if the Argies were as fanatical and prepared to back their boasts as they seemed, there would be nothing left of the town.

The Argentinians said from the very beginning that there would be no fighting in town, but actions always speak louder than words and as machine gun posts started to appear, local people began to leave for the countryside, known as camp.

The initial aim of the Argentinians was for the Islanders to resume normal life and for the local populous to understand they were somehow doing us a favour. On the days of the invasion, a few people had somehow missed the news and went off to work – only to be sent straight home again.

The schools closed down for a number of reasons, with many of the expatriate teachers leaving and most parents unwilling to have their children go to school with foreign troops milling around in town.

The Falkland Island Company jetty gang wasn't allowed anywhere near the jetty. The Grasslands Trials Unit closed down. Shops shut or greatly reduced their opening times. The police force dissolved as the Argy Military Police took over.

Andy Clarke had left town on the day before the invasion. He was cock-a-hoop thinking he had avoided the trouble when he called us on the 2 meter radio set to see if we were all right. A few days later, Goose Green, the settlement where he was working, was garrisoned by a large number of Argentinian troops. He spent most of the conflict locked up in the community hall with the rest of the people at Goose Green.

What follows is my transcribed diary entries from this period.

Monday 5 April

8,000 miles away, the British task force weighed anchor for the Falklands. In Stanley, Toni, her brother Derek, Bozo my dog, and I left town and headed for camp. Derek took Toni on his motorbike and I took Toni's motorbike. Bozo ran along behind.

It was an emotional goodbye. Toni was especially upset about leaving her parents and her horses. No one was allowed on to the Common to see if the horses were OK. We arranged 2 meter radios to listen to at different times to communicate. We didn't know what restrictions would evolve.

We went out of town over Wall Mountain, a track we wouldn't normally use, and one which became occupied by Argentines. We steered clear of the usual tracks because we weren't sure how the Argies would view these pilgrimages.

Estancia was the first stop. Toni and Derek's uncle and aunt, Tony and Ailsa Heathman, owned this farm. We stayed the night with two other refugees from Stanley. Tony, Toni's uncle, had an FRG7, an amateur radio receiver, tuned into the World Service, which was talking about what the British were going to do to the Argies and how long it would take them.

Most people had heard the invasion over the radio and having no first-hand knowledge, feared the Argies would come out to camp. No one really knew, but in town there had seemed no urgency in their movements out of town to occupy the whole country.

As the tracks were still remarkably dry, Toni and I decided that we would travel to Green Patch and then on to Rincon, the next day. Toni, who was very upset at having been forced by circumstances out of Stanley, pulled her head up and looked on it as a kind of adventure.

Tuesday 6 April

Derek again took Toni on his bike, as it was a powerful Suzuki SP400cc, I kept up comfortably on Toni's bike, which was a Honda 185cc trial bike.

We went into Green Patch to see how everyone was. Unbeknown to us at this time, we were about to get involved in a small drama.

During the summer months when *HMS Endurance* was in and around the Falkland Islands waters, a naval party was put ashore as part of a survey team, which charts a specific area of the sea. This year, the survey was taking place in Berkeley Sound, off Green Patch. They had survey flags at the top of Long Island Mountain and on Long Island, an island off the beach and at the head of Berkeley Sound. Tidal readings were being taken at the Green Patch jetty. The survey party were based at Green Patch.

When *the Endurance* shot off to South Georgia, during the scrap-dealer incident, a man was left at Green Patch to finish the recordings of the tides.

The Argentinian authorities knew this chap was at Green Patch and when Toni and I paid a visit to Carol and Terence Phillips, who owned Mount Kent Farm in the area, we also found Steve, the man *the Endurance* had left holding the fort. He was understandably rather apprehensive not knowing what the Argies were going to do.

Carol was visibly upset about the recent events and on top of that, concerned for Steve. Terence kept his cards close to his chest.

There we all were anyway, giving our opinions of the Argies and looking into the not-too-distant future, when the phone rang. The people from Long Island, a few miles to the east, had phoned to say that an Argy helicopter was on its way.

Steve had already got his gear together. Carol, Terence and Steve must have discussed at length the procedure once the Argies came to arrest Steve.

The first sign of an Argentinian presence at Green Patch was the noise of a helicopter to the southeast and three Argy soldiers sneaking over the ridge behind the settlement from the southeast. The helicopter also dropped men to the southwest. These troops came in running from cover to cover, building to building until they arrived at the back door.

Steve went out and so did Carol and Terence. Their three children watched from various vantage points. The Argentinian soldiers, decided to come in and look at the firearms. They showed a lot of interest in the .22 rifle, but handed the shotgun straight back. One of the chaps spoke fairly good English and asked if there were any other guns. Terence said 'no'. They then handed the rifle back, apologised profusely about the inconvenience and went out.

They kept telling Steve not to worry as they led him away. He remained remarkably cool but noticeably wary.

As the Argy troops did their bit, the helicopter flew above the settlement at 50 to 100 feet. The ground troops reassembled up by the corral and the helicopter picked them all up.

We all had a stiff drink and began reassuring each other that Steve would be all right. No one trusted the Argentinians, so all arguments supporting Steve's safe repatriation had an eggshell bottom.

Toni and I then left to go to Rincon, where I was teaching at the time. I was used to driving with a passenger over camp, so I soon settled down to a comfortable trip.

That night I learnt that Sally, my sister, had broadcast a message to me on the World Service saying she didn't realise teaching was so dangerous. Tony, Toni's uncle, played the recording of Sally's broadcast over the 2 meter set.

It was at this time that we heard about yet another edict, which forbade anyone to speak on the 2 meter sets. This was another blow, but not that unexpected. I had hoped, especially for Toni's sake, we could keep in touch with her parents in Stanley.

Wednesday 7 April

The Spanish part of the Falkland Radio had become much longer with a daily link with mainland stations. The music was far from our taste and the Argentine National Anthem, which was played before programmes, seemed morbid and more in keeping with a requiem.

There were two announcers on the radio by then, an Argentinian one and our own local announcer. Patrick came on first and then an Argentinian was next, spewing out propaganda. The studio used to broadcast BBC news, but the Argentinians had stopped this – however, they then reintroduced the BBC Sports round-up. At least that was something.

Toni and I weren't able to listen to the World Service direct at Rincon because my tape-playing transistor radio could only pick the signal up if the conditions were good and in the winter they rarely were. My FRG 7, an expensive receiver, was in Stanley, because I took it to Great Island when a friend and I had searched for a wreck in the Falkland Sound. Some people felt that the BBC signal was being interfered with because funny noises would come on from time to time.

Dave, my diving partner, phoned – we still had this link with town – and told me that one of the Argentinian warships had become entangled with a Polish fishing vessel's anchor chain. He felt we might be approached to free the two vessels. I couldn't believe the Argentinians were disorganised to such an extent that they didn't have any divers. I told Dave that I would only be prepared to dive if the Polish vessel was in serious trouble.

Thursday 8 April

Rincon and all the North Camp were relying on *the Monsunen's* impending voyage to replenish essential supplies. Diesel was one of the most important commodities. The generators, supplying power to all the houses, ran on diesel and many people would find it difficult to live without conveniences like lights, washing machines, deep freezes and the like.

Most farms ordered enough of the fuel to last between boats, usually a few months, plus enough for any reasonable delays. Now that the Argentinians had taken over coastal shipping people had to start looking elsewhere.

Pat Whitney, a chap living in town and owner of a long wheel base Land Rover had already brought out a considerable number of people from Stanley to camp. His trips began to form a link with town, especially for stores and mail, which was a considerable morale booster.

Pat was an experienced camp driver and he would load his Land Rover up to capacity in town and head out. The Argentinian troops knew his vehicle and sometimes gave him an easy time, although he did have some problems. At first, his Land Rover was in camouflage colours, exactly the same as the Royal Marines, but he wisely painted it blue with big white squares on the sides and top to be clearly identified, and also carried a tin of red paint and a paint brush to paint red crosses on the side, to look like a medical vehicle, if things got out of hand.

The Land Rover took some big loads out of Stanley and into camp and on some of his later journeys he was searched two or three times on the Two Sisters track. He was even stopped a few times on the camp tracks, miles from town.

As time went on Pat found it increasingly difficult to carry on this community service. He eventually had to get a pass for every trip out of town. He had split responsibilities between some of his family in camp and his wife in town.

Friday 9 April

After one week occupied by the Argentinians, the weather was still extremely kind.

The generators ran all day at the top and bottom settlements. The children weren't allowed to wander too far and didn't have school to occupy their minds, so many hours were consumed watching old videos.

My Honda motorbike lay in the shed stripped down, but it hardly felt worth rebuilding it for the Argies to take.

Toni started to think about her horses on the Common, worried they would be hurt, and the plans of her mother and others to round them up and take them out of harm's way, seemed to have come to nothing. We heard the Argentinians had already started to lay mines in the Stanley area, which was more bad news for horse owners.

Saturday 10 April

The Argentinians stopped the use of the 2 meter radios by broadcasting an edict which stated all 2 meter sets in Stanley must be handed in to the authorities. People in camp had to dismantle their beams and remove the valves (the latter being a rather difficult procedure with transistorised circuits). The valves had to be placed one mile from the transmitter.

There had been a lot of confusion when the earlier edict on Tuesday the 6th had come out. Some people said it meant one sort of radio and not others and I think this action to confiscate town sets and incapacitate camp radios was to implement the original edict.

Toni and I packed a rucksack and left for Brookfield Farm, taking some video tapes to exchange. The conversation at Brookfield centred on the Argentinians.

June, a teaching colleague who worked at Green Patch, was living at Brookfield. I had never heard June swear before, or even get slightly ruffled, but this all changed when she gave her opinion on our unwanted guests.

We carried on to Green Patch and met Derek who was at Carol and Terence's home. A few other refugees had also arrived – Peter Gilding, the Senior School headteacher, his wife Jaqui and their children Debbie and Sarah. Peter was lifting everyone's spirits with his quick wit and plans of different events to be carried out during our occupation.

However, Peter did also have a serious strategy and with Terence, during the hours of darkness, hid the rations left by the survey party.

Sunday 11 April

The night was not too peaceful. While the weather was clear, bright and calm, the Argentinians took full advantage. Planes droned in and out constantly. Not only

LADE but also Argentinian civilian airlines were flying in all kinds of jet planes including 727s.

It turned out to be a very slow day for us. We all seemed to be waiting for something to happen. Every hour we listened to the BBC World Service news to hear how the talks were going. None of us felt the Argentinians would withdraw, whatever happened talk-wise. They seemed to be rigid in their demands.

Monday 12 April

Despite the worry of the invasion, nearly everyone from Green Patch turned out to go on a fishing trip. The venue was Monte Deans and the tackle – one net.

Derek took two youngsters and I took Toni and two youngsters on our bikes. We went ahead for gate opening duties amongst other things. Two Land Rovers came behind with the rest of the contingent.

Monte Deans was a creek with high-sided banks. A small stream ran into the creek head. Driving down the steep bank was great fun and the squeals from the passengers confirmed that they enjoyed it too.

The Land Rovers caught us up and we untangled the net ready for use. Sadly, the fishing experts, primed with local knowledge and wisdom foretold of a disappointing catch. We had arrived rather late.

Having thigh boots on, I grabbed one end and went into the water and with Derek on the other end we began to drag the net up the creek. No joy and no fish either. We carried on down to another location below the dip but it was obvious that we weren't going to catch fish there. However, we did take our minds off the Argentinians for a few hours and got some fresh air into our lungs.

Meanwhile the American Secretary of State, Alexander Haig, arrived back in London, as he shuttled between the main protagonists.

We heard that Bill Luxton, a farm owner and local politician, was leaving the Islands via the jackboot of the Argentinians. He was an 'undesirable'. No one seemed to know what he'd done or why. Rumour had it that he demanded to fly his plane back to Chartres, his farm on the West Falklands, from Stanley. I felt it might be deeper than this. Bill was one of the biggest private landowners in the Islands and perhaps they mistook this large ownership as a symbol of leadership. As a local politician however, Bill had also never shied away from criticising Argentina.

Tuesday 13 April

The BBC told us that Haig went back to Washington to allow Britain and Argentina some thinking space. They also hinted that the Russians might have been giving the enemy intelligence information.

It seemed ridiculous that a right-wing Junta and the Russians could strike up a relationship, particularly as the Argentinian police had shot communist demonstrators in Mendoza a very short time beforehand. It must have had something to do with commercial sales between the two countries.

A large contingent of Toni's Grassland Trails colleagues left Stanley to journey back to the UK.

We then went back to the Estancia. No one was staying there apart from Toni and I. Tony and Ailsa asked us to stay.

Wednesday 14 April

We listened to the World Service. It was becoming a ritual. It told us twenty more Harriers were coming down on the container vessel the Atlantic Conveyor. The British government thought there was going to be a fight and that there was a possibility, because of the threat to the Task Force from the mainland, we would lose some planes.

We did hear a few planes, but really you wouldn't have thought there was a war on at this point.

Friday 16 April

Tony and I went out to the old shearing shed and looked at the new peat stove he had bought. The difference between this stove and a Rayburn was that the new stove was designed to heat a number of radiators. The firebox was quite a bit bigger and its sides worked like a water jacket that heats the water for the domestic hot water and the radiators. We were discussing the pros and cons of both new and old when we heard a helicopter. It must have flown exceptionally low, because although we could hear that it was in the next valley, flying towards the house, we couldn't see it.

Tony climbed up on to the roof, because he was sure it had landed a few times and he wondered if it was dropping off troops. He eventually saw it. It was a smallish thing and it had landed in the Peat Bog Paddock, but no one got out.

As Tony was watching, it took off towards the house. Tony jumped down and we ran back to the house. The helicopter landed beside the farm's pig – to its great consternation. Instead of people getting out, it just took off again. The people in the back waved to us, but we didn't wave back. It was very strange behaviour as though they were sightseeing.

At this time we weren't 100 per cent sure how the Argentinians viewed radios. Ailsa also had a revolver that would have been found during the most half-hearted search. While the helicopter was buzzing around, Ailsa was busy hiding the radio and other bits and pieces.

This was Tony and Ailsa's first encounter with the enemy. I think Ailsa had been beginning to relax, but after that she seemed to be a bit on edge.

Saturday 17 April

Ailsa and Tony's daughter Nyree, not even a year old, had a plaster cast on her leg for several weeks to try and straighten a twisted ankle. War doesn't take into account medical problems and their cures. Ailsa spoke to the doctor in Stanley, who recommended removing the cast and inspecting the ankle.

This was no problem – apart from no roads and the route being infested with our unwelcome visitors. Derek offered to take Ailsa on his bike with Nyree in a papoose on her back. Toni and I decided to go along to give assistance and moral support.

The track had softened over the previous few weeks, but it wasn't too bad using the track across the Murrell Bridge and over the Two Sisters Flat and down the Two Sisters Road. We didn't meet anyone, friend or foe, until we reached the Two Sisters gate. From the gate the Two Sisters Road was a rocky, stone-strewn road, which led to the west end of Stanley harbour. It was far easier on a bike to get off this rough, uneven surface and stay on the grass.

We started to see members of the Argentinian army on the sides of Mount Longdon on the left and the Two Sisters on the right. We were looking this way and that as we drove along. Some of the positions in Moody Valley were really quite hard to pick out from their surroundings, but the trenches on the ridges stood out clearly as you could see the lines of peat which they had dug out.

Toni pointed out some tents I couldn't see. Then the inevitable happened as I was scanning the hills. The bike hit a big black hole at the wrong angle and we were left in a heap.

Stanley was quiet as a lot of people had gone to camp. The Argentinian officers who had strutted around town with a couple of bodyguards, now swaggered round quite unattended. Groups of civilians lounged around talking. The whole atmosphere in town was strange.

A lot of people had been evacuated from Davis Street and there were also many 'no go' areas behind town, although some people still remained. Most of the expatriate teachers were planning to leave over the next few days.

Dave was in a state. His boat, *the Penguin*, had been sunk and he'd had some rough treatment from the authorities. When he went down to see the vessel they took his camera away and destroyed the film. I didn't stay long in town, but it was depressing news to leave with.

A large Argentinian boat had made it to Stanley. Loads of motorbikes were part of the cargo and we met an Argentinian soldier battling with a small Kawasaki as we left. There were also two small, armed patrol boats steaming up and down the harbour.

We left Stanley and decided to go out via Wall Mountain rather than up through the Two Sisters, but were stopped by some Argies not far from town, along the Darwin Road. They refused to let us pass and so we doubled back and headed back out the way we came in via the Two Sisters.

We were stopped again a few times, but each time we were allowed to proceed. The last time we were stopped a soldier asked Derek if he spoke Spanish? Derek said no, but when the soldier asked if the Argy at Moody Brook had said we could go, in Spanish, Derek said 'Yes'.

Sunday 18 April

Most farms had stopped work except for essential day-to-day functions.

The water to the Estancia house came from a catchment area 500 yards from the taps. The catchment area was higher than the house as the water was gravity-fed to the farm. The pipe left the catchment area, travelled down the hill to the creek, crossed it, and then climbed the gradual slope to the house.

Some of this pipe had somehow come to the surface because it hadn't been put in properly, so Tony and I went over to the other side of the creek to bury it.

Derek and Toni had a bike maintenance session behind the house out of the wind. The bikes were showing the wear and tear of non-stop use since the invasion and were in desperate need of some work. Chains were tightened and oiled, brakes were adjusted and oil levels checked.

We had heard from some travellers on the track. Alan Miller from Port San Carlos drove in with a couple of passengers. He told us that a helicopter landed there looking for Bill Luxton. He went out to meet the soldiers and one hit him in the stomach with his rifle butt, pushing him up against the store and banging his head against it. This was the first time we had heard of the Argentinians using physical force and intimidation tactics on the civilian population.

Alan Miller also had very strong views about the Argentinians after the invasion and had aired them on the 2 meter frequencies. It was possible that someone had overheard him.

Derek, Toni and I finished off the day with another leisurely fishing expedition. It wasn't much of a catch, perhaps the fish were suffering from the pressures of war.

Monday 19 April

There was nothing startling on the news, so Tony and I finished burying the pipe. It was difficult stopping the water from the tank with a wooden bung. The weather was very cold.

Derek came home with a monstrous trout, which weighed 9lbs and was a good-looking fish. It seemed a shame to catch and kill such a healthy, strong specimen.

Toni and I decided to take a run up to Rincon to see how Bozo was doing and to pick up a few bits and pieces like a fishing rod. Bozo was pleased to see us and was glad of a good run.

We intended to get back to the Estancia, but we had left it rather late and thought that night travel would be pushing our luck. Paul Watson, from Long Island, was on the track and had left Horseshoe Bay a few minutes before us, so we had to race to catch him up so that we could travel up to Green Patch together.

Terence and Carol's house was suddenly overflowing, but they found us a corner for the night. They still hadn't heard from Steve, the chap that the Argentinians picked up from Green Patch. He had promised to send them a telegram when he got back to the UK.

Tuesday 20 April

Toni, Bozo and I went to Johnsons Harbour to see Toni's aunt and uncle Jenny and George Smith, and to see if Bozo was as big as his father, their pure-bred Huntaway. Bozo ran well and led the bike for a lot of the time, showing that he hadn't suffered at all for his enforced rest.

The Smiths were very well and gave us a hearty lunch and an Argentinian-dominated chat. None of it was good. They hadn't had much contact with the Argentinian forces, but they had witnessed a stream of aircraft flying overhead into Stanley.

Bozo was introduced to his father and although Bozo was a big dog in Falklands terms, he wasn't as big as his dad.

We had to be careful on this occasion to allow time to get back to the Estancia, but we made time to go to the store and buy a few bits and pieces for various people along the track. Johnsons had a good reserve of fuel so while we were there, I asked Osmund Smith, the manager owner, if Rincon could have diesel because they were getting quite short. Here was the Falklands community at its best helping one another through a crisis.

Bozo ran back to Green Patch where we had to leave him. We dropped off some stores and headed back to the Estancia.

The ranks had swelled substantially at the Estancia. The Davidsons, who ran a hotel and market garden in Stanley, had arrived for the duration and their escorts – the Duncans and Peter Clement – were just staying the night.

Heather, Toni's Mum, rang to unsettle us all by announcing that both Derek and Toni must be ready to go to town, because they were preparing to go to the UK. Toni was really upset. I unintentionally rubbed salt into the wound by telling her I wasn't prepared to leave.

A lot of people, Falkland Islanders and expatriates, left on that day to fly to England, but the Petterssons decided to stay where they were.

Wednesday 21 April

It wasn't total drudgery, but Don, Toni and I went fishing up in one of the smaller streams. We got nothing. We were just hanging around waiting for something to happen.

Sometimes it was as if the war was somewhere else. Not a sign of the Argies as we nonchalantly picked dry fern for the pig's bed.

There were more 'pleasantries', over the radio, from our occupying forces. Edict number something-or-other said we must observe a blackout protocol.

We at the Estancia had a bloody good laugh. With modern technology British forces wouldn't rely on the lights of Stanley, even less the odd farm settlement or outside house to guide them in on Falklands targets.

We often listened to Radio Rye, an English language Argentinian broadcasting station. It broadcasted propaganda – there was no other word for it. Listening to Radio Rye you would have thought it was only the Argentinians who lived in the modern world. They were quite insulting about the British Task Force calling it scrap metal and saying that most of it would sink on the way down here. How pathetic.

Stanley was given an air raid schedule. A minute's alarm time would be given for people to take shelter and then an all-clear would sound. The fire siren would be used.

Thursday 22 April

An Argy 707 flew over the British Task Force and a jump jet was scrambled to intercept it – so the BBC World Service told us as we sat around the radio. The pilot was told only to shoot in self-defence. Although there was nothing much in this report, everyone at the Estancia was delighted that something was happening. It was contact between the two forces. We debated how the Argentinians had found the Task Force in the middle of the South Atlantic. Was it by enemy submarines or Soviet satellites?

The Argentinians celebrated the sightings with more edicts. The first asked people travelling between Stanley and camp to get a pass from the Police Station. The next informed members of the public that the police force was made up entirely of (Argentinian) military personnel. Islander Anton Livermore (who was a local police officer), however, was available to advise the civilian population. The last edict told the local fire brigade and medical staff where they were expected to be.

President Galtieri was meant to have visited the Islands, but no one that I knew saw him. I don't think many, if any, local people were that interested. I was sure the Argentinian press and especially Radio Rye would make the most of it.

Heather talked to Toni on the phone with the news she had been longing to hear and that lifted her spirits. If all went well the horses would be ready for us to collect the next day.

Elephant Seal on the beach at the south beach, Sea Lion Island.

Elephant Seal pup a few days old.

Marie Clifton by a pond with Magellanic (Jackass) penguins Sea Lion Island

Don Otto bus, South America.

South American ferry on our travels.

View of Machu Picchu from Huayna Picchu.

Arthur and Andrea Turner trying to remove one of the Shetland ponies from the back porch Rincon Grande.

Me untying the ropes from Dave Eynon's inflatable, ready for the journey to Great Island. Photo courtesy Dave Eynon

Dave, Leeann and Christopher Eynon, the inflatable loaded with stores including a 45 gallon drum of petrol for Great Island. Photo courtesy Dave Eynon

Dave Eynon filling diving bottles on the beach at Great Island.

39. Me at the site of the wreck Conquimbana with the copper ingots visible in the background. Photo courtesy Dave Eynon

Me with one of the recovered copper ingots on the beach at Great Island.

Dick Baker Chief Secretary, heading to Government House with our uninvited guests on the morning of April 2 1982.

Argentine Armoured Personnel Carriers out side Police Cottages 2nd April 1982.

Smoke from damaged Argentine helicopters after Harriers attack Mount Kent.

Argentines being returned to their camp at Estancia Mountain by Tony Heathman in his tractor accompanied by Don Davidson.

'eal Inlet tractor stuck in the creek at the Estancia.

Blues and Royals in tank at Estancia

Loading troops and equipment into trailer at Estancia.

Line of tractors and trailers ready to move men and equipment at Estancia.

Tractor with sleigh loaded with Milan missiles and other kit at Estancia.

Army Air Corps Gazelle at Estancia, with their camp visible to middle left of photo.

Wessex with under slung load at Estancia.

Wessex, Gazelle, tractor and rover at Estancia.

Estancia taken from across the creek, with smoke from burning drums drifting across.

Toni standing behind bomb crater east of Stanley after the war.

Rescuing Dave Eynon's boat the Penguin after the war.

Dave Eynon, Peter Clement in inflatable, engineer on beach and MV Forrest in background during seismic survey at Mare Harbour.

Dave Eynon, Billy Duncan and Eric Spink laying the hydrophones from the MV Forrest.

Diving gear on the hatch of MV Forrest.

Machinery lined up at Mare Harbour ready to start work on construction of Mount Pleasant Airfield.

Me lying in bucket of machine to give scale to the size.

Toni and I on our wedding day.

Vehicle with Giles Mercer getting ready for our epic trip to Port Sussex after our wedding, to show my father the farm we were buying.

Friday 23 April

Flat calm. Once again the consensus of opinion was that the weather was being exceptionally kind to the Argentinians. Most Falkland Islanders were hoping for a nice southerly gale, which would be ideal weather with some rain.

Heather phoned early in the morning to say the evacuation of the horses was on. Toni made a few sandwiches and a flask of coffee and we all piled into a Land Rover and headed towards town. We went on the old fisherman's track, which was to the north of the usual route. It was surprisingly good, which shows how dry it was and how little traffic it had seen recently. We didn't have any problems.

We got to the Two Sisters gate, but the horses hadn't arrived. We drove up on to a peat bank so that we had a clear view into town.

The following is the document issued to Heather Pettersson to allow her and others to walk the horses out of Stanley and meet us at the Two Sisters Gate for us to take them to Estancia.

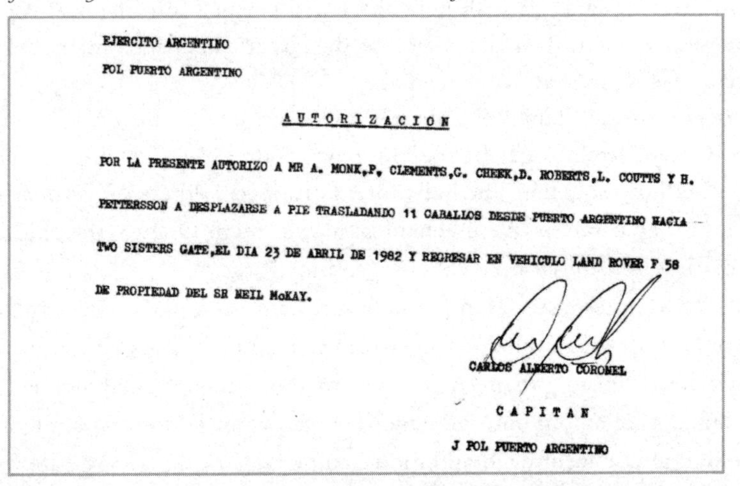

EJERCITO ARGENTINO

POL PUERTO ARGENTINO

AUTORIZACION

POR LA PRESENTE AUTORIZO A MR A. MONK,P, CLEMENTS,G. CHEEK,D. ROBERTS,L. COUTTS Y H. PETTERSSON A DESPLAZARSE A PIE TRASLADANDO 11 CABALLOS DESDE PUERTO ARGENTINO HACIA TWO SISTERS GATE,EL DIA 23 DE ABRIL DE 1982 Y REGRESAR EN VEHICULO LAND ROVER F 58 DE PROPIEDAD DEL SR NEIL McKAY.

CARLOS ALBERTO CORONEL

CAPITAN

J POL PUERTO ARGENTINO

A Land Rover arrived with a generator for the Estancia and horse gear for Toni and me. We could see the horses about half a mile away with quite a few people leading them.

Four Mirage jets flew over town. We thought they were Harriers, but unfortunately that was wishful thinking and Tony was able to look at them through a telescope, which made it clear that they were Argentinian.

Several helicopters appeared from the Darwin direction, noisy brutes. Helicopters going the other way were flashing their lights to the soldiers on the ground.

Eleven horses in all came up to the Two Sisters gate. Toni decided to ride Silver Blaze and lead Granny Arab, and a bay-coloured mare. I rode Nicky Nanny and led a brown horse and Bluey. The rest of the horses would follow our lead.

As we were readying the horses to leave, we saw Argentinian Pucarás – twin-engined, propeller-driven, ground attack aircraft – diving in and around the Estancia. We could hear the engines screaming as they swooped down. We could also hear helicopters and we began to worry and wonder what was going on.

We had a good ride back to the Estancia. The weather couldn't have been better for the time of year. It wasn't an occasion where we could forget about the war though, because as we rode along there were continuous bangs from town. Something was happening, but we could only guess at what it was.

We took the horses to Stud Rincon. Tony came and picked us up and shot a few geese for the pig while he was at it.

We heard over the World Service that the British fleet was off South Georgia in very rough weather. So rough, the Argentinians said that the British wouldn't attack. The Argentinians were appealing to the Organisation of American States. I could imagine the emotional begging that would be going on.

Saturday, 24 April

The World Service said a British helicopter had crashed into the sea. An officer was lost, but the pilot was saved. It also said that the Americans had some new ideas for the British Foreign Secretary Pym to consider.

On the local front, in Stanley the air raid sirens were to be tested.

I went to Green Patch to get Bozo. The news from Green Patch was that they have suffered another house search. The helicopters dropped soldiers off at both ends of the settlement and they came in like mechanical action men. One of the soldiers told the people in the first house that they were 'surrounded'.

Other stories were told. Apparently the family living at the Murrell Farm saw soldiers killing sheep. Not for meat, but running after them and just stabbing them with a knife, or indiscriminately shooting them. A member of the family phoned Stanley to complain about the soldier's behaviour and the Argentinians promised to send someone over, but instead, the phone line went dead and didn't come back on.

A helicopter landed at Brookfield at some time and gave them permission to use their 2 meter sets in times of medical need. Roddy McKay, who worked there, was told to be careful, however, because they knew he had sons in Stanley.

People in town seem to be sticking up for themselves – ordering the Argy soldiers out of their houses and sheds. The soldiers seem to accept it, although rumour control said one local was told that he would have his throat cut if he didn't look out.

True or not, these stories gave everyone something to talk about and do between listening to the World Service.

Bozo and I got back in time for Toni and I to go fishing. I caught an 'occupation special' in the shape of a 5lb trout.

Sunday 25 April

I forgot again that there was no BBC World Service Newsreel on Sunday at 8pm, like the rest of the week. I cursed for the third successive Sunday.

When the World Service did come on it was an eye-opener. An attack had been carried out by helicopters of the Task Force which found an Argentinian submarine on the surface off South Georgia.

The so-called local broadcasting station continued to bore and insult us with its rubbish. The Argy name, for what had been the Falkland Radio, LR60, was said every other word and some so-called 'friend' gave us the weather. Needless to say, no Falkland Islander or British civilian had anything to do with its production. One of the so-called friends was the Argy Spanish teacher who had already shown her true colours – light blue like the Argy flag.

British troops were on South Georgia. Toni and I took Bozo for a walk – anything to fill in time. Toni and I were scrambling through an expanse of rock, locally called a stone run, on the other side of the creek when Tony came down to the other side to shout 'the Argies have surrendered in South Georgia'. We both rushed back to the house. It was just after 4pm.

The BBC gave the details. There was limited resistance and no casualties on the British side.

We talked about the day's events. The British had started to fight.

Monday 26 April

Argentinian helicopters gave a display of strength as five flew up the Estancia side of the mountain. My kingdom for a Harrier!

A funny-looking plane that we had christened the box cart (Skyvan) appeared. It was a fat twin-engined plane, which had passed the house several times heading west and returning from the same direction. The pilot must have been very confident, because he flew so low in the valleys we couldn't see him until he was on top of us.

Tony wasn't going to take this effrontery lying down and on the plane's second or third excursion, he ran down the green and hurled a rock at it. It was an action that brought great humour and light relief, but fear as well, that the Argentinians who were up in the hills might misinterpret Tony's madness and come down and beat the crap out of us.

Tony and I dug out the meat house foundations while listening to morning news and Radio Newsreel at 11am. The air traffic had been continuous.

The Argentinian Radio Rye broadcasted some dramatic news, saying its troops were heroically resisting in South Georgia and its special forces would withdraw into the Island, never to surrender, instead fighting an everlasting rear-guard action. Rye didn't fool anyone at the Estancia.

Our local radio had begun broadcasting to the troops. The Argentine commander, General Menendez, gave a speech to fill his troops with pride: 'Argentinian airmen, sailors and soldiers who defended the national sovereignty and the honour of the flag in Islas Malvinas (the name they gave the Falkland Islands): the hour of battle has arrived.

'Destiny has wanted to trust us the honour of the nation and the responsibility to preserve this ground as Argentinian, as the land where each of us was born.

'In the place of honour, which each one has, there shall be a lion in the battle. Ready to shoot to kill, nearing to fight hand to hand with the courage of Cabral and Ciachina.

'Let's honour our oath of fidelity to the flag and give a new page of glory to our Fatherland arms, defeating the third English invasion.

'The whole world is watching us. Invoking the protection of God and the Blessed Virgin, protection of our arms, we shall go to battle carrying in our hearts the firm decision of victory or death.'

Toni, Tony and I were not impressed. We went fishing and shooting. The teal duck had wisely left the war zone and the fish weren't biting. I tried to get Bozo to chase some sheep, also unsuccessfully.

Tuesday 27 April

Alexander Haig told the Organisation of American States that the Argentinians were the aggressors and there was no reason why they should invoke the Rio Treaty, which would have meant the rest of the Americas would have supported the Argy cause.

Radio Rye was still telling the world that its troops were continuing to fight on South Georgia.

General Menendez in 'Puerto Soledad' (in other words Port Stanley) spoke to the troops. Everything was said in Spanish, but it sounded typically emotional. I could picture the Argentinian troops grouped around the brigade's radio bawling their eyes out.

I went to Green Patch in an attempt to get a letter to town. I missed Pat by two hours. I thought there could be troops in the camp around Green Hill. The sheep that usually abound in and around the green grass of the sheep pens were ominously absent.

I got roped into killing a steer. A gang of us went, so it wasn't a long process. It was not a bad job when there are loads of people who are willing, joking and working.

Pat was due back in the afternoon. I waited for a few hours, but at 4pm Ron Turner phoned from Rincon to say that a blackout for camp had been announced on the radio.

Terence and I chased the remaining bullock out of the settlement and through the Pond Paddock. I then left and made a swift journey to the Estancia, because I was certain they wouldn't have heard the edict. I arrived to find that they had.

We tacked up blankets in a half-hearted effort at a blackout. The foggy, overcast nights did a lot for us, plus the fact that the Estancia was hidden because it lies below the average lay of the land.

Wednesday 28 April

The BBC said that an Argentinian prisoner had died in captivity in South Georgia. They referred to it as a serious incident, but didn't elucidate. They also announced the forthcoming air blockade from 7pm camp time – 11.00 GMT. Things were hotting up.

Toni and I went to Green Patch. An Argentinian helicopter was hovering over Long Island Mountain, but we couldn't really see what it was up to. We speculated that it may be moving troops or searching for British Special Forces which were rumoured to be in the Islands already.

Pat could no longer travel in and out of town. He had been threatened by the Argies. They told him to be back that night, but he intended to remain in camp and disable his Land Rover as he was worried the Argies were becoming more difficult. He told us that the day before, the Argies had rounded up several youths, most of who were involved with the Falkland Island Defence Force.

That effectively closed the source of news from town, but we were still able to use the phone from the Estancia.

Ailsa tried to persuade Toni's parents and granny to come out to camp, but the answer was to wait and see. I was worried because I knew the phone wouldn't last forever. It didn't need the Argies to cut it, because a decent wind often damaged the line. Once there was no communication we would be worrying about each other. People felt there were disadvantages to leaving their homes, but I felt they outweighed the possible loss of life if it got hot in town.

The Brits attacked, but the Argy and British versions of events differed. Britain said all the planes returned safely, but the Argies said two Harriers were shot down and one pilot ejected. A British journalist, Brian Hanrahan, confirmed that all the Harriers returned safely, although one did have a bullet hole in its tail, which was quickly repaired.

At 11am camp time, 15.00 GMT, the aircraft carrier Hermes came on 4.5, the frequency used internally on the Islands to communicate with Stanley. Everyone's ears were pinned back. Both Rob Pitaluga at Salvador settlement and Jimmy Forster at Dunnose Head farm tried to contact someone in Stanley. Eventually a message was transmitted to the Argentinians and a reply returned. Unfortunately for the listeners at the Estancia, it was in morse code.

The sky above Stanley was lit up as anti-aircraft fire burst in the air. We presumed the British were attacking, but could only guess at what was happening. Big bangs could also be heard clearly coming from town.

Scanning the radio bands we heard the British Fleet. From all accounts they were at action stations. They came under a heavy attack from hostile planes. We could hear them on their radios, where they referred to the enemy as 'hostiles' and then gave a bearing, read out with a range and a speed. One ship said: 'It got a little too hot in there so we had to withdraw.' When the hostiles left they were ordered back in 'to complete their task'.

Harriers were giving them air cover which they referred to as 'caps'. One radio operator came on because a cap had flown straight at them at high speed and frightened the life out of him. The operators also co-ordinated the positions of the 'caps', which they also termed as 'friendlies'.

One ship was hit during this fight, but by what they didn't say. No names of ships were mentioned. It was exciting and at the same time frightening to hear the Royal Navy in action. It gave me a feeling of security to hear the men's voices cool, calm and collected with even a hint of humour, which in itself suggested a high level of confidence.

Later that day the BBC World Service confirmed the action we had been listening to, saying that the ships of the Task Force were shelling Argentinian positions around Stanley when they were attacked by Argentinian aircraft.

Two aircraft, a Canberra and a Mirage, were said to have been shot down. They also believed that the Argentinian ground forces shot one of their own planes down.

We had a feeling we saw the plane heading into town. A Mirage came flying in low, but not that fast, from the west. It flew around the back of Mount Estancia. We could hear it clearly and then there was an almighty explosion and we couldn't hear it any more.

We saw more flashes late in the afternoon. Two Pucarás busily flew around. They flew up the valley between Mount Kent and the Estancia Mountain and then turned counter-clockwise right around the mountains and then they'd appear from the Green Hill direction, to the north, and around they would go again.

This went on for some time, so we had time to study them in some detail. They had rockets with black heads under the wings. I am not sure whether they were taking part in some kind of action, but no one could see them posing any great threat to the Harriers.

After spending days and weeks waiting for something to happen we were now, or I should say the Argies were now, receiving the full attention of the British Task Force.

After all the action, there was nothing to do. The evening was spent with Toni making a rug, Margaret spinning and Ailsa writing her diary.

Thursday 29 April

Ailsa received some bad news from Granny Johnson on the phone to say that her mother and father, along with other so called 'anti Argentine' locals, had been taken to Fox Bay. There were 14 in total. Ailsa's parents. Velma and George Malcolm, Dr Haines and his wife Hilary and three children, Stuart and Lillian Wallace and their two children, Gerald Cheek, Owen Summers and finally Brian Summers.

Grizelda Cockwell got on 4.5 and asked for the aforementioned peoples' mail to be sent to Fox Bay East thus telling people where they were. However Heather, Toni's mum, had already told Granny Johnson where they were because she had been told by Dr Mario who she knew while working at the Upland Goose Hotel.

A lot of horses had been evacuated from town in several large parties. There was an increasing danger of mines and people didn't want their animals in and around Stanley.

Toni received a phone call from Rene Duncan, in Stanley, who wanted to evacuate a mare and foal to camp. Toni arranged that we would meet them on the track and walk them to Long Island.

I fuelled up the bike and noted we were getting low on stored fuel.

When we arrived at the rendezvous, there was nobody there. We checked the Caravan Track and Riding Track passes, but there wasn't a sign anyone had been there recently. We slowly made our way along in the direction of town searching for signs of people on the track because we didn't want to miss them.

With all the Argies out in the camp, we couldn't be sure they were safe. We travelled to the top of the first rise. Nothing. Over a flat, and the next rise and still nothing. We weren't late, but I had an uneasy feeling that we had missed them somehow – or worse. We stopped the bike and we guzzled a can of Coke between us. I decided to sit tight, but it was extremely difficult to do because time drags in situations like this. After what seemed like ages, over the hill came Rene leading the mare with the foal following, her husband Billy following in the Land Rover.

We swapped stories and I asked them to convey to Toni's mum and dad that they could always replace or get new possessions, but you could never replace a life.

The period of not being sure if we were in the middle of a war zone, or not, had ended. We were. Helicopters are going this way and that, some so low that you couldn't see them a lot of the time. The Pucarás were howling along at low level, like angry, giant insects.

I drove in front as Toni led the mare and foal. I was sure from all the activity that eventually we would be stopped. Toni wanted me to tear ahead and get someone from Long Island to come and meet her, because it was a long slog in the middle of winter.

I didn't dare go, because I was worried that Toni might bump into an Argy patrol, if there were such things, and as it was heating up, you would have thought there would be. As it was, my fears were unfounded and nothing happened. Toni ended up walking all the way.

We met Neil, Paul and Lisa Watson, from Long Island Farm, on the sand beach just before the house. They were preoccupied with Argy spotting when we arrived. Up on the side of Long Island Mountain was a group of Argentinian soldiers. About forty of them looked as if they were on parade, but you could also see isolated ones and twos searching the rocks.

Neil and Lisa took the mare and foal and led them up towards the house. We became aware that one of the Argentinian soldiers was a little too close for comfort. As we were about to leave we saw a bike heading along the track towards the bottom of the mountain and heading towards Stanley.

We popped in for a quick cuppa, and as with most places they were playing host to a number of Stanley residents, so we all had a jolly good chinwag.

We had left it a bit late, but we thought we should try and get back to the Estancia as all the houses were full of refugees from town.

As we turned left to head towards the Estancia, I put on our lights. As we began to climb we saw a helicopter coming over the Long Island Mountain heading our way with its searchlight sweeping the ground.

As we were meant to be obeying a curfew it was a bit of a shock. Had the Argentinian troops on the hills reported us? Were we what the helicopter was looking for? I flicked off the lights and we went for it as fast as I dared. If they had seen us, I doubted if we would get very far before they would be overhead.

In the dark, we were wandering all over the track and had a couple of near crashes as we blindly drove along thinking that at any moment we would hear the helicopter. Just outside the Estancia we hit something with a hell of a bang, but we were still going.

The helicopter didn't materialise, but we were mightily relieved when we walked into the house. Whatever we hit put a large dent in the wheel rim and was evidence of our rather hasty trip in the dark.

Toni's mum Heather was on the phone that night and gave Toni a severe roasting about being irresponsible and of course she was not wrong. With this episode came the end of our gallivanting about in the North Camp even though this last effort had been for a good cause.

Back at the Estancia we listened to the World Service news. The Argentinians have countered the British blockade with one of their own.

Jack and Kay McCullum, from Stanley, arrived to spend the rest of the war with us. Their Land Rover broke down on the way, so Tony went out to tow them to the Estancia with the tractor.

All-out war was imminent. Nobody in Estancia thought it could be averted, and felt the sooner the British removed the Argentinians the better.

During the occupation I had been bewildered by the USA's foreign policy. Argentina had some modern technology withheld by previous president Jimmy Carter for violation of human rights, but Reagan sat on the fence. If an international discussion or law went against the Argentinians, their delegates left in a self-righteous manner yet this behaviour was ignored. If, however, they have a ruling, which supported them, they clamoured, like children, for immediate implementation.

However, Radio Newsreel announced at 8am local time that the United States of America had come down on the side of Britain. Logistical support and materials would be given.

That was a slap in the face to Argentina. They hadn't commented yet, but when they did, I was sure it would be with unparalleled outrage and indignation.

Sunday 2 May

Conflicting reports of yesterday's action poured in. The Argentinians claimed to have shot down five Harriers and said several more had been so badly damaged that they didn't return to their carriers. They also claimed to have damaged the Hermes and a frigate. They admitted that a Mirage and Canberra bomber were shot down.

Radio Rye went over the top completely, saying seven Harriers had been shot down and several warships destroyed. It was pathetic. We listened to Radio Rye to boost our morale and have a good belly laugh.

At 11am local time, the Ministry of Defence announced on the World Service, that a British submarine had attacked the Argentinian cruiser the *General Belgrano*. More than one torpedo was used. The Argentinians agreed that the ship had been attacked, but said it had been slightly damaged.

After all the Argy propaganda about British ships and planes destroyed, it showed that action spoke louder than words.

Monday 3 May

An Argentinian patrol boat fired on a Sea King helicopter on anti-submarine patrol. British missile-carrying helicopters sunk one patrol boat and attacked another.

The Argentinians were jamming the BBC Spanish broadcasts to South America. They must have realised the effect these broadcasts would have in the future, even if no one in Argentina believed what the BBC were broadcasting. The Argentine military's propaganda would be exposed when the BBC were proved to be reliable.

The Argentinians said that the *Belgrano* had disappeared from their radar screens, which must have been the best way for them of saying it had sunk. The minor damage they reported must have been a little more serious than they suggested. An air search started and boats were standing by.

No one seemed to know how many sailors were on board. Estimates ranged from 700 to more than one thousand. People had begun to die in large numbers, which was a prelude to out-and-out fighting.

Tuesday 4 May

On the day Nyree, Tony and Ailsa's daughter, learned to walk, the first British casualties due to Argentinian action were counted.

The Ministry of Defence announced that when the *Belgrano* was attacked, it was in the company of two other ships. What happened to them when the *Belgrano* was hit? Did they chase after the sub, stay to pick up survivors or run away?

Later in the day the British attacked a submarine, but details seemed rather vague. Surely with all this sophisticated sonar they must have known whether they hit it or not.

We heard Stanley Airport getting some more attention from British planes with large bangs and the sound of anti-aircraft fire.

Disaster for the Task Force. The BBC interrupted a programme just before 5pm local time, to say that the destroyer, *Sheffield*, had been hit by an Argentinian missile and gutted by fire. There were more casualties, including at least twelve dead. This was a blow to everyone.

The British public would now know that it wasn't going to be a walkover. The Argies could fight and their weaponry wasn't to be sniffed at.

The Sheffield was afloat but it sounded as if it was a write-off.

Wednesday 5 May

How depressing, we heard 30 were now presumed dead. A French-made Exocet missile, fired from a Super Étendard plane, 20 miles away, hit the *Sheffield.* How many more had the Argentinians got?

Diplomatic efforts were given another chance, with Peru offering a solution. I couldn't see the Argentinians accepting anything except total sovereignty. They might have gone through the motions of negotiations, but they didn't fool me.

Argentina then said the sovereignty wasn't negotiable, so the fight was still on.

Thursday 6 May

The men left the Estancia with a packed lunch to erect a fence. We fuelled up the tractor, loaded the transport box and hitched up the sleigh, a large trailer with runners rather than wheels, with more fencing material.

It was another beautiful winter's day – flat, calm and relatively warm. It had been a record-beating year for good weather, ruined by our unwanted guests from the South American mainland.

The fence would not be a masterpiece, but it would do the job. We built triangular crates and filled them with rocks from the beach. The crates supported the fence into the sea, remaining in the water during the lowest tides so that sheep or cattle couldn't walk around the end.

Argentinian helicopters were up on the hill and we saw and heard a lot more. Just after we finished building the crates Toni appeared, running over the hill, which was quite a surprise considering we were miles away from the Estancia. Toni had ridden her bike most of the way, but was unable to get across the last ditch.

There was great excitement at the farm, because a solitary Argentinian soldier had wandered in from the hill, apparently lost.

Don and Tony returned to the farm and Jack and I carried on with the fence. Don spoke a little Spanish, which made him an important asset, and Tony wanted to have a close look at an Argentinian. Toni stayed behind with us and shot some duck and a goose.

Jack and I managed to stitch the fence together although we didn't manage to finish it completely. We didn't want to stay too long because we weren't sure what was happening back at the Estancia.

By the time we got back, however, Tony and Don had taken the Argy back along the track to the nearest known Argentinian position, which was Long Island Mountain.

The women felt sorry for the Argy, who looked a bit frail and out of sorts. Living in the mountain in the middle of winter would have that effect on most people, so they had given him some food and a drink. He wouldn't enter the house, but he didn't refuse refreshments.

He didn't know where he came from, but spoke of a road and some machines, so we decided he had come from the Darwin Road.

When our Argentinian stray had staggered in, he'd said that he'd had nothing to eat or drink for three days. Once he'd eaten, his strength and vitality returned and he offered to hoe the garden in return for the women's kindness.

No one took up his offer of hoeing – not because they wanted him to retain enough strength to walk off the farm, but because buried in the garden was the shot gun and .303 rifle, as well as some .303 bullets.

Don had done remarkably well, considering he was supposed to know only a 'little' Spanish. Apparently this chap came from the northern part of Argentina, where their minimum lowest temperature in winter was hotter than our hottest summer day.

Don worked on the weather aspect, telling him how mild the weather had been and how he should be prepared for some cold howling winter gales, driving sleet and snow. Don followed this by an enthusiastic, if somewhat inaccurate, reference to how many degrees below zero the temperature would go. I wasn't there but I am told the soldier paled visibly at this information.

When Tony, Don and the Argy arrived at Long Island, the Argentinian soldier apparently made a great performance of staggering bravely up the hill to meet his mates.

The BBC World Service said two Harriers were missing, but not due to enemy action. They had disappeared simultaneously from the radar. It sounded as though they had crashed into each other.

Friday 7 May

We heard that Nimrods were on their way down to provide some kind of early warning. Harriers were also on the way thanks to air-to-air refuelling.

British forces warned the Argentinians that anything further than twelve miles from the Argentinian coast would be treated as hostile.

We felt the new zone must have been an attempt to give the Task Force a bigger buffer zone between the Argentinians and the fleet after the attack on the *Sheffield*, but the problem for them was how to enforce it.

We loaded up a Land Rover and headed back to the fence. We tightened up the wires and piled rocks in where the ground was uneven, or where there were gaps under the bottom wire. On the way back we patched and tightened another fence.

As we were working we saw several Argy helicopters and a couple of Pucarás whizzing up the valley at ground level.

On most evenings we walked up the hill, or even just behind the house, listening for the slightest noise or looking for anything which might mean that the British Special Forces were about. We felt that with all the activity, British forces were bound to be on the Falklands and we were just willing something to happen.

I blamed the visiting Argy for giving me a stinking cold. They were not content with digging up the countryside and Stanley, they had dabbled in germ warfare too!

Saturday 8 May

BBC World Service said a Harrier Jump Jet had set a world record for its type of plane, by flying non-stop from Ascension Island in nine hours. It had refuelled in the air.

The UN said progress had been made in brokering a peace settlement. I doubted this somehow. With the Argentinians losing the *Belgrano* and the Brits the *Sheffield* I couldn't see either side climbing down.

Both Britain and Argentina said that there have been no reports of any action. This statement meant very little.

Toni and I heard some big bangs in the afternoon and evening. If it was not action, the Argentinians must have been taking their training very seriously.

There was a huge bang in the evening, which had Toni leaping out of bed. I didn't know what had been hit, but perhaps it was something like a fuel or ammunition dump.

Sunday 9 May

The Argentinians reported that their positions in Stanley had been attacked and British helicopters also attacked them in Goose Green.

Later in the day, the Argentinians said British Harriers not only attacked a fishing boat, but also strafed the crew as they took to the lifeboats. The latter part of their accusation was insulting and I was sure few people would believe such outlandish claims.

The fishing boat turned out to be an Argentinian fishing boat, which was spying on the Task Force. Despite being told to remain outside the exclusion zone, it had remained close to the fleet. The vessel was then attacked and captured by the Royal Navy. Members of the crew were injured in the attack, but it was proved conclusively that the vessel was spying.

Radio Rye was broadcasting an alternative view, which everyone felt was very insulting. Unfortunately, I could imagine some Argentinians would have believed it. I hoped it could be proved after the war that Britain had conducted the war in keeping within the terms of the Geneva Convention.

Monday 10 May

At 2am we heard some big bangs from the Stanley direction. We all heard them, but only Jack counted fifteen bangs in close succession.

In the morning, the BBC said that all was quiet and there hadn't been any action since Sunday. The Argies must have been playing in one of their minefields. However, we later found out that it was the British Vulcan bombers mounting a bombing raid on Stanley airstrip.

Radio Newsreel was interesting later in the day, with a report from HMS *Hermes*. The Argentinian fishing vessel was found to have an unexploded bomb in her bow when the crew went on board, and she sank during the night. The *Sheffield* also sank in rough seas.

My mother spoke on the radio on the *Calling the Falklands* programme from the UK. We were having major problems tuning in to these frequencies. Tony thought the BBC would do better if it broadcast on the frequencies they used on our normal weekly programme on Sunday. I thought the Argies were interfering with the signal in some way, because the BBC had been clear during the first few days of the invasion.

People were saying that Stella Perry's house had been shot up. She lived in the middle of town and the talk was that the Argentinians were getting itchy fingers and beginning to get jumpy.

The weather had been continuously foggy and overcast. Not much fun for the men of the Task Force, although it may have restricted the activities of the Argentinian air force. It didn't stop Argentinian helicopters flying in and setting up a base in a stone run between the Estancia and Mount Kent Mountains.

The men folk started work on the new shearing shed. Jack was the technical advisor, Tony the foreman and I was the gofer, passing bits and pieces to the workers.

Tuesday 11 May

Action in the Falkland Sound. A Royal Navy ship, patrolling in the Sound, sighted an Argentinian ship and asked it to stop. The Argentinians started to move off, so the Royal Navy opened fire with her 4.5 gun. There was a huge ball of fire and then nothing. It was reported that the flames broke through the cloud cover. It must have been a quick end for the sailors on the Argentinian vessel.

The Argentinians extended their exclusion zone to cover the whole of the Atlantic Ocean. I was not sure if this was a subtle threat to ships travelling in this zone, or a warning.

The weather was pretty foul with rain all day and low cloud. We amused ourselves at the Estancia by looking at the troops in the stone run and speculating at the level of their discomfort. Two helicopters were parked there all day.

A few bangs were heard towards Stanley. The frigates and destroyers were possibly bombarding Argentinian positions again to keep them on their toes.

Wednesday 12 May

On the whole, we had been blessed with exceptionally calm weather, which allowed us to hear the Argentinian activities. Today, however, was not one of those days and the wind got up and drowned out the noises of the planes and helicopters.

We spotted vapour trails in the sky, but they were much too high to identify. Whoever they were, they were shifting along at a fair old pace.

We heard on the news that a ship of the Task Force had shot down two Argy Skyhawks on the west of the Islands. The Argies attacked again, but there were no losses from this action.

A Sea King went into the sea, but the crew was rescued. These helicopters didn't seem to be the most reliable bit of kit, but it was probably doing more work than the other types.

Thursday 13 May

It was Nyree's first birthday, Ailsa dressed her in her party best and she dived into her presents with great gusto. I think she was interested more in the crunchy qualities of the wrapping paper than the actual gifts. It gave us all five minutes away from thinking about the war.

The BBC clarified Wednesday's action by saying that three Sky Hawks were destroyed, as three waves of four Sky Hawks attacked two Royal Navy vessels. Two Sky Hawks were shot down using Sea Dart missiles and another plane crashed into the sea avoiding another missile. One of the British ships was damaged when a bomb passed through it horizontally. The report went on to say that the last wave of four decided not to engage, after seeing the losses inflicted on their fellow pilots.

Friday 14 May

British planes attacked Stanley Airport. Tony, Ailsa, Hamish (Don and Margaret's son), Toni and I went to Brookfield, on the way to Rincon, to collect food, clothes and other vital items.

Everyone at Brookfield was talking about the Harriers that they had seen. They whistled past the house, barely off the ground. Everyone took cover and those who were still standing, looked into the cockpits of the planes

Trudi, one of four who lived at Brookfield, drove the Land Rover up to Rincon and Tony stayed behind at Brookfield.

I was surprised to find two cats in my back kitchen at Rincon, where I had been living and working before the invasion. I soon found out the reason for this. An epidemic was sweeping through the cats at Rincon and a number of otherwise healthy animals had died as a result of being infected – as if it wasn't enough having the Argentinians causing havoc in the land.

Just before I left Rincon to go to Stanley, prior to the invasion, to attend the camp teachers' seminar, I was in the process of rejuvenating my motorbike.

I had removed and painted the tank where my thigh boots had rubbed the paint from large areas of both sides. (This job was done in the scullery.) I had intended replacing the last section of my exhaust pipe, but had found out it would cost at least £90. This made me reassess the old pipe, and I planned resurrection.

Thus, the scullery was littered with petrol tank and fittings, a battered and repainted silencer with jagged rust holes and its assorted fittings along with spanners, paints, brushes and sundry other items. This mess represented the freedom of a bachelor's abode.

Toni and I went to see how Ron and Diana Turner were getting on.

They gave us lunch and we had time to swap stories and strongly criticise the Argies. Some troops had appeared up on a hill known as the French Wreck, obviously watching for a landing on the north coast and to keep an eye on the settlements in the Salvador Waters, which were all clearly visible from this vantage point. They hadn't been down to Rincon thankfully.

Before we left Rincon, Keith Whitney, who worked for the Turners, told us he had heard that the plane everyone referred to as the box cart had taken a nosedive on the race course in Stanley. No one knew whether it crashed on landing or take off, but it seemed certain that it was no longer serviceable.

The trip back to the Estancia went without any outstanding events, although we had plenty to think about with the troops on the French Wreck and the box cart crashing.

Saturday 15 May

Everyone heard a noise in the night, which we assumed was another attack on Stanley Airport.

At 10am, the Ministry of Defence announced that a raiding party had attacked Argentinian positions on an island off the West Falklands.

Radio Newsreel at 11am named the island attacked by British forces as Pebble Island. A number of planes were said to have been destroyed including the ground attack Pucarás and one of the familiar Skyvans. Unidentified Argentine planes were also destroyed.

An ammunition dump was also destroyed and a radar installation damaged. The British Commando Force suffered two minor casualties. The BBC also confirmed that Harriers had attacked Stanley Airport.

This latest action had us speculating on the Task Force's next move. Was this the final warning to the Argentinians telling them to get out before the fighting started in earnest? Tony felt that the Task Force would take a direct line and attack Stanley in an all-out bid, or land relatively close to Stanley and then attack. Don favoured taking the West and building a bridgehead where such a position would lead to a negotiated settlement or a jump-off point for an attack.

Jack was undecided apart from an ultimate British victory. I thought the Task Force would land on the East, possibly at North Arm or there about, and sweep towards Stanley, taking Goose Green on the way. I also thought of Port San Carlos, because of the deep-water jetty, but I didn't consider San Carlos or Ajax Bay.

I didn't rule out a landing on the east side of Salvador Waters, but thought the bottleneck at Green Patch might be a weakness in this approach.

Things were really hotting up. A big bang just after lunch shook the house. Heavy bangs came from many directions throughout the afternoon.

All day I had had a feeling that something was imminent. I took an extra few minutes at dusk that night, listening and peering into the gloom for any sight or sound of British forces.

Sunday 16 May

It was another very cold and calm day – one for hearing bangs and seeing planes scurry about in the sky. We thought they were Harriers, because they flew in pairs high over town to a chorus of bangs, which we took to be bombs going down and fire going up from the air defence.

Tony and I went off to gather sheep in a piece of camp to the west of the house. Bozo worked well. I showed him the direction with the bike and then let him get on with it. Bozo had been sharing kennels and not getting the exercise that he was used to. He took this opportunity to display his stamina as he loped along at a healthy pace going ahead, while I negotiated a tricky ditch or other obstacle.

A three-legged sheep appeared from somewhere, a roughie at that. (A roughie is a sheep with a full coat of wool.) This slowed our progress as all the sheep came together. Tony was screaming at his dogs to stop them rushing the three-legged sheep.

Eventually, Tony abandoned the bike to administer more authority among his enthusiastic pack.

Don was meant to come and meet us in the Land Rover, but never materialised. When we returned we found he had attempted to come, but had got stuck in the muddy ground.

While he had been deciding what to do, a sinister Argentinian helicopter buzzed him at a very low level. It was a dark-coloured machine that was rarely seen, with guns protruding from the front. This put the wind up Don who high-tailed it back to the house. Jack went and towed Don out, but by this time it was too late to for him to come and help us with the sheep.

The day's news was more impressive than usual, mainly because I heard it in one sitting rather than listening to it in dribs and drabs all day. British Harriers had attacked two supply ships, one in Port King and one at Fox Bay. Attacks were also reported to have taken place on Stanley Airport and other Argentinian military installations.

At 10pm, the sky over Stanley was lit up with flashes in the sky. Don spent a long time outside listening to the sounds of the night.

Monday 17 May

Today started as any other for me. I got up in time to hear Radio Newsreel at 8am, then, after a cup of coffee, I went outside to find something to do. I saw a Harrier flying east through the binoculars.

Tony, Jack and I started sorting the sheep in the pens. Tony went off to open or shut a gate as Jack and I stood talking. Tony started bawling and I couldn't make out what on earth he was saying. Jack thought it was something about the dogs, so I went over to the kennel to let Kester and Sky out. Just as I got to the kennels, someone else started shouting.

We could hear shouting coming from the direction of the stream that runs southeast, away from the creek in front of the house. Tony must have got an awesome scare, because he started shouting like a mad man telling whoever it was that they would have to come up to him because he wasn't going to them.

More shouts were exchanged as Tony retreated towards us along the fence as we went to meet him. Four Argies rose from the grass and walked towards the house. One of the men spoke a little English, but I had already worked out that it couldn't be that great, because if he had fully understood Tony's aggressive adjectives, we would already have been shot. Tony's behaviour was a morale booster after the event, but during these and other potentially tricky situations, it became rather frightening.

Don became chief interpreter and talked to the officer who looked like an aggressive little man. Tony would interject with pigeon Spanish that would have made Manuel from *Fawlty Towers* seem articulate in English.

Ailsa, Margaret and Kay rustled up some dry bread and a few meat bones and a large container of coffee. Margaret took the food out and supported Don's struggle communicating with the Argy officer.

The officer amazed us all by refusing the coffee saying they didn't drink such things in Argentina. He must have thought it was poisoned.

As Don and Tony talked, a fifth Argentinian appeared. He had been lying in the grass covering his comrades with his rifle. He walked up and joined the group.

Don took it upon himself once more to tell them about the realities of the Falklands winter. Plummeting temperatures, howling winds, endless deep snow and when there was a break in all of that, rain.

As if there wasn't enough going on, one of Tony's pigs escaped from its enclosure by deftly walking over the electric fence and came trotting down to be introduced. I thought this might cause a bit of fun, but the Argentinian soldiers took the behaviour of this pig in their stride and totally ignored it. I was hoping at least one city boy would throw down his gun and run off.

We pointed out where the Argentinians had a base on the side of Mount Kent. These guys were professionals and I wondered how long they had been watching us and how many times that fifth guy had run each of us civilians through his gun sights. They were finally persuaded to get into the transport box on the back of the tractor, and Tony and Don took them to the base at Mount Kent. They must have thought we were taking them to the British, hence their reluctance, because when they met up with their comrades one of them offered Tony some Argentine pesos and another offered his rosary beads.

A jet flew out of town at 11.40am. It was a small plane with two engines, probably a Lear jet. Later, a Hercules flew into town low over Mount Kent below its peak on the north side. I didn't admire the courage of the Argentinian pilots. I was too busy explaining away the failure of the British blockade. It was a calm crystal clear day – where were the Brits?

No one seemed to feel this Argy affront as keenly as I did. Was the fleet incapable of picking up a plane the size of a Hercules flying into the Islands? Had the Russians told the Argentinians the position of the fleet, giving optimum times for attacks and flying essentials into the Islands?

Tuesday 18 May

We heard the Argentinian Foreign Minister, Pérez de Cuéllar, had postponed peace negotiations for 24 hours. Argentina had received Britain's proposals and submitted more of its own. Margaret Thatcher told the world that Britain wouldn't stand for Argentina's continuous delaying tactics.

It was announced later in the day that yet another Sea King had ditched in the sea. This brought Sea King losses to four. Conditions and pilot fatigue were blamed. The crew of this latest Sea King crash were rescued.

Wednesday 19 May

The BBC told us that Thatcher rejected the Argentinian proposals. It went on to say that the government had taken over one of the BBC transmitters on Ascension Island to broadcast propaganda to the Argentinians.

A few farms had been allowed to use their 2 meter sets to speak to the doctor in the mornings. While Ron Binnie, manager of Fitzroy farm, was speaking to the doctor in Stanley, a huge explosion rocked the Estancia. As the bang was heard Ron paused: 'A shell has just burst over Mount Challenger.' The doctor replied: 'But still, carry on.' And Ron did.

There was nothing dramatic in the news, although it was obvious that the peace negotiations had fallen through. Mr Pérez de Cuéllar called a Security Council meeting.

The weather was calm but fairly foggy and overcast. Not very suitable weather for launching Harriers from the carriers, but equally, once more, it must have been difficult for the Argentinians to fly planes into the Falklands or against British forces.

Tony and Jack took advantage of the calm weather to take the flat iron off the west end of the house and replace some of the rough boarding that was rotten. I had a tidying crusade, chopping up all the odd pieces of wood for kindling. I built a fire in a 45-gallon drum, which raged with all the rubbish I had accumulated.

Rain came to end the play for another day although it wasn't quite the end. Thank

God for Radio Rye and its efforts to raise our spirits. Its propaganda was now delivered through the husky voice of a woman calling herself 'Liberty'. She told the British Task Force that Admiral Sandy Woodward had committed suicide. What a brazen tart.

Thursday 20 May

We heard Pérez de Cuéllar had submitted his ideas for a peaceful settlement. Meanwhile, the Argentinians informed the world they have caught seven British soldiers. No one else seems to know anything about this boast.

Trudi McPhee came over from Brookfield to borrow Tony's tractor to take a large tank home. Most farms had experienced a vast increase in their population due to the refugees from town. Brookfield was suffering from a water shortage because its water system was never designed to cater for so many.

It had been reported that Harriers had been in action again and British ships had bombarded Argy positions, again.

As Pérez de Cuéllar admitted his peace initiative failed, a British helicopter was found in Chile, just outside Punta Arenas.

The helicopter was said to be burnt out and a tent was found close by. I don't believe the official explanation submitted by the British. The Ministry of Defence said that the helicopter was lost due to faulty navigation equipment. Something fishy was going on. It was clear it was a troop-carrying Sea King.

Friday 21 May

At 7.30am Harriers attacked the Argentinian positions between Mount Kent and Mount Estancia. These positions were clearly visible from the house. Jack was the first to realise that something was going on. He shouted to Tony and me that something was happening.

I threw my clothes on and rushed to the door. Above the Argentinian position I could see two small dots, which turned and climbed at very tight angles. One plane rushed in and flew out towards the east, behind Mount Estancia, heading towards Long Island. A second plane flew straight down the valley strafing the Argy positions with cannon fire.

Big puffs of smoke and dirt erupted along the south side of the stone run. As the plane came closer to the house we could see clearly the unmistakable contours of the Harrier. What a beautiful sight. The plane looked like a bee with the air intakes looking like eyes, while the drooped wings accentuated this insect effect. One went out of sight in the valley that ran east to west to the north of the mountains. One then rose up, turning to fly northeast along this side of Mount Estancia towards Long Island, in the same direction that the other Harrier had gone, but on this side of the mountains.

This was the first close-up of the Harrier we'd had and were all really excited and full of praise for it and the bravery of the pilots.

Two big, billowing clouds of dense black smoke poured into the sky. The Harriers hadn't been with us (or the Argies) for very long, but the effects were plain to see. It was only half light when the attack began, but in the clear light of day, we could savour the apparent damage.

We could see the Argentinians up on the mountain, where they had all gathered on the skyline and appeared to be looking towards Stanley. We all wondered what had happened up there, although there wasn't a lot of sympathy for them.

The BBC news wasn't that cheering. The Task Force had lost another Sea King.

Two Argentinians approached the house. Luckily they were spotted some way off and everyone was prepared for the visit. There was none of the cautious hiding in the grass, or leaving one man to cover the others this time. They just strolled in, seemingly without a care, or a fear in the world.

We waited by the back door as the Argentinians walked down along the telephone line. The soldier who led this pair was armed with a pistol. He wore a cap and a grey jacket and trousers with typical army boots. The other soldier wore a grey combat jacket, trousers and boots, but he wore a helmet with netting on it entwined with pieces of grass. He also carried a rifle very like the ones used by the British Royal Marines. The second guy had a dark complexion, and was strongly built, being tall and broad.

The foreign delegation stopped at the end of the house where we all stood. The leader was a lieutenant with two stars on a tab that buttoned on to his top pocket. He wasn't very big, but his manner was confident and he spoke good English. Apparently, his wife was an English doctor.

He asked for a Land Rover, but it wasn't really a request and there really wasn't a choice. He also wanted the best one.

He said he needed it to charge the battery for his radio up on the side of the mountain. Tony couldn't help himself and asked what had happened up on the mountain. The soldier said that they were attacked just as they were leaving to walk down. He was quite open about the fact that three helicopters had been hit and put out of action and there were many casualties. He wanted to get back quickly to help.

As we were talking I noticed the other guy walking around one of the Land Rovers running his hand along the surfaces and studying the interior with a look of awe.

The Lieutenant insisted that one of us drive the Land Rover up to his camp, so Tony with his driving skills and Don, because of his small knowledge of Spanish, went, although with the officer present it would be doubtful that the latter skill would be needed. We did mention that we thought making us drive the Land Rover was against the Geneva Convention, but he didn't get nasty or aggressive.

As they drove up the mountain the Lieutenant told Tony that it wasn't much fun when the British attacked their positions early in the morning. 'It makes a good alarm clock though,' answered Tony.

'I see you have a sense of humour,' the officer replied. I bet he had his tongue between his teeth when he said that.

Surely he didn't think that he would get some sympathy. At that stage we knew people on both sides were getting killed and injured, but the Argentinians were the enemy and so we didn't consider their feelings.

At the camp, Tony and Don saw a burnt-out helicopter and two others which were damaged by cannon fire. One was beyond repair.

Toni and I took the farm's horses away to better pastures. We took an exceptionally long, short-cut managing to lose Tony and Ailsa's telescope in the process.

Trudi McPhee and Derek arrived with the tractor, stores and mail.

The Ministry of Defence announced there had been a substantial landing at Port San Carlos. Five ships had been attacked and two seriously damaged. Seventeen Argy planes and two helicopters had been attacked and destroyed. This was the beginning of the British return to the Falklands.

The day was calm and clear after a period of overcast conditions. This must have helped the pilots of the Argentinian air force.

Saturday 22 May

Everyone was up exceptionally early, but there was no rerun of yesterday's Harrier attacks and no sign of British Special Forces spearheading the British advance.

The sky seemed to have a couple of planes travelling east and west constantly. Two planes together usually meant Harriers, so we deduced that they were flying missions from the Task Force. Because it was so calm, plane spotting was easy.

The wind got up later and spoilt this activity because we couldn't hear them. It was a lot harder to be continually sweeping the skies for a vapour trail.

The Ministry announced there had been no attacks on British land forces by Argentinian planes. It went on to say that a Harrier had been shot down near Darwin. Five thousand British troops were now said to be on the shore.

An Argy helicopter visited the camp up in the mountains and dropped off spare motors for those damaged by the Harrier attack yesterday.

HMS *Ardent* sank with the death of twenty. The ship was attacked by a number of Argy planes and it was reported that the NAAFI manager (the NAAFI being the forces' shop), manned one of the machine guns in the ship as a last defiant gesture.

Sunday 23 May

The BBC broadcast a special Radio Newsreel, which described the Argentinian attacks. In one, it said two Skyhawks attacked and one dropped its bomb in the sea while the other just turned tail.

There was a bit of air traffic in the morning, which we think was British, because of the formation of twos.

The radio telephone, which had kept the camp in touch with the goings-on didn't come on the air until an hour after the normal time. It was a frightening feeling, because it was the one internal link that let everyone know everything and everyone, Island-wide, was okay. Kay was our avid listener and these increasing delays, as the days went on, distressed her. It was her only link with one of her two sons, one in Stanley and the other on Carcass.

There was hearty news from Hill Cove. We were told that an Argentinian pilot had arrived there with an injured arm and supposedly spent many hours in the sea. There was also horrific news from Dunnose Head. The settlement came under attack from unknown planes. Bombs had flattened buildings and one of the residents was badly wounded. This was grim news for us to digest.

It was obvious that the grass airstrip has been bombed. It was supposed to be very good in the summer, but at that time of year it would be totally useless in military terms for fixed wing aircraft. Had the Argentinians attacked because they'd discovered British forces there? We later learnt that the British had dropped the bombs as they believed this to be a viable airstrip.

The BBC gave us more news on the air-war. Five Mirages and a Skyhawk had been shot down. One Puma exploded in mid-air and another landed in flames. British troops were now harassing the Argentinians around Goose Green.

Monday 24 May

The BBC gave us the latest news. The Argies were attacking in force and seven planes had been shot down. A Harrier crashed on take-off and the pilot died in the accident. The *Antelope* sank after being hit by a bomb the day before.

Britain reinforced the Task Force. A few supply ships had been damaged. A correspondent on board one of the vessels broadcast one of the Argentinian attacks and it sounded really hairy.

We listened to the frequency the Brits are working on. Air warning reds and the direction of attack and the distance of hostile aircraft. It all sounded very busy.

We heard through the telephone that the Argies had arrived at Douglas, a big farm between where the British had landed at Port San Carlos and us. They were forcing two youths to drive them to Stanley. The Estancia was on the route of this convoy, so we got a call. Due to one of the two Land Rovers breaking down after they left Douglas they had 'borrowed' a County tractor from Teal Inlet.

They finally arrived. Patrick Minto from Douglas was driving the County and Clive Newman his father's Land Rover. With them were two Argentinian soldiers. One of the soldiers was a cocky European-looking chap. He was wearing a military jumper with patches on the shoulders and elbows and had two torches hooked into the breast pockets of his jacket. He was strutting around like an immature schoolboy. The other chap was a Latin American, with a sallow complexion and uneasy eyes.

Patrick gave us a run-down. Apparently the Argentinian troops had poured in from the Port San Carlos direction and forced people in the Douglas settlement into the community hall. The soldiers then got into the houses and started helping themselves.

They reckoned there were at least 40 soldiers and they were the lookouts from Fanning's Head, which over-looked the entrance into San Carlos Water, and had run away after the British attacked them.

Tuesday 25 May

We listened to the Brits going through their paces by listening in on their frequency. It was very exciting listening to the operators giving out red alerts and co-ordinates as well as talking about numbers of hostiles down.

North Arm came up on the radio phone and spoke to the authorities in Stanley about an Argentinian who had had been found in their area.

While the war was being fought, Tony, Jack and I made some blocks out of concrete in a machine. The wind made it difficult to hear plane activity, but we saw a few tell-tale vapour trails.

Patrick and Clive arrived back with the two disgruntled Argies. They hadn't got the helicopters they expected for evacuating their section from Douglas. They had managed to get some provisions.

Patrick was full of the news from Stanley including a story of a day in town when a plane flew over really low. The Argentinians opened up and shot it down and went mad celebrating, shouting and cheering wildly. Then a quiet spread over the anti-aircraft positions, as they were told that it was one of their own. He went on to say that later two Harriers flew over, thousands of feet up and the Argies in their frustration opened up with everything they had even their rifles.

Tony explained the route to and through the Low Pass and Clive, Patrick and their two Argentinian soldiers moved off. Minutes later the Land Rover, which left with crunches and bangs, came roaring back along the beach. Patrick had managed to bog the County tractor at a place called the Tarbarrel with the tide rising, which meant that it was only a matter of time before it disappeared under the sea.

Tony was absolutely furious, because he had spent the day before hiding his tractor to prevent the Argies taking it. He went totally mad, screaming and shouting and swearing and even leaping up and down. It was hilarious in retrospect, but at the time I thought he was going to have some kind of breakdown. Eventually the red mist cleared and he went off to retrieve the tractor.

We went down to the Tarbarrel where the tractor was certainly bogged and the engine was still running. Tony got him to switch it off because he was frightened the engine would suck in salt water. The water was already well over the sump and rising.

Tony hitched up for a pull with a rope from the County to his tractor. We were running out of time. Not only was the tide coming in, but the light was rapidly fading.

Tony drove forwards and the rope tightened, his tractor slid to one side with all its wheels spinning on the rocks. The County didn't even make a ripple in the water as it was stuck fast. The County engine wouldn't restart, so Tony was pulling a dead weight. After several futile attempts it was clear that the tractor was going to stay the night and go under the incoming tide.

BBC news reported another destroyer badly damaged and the British ground forces chasing some Argies as they advanced. The Chilean authorities found three of the crewmen from the Sea King that mysteriously landed there.

The Argies spoke to Patrick. The thinner of the two said that if they were not back at Douglas by 8pm, the remaining troops there would shoot the civilians in the hall. It was hard to judge how serious this threat was, but Tony phoned up the track to ask if people in the house just outside Douglas would get a message into the settlement. However, these folk, fearing for their own safety, refused.

The Argies and their guides returned to the Estancia and spent the night in a shed. The Argy in the jumper decked out with two torches spent a considerable amount of time sitting in the Land Rover on guard.

Wednesday 26 May

Tony took the Argies, Patrick and Clive along the track towards Teal Inlet early in the morning. They were met by Rex McKay, from Teal Inlet, who took over the transportation. Tony had overslept and I had to wake him when I heard hammering on the door of those wanting to leave.

The destroyer in difficulties turned out to be the *Coventry*. She was hit by a number of bombs and sank. The merchant ship, the *Atlantic Conveyor*, had been hit by two Exocet missiles and sunk.

An Argy helicopter – a Bell Huey – full of troops searched the Estancia Creek and the surrounding area. We watched it as it swept to and fro. I wouldn't have liked to be in the helicopter if they did find elements of the British forces, especially the SAS or SBS units.

Four Argy helicopters flew past the Estancia heading towards Douglas Station. I surmised that they were off to help the Argy soldiers retreat more efficiently. Not long afterwards, Tony returned from his jaunt, the four helicopters returned flying up the valley to the south. Douglas Station was soon on the phone to tell us that the Argentinian troops had left.

Terry Peck, who was the former Chief of Police, was a fugitive from the Argentinians and he had been hiding from them in various parts of the camp. He would have been another candidate to be exiled or flown into local internment at Fox Bay. He started walking from Brookfield to Port San Carlos to meet the British.

It became clear that the people of Douglas had been locked up since Sunday morning in their community hall. The Argies arrived in the settlement before a lot of people were up. Everyone had been made to leave their houses and to congregate at the hall. Once the Argentinians had left, the people returned to find their houses abused beyond description.

The Argentinians had behaved appallingly, such as using the beds with their boots on. Clothes, food and personal possessions had been stolen.

Toni and I walked down to the Tarbarrel to see if the tide was over the tractor. As we walked we were sure we could hear the sound of jets. We dashed up on to the bank, which was perhaps three metres high, but gave a good 360-degree view. Unless the plane or helicopter was flying really low in the valley, running along the side of the mountain, we should have seen something. I thought there must be something happening behind Mount Kent or Harriet so I went back down onto the beach.

Toni remained on the bank and let out an excited yell. Two Harriers shot to the east of the Estancia going up Princes Street – a large stone run on the east of Mount Estancia. They must have travelled behind Mount Estancia on the east side because they hit the Argentinian position on the mountain again. They then shot out from between Mount Kent and Estancia and looked as if they had finished, disappearing towards the San Carlos area. However, they came screaming back east in the deep valley. One flew over the Argentinians as the other turned in between the two mountains and flew towards Long Island, which was a tight manoeuvre for a fast jet.

Toni and I stood on the bank waving and shouting for all we were worth. More smoke poured from the Argentinian positions. We couldn't stop talking about the raid back at the house. The total submersion of the Teal Inlet tractor was no longer really newsworthy.

We spent more time at night listening for the sounds of British forces. I didn't know what we expected, possibly a patrol or something that wasn't Argentinian. This night Tony didn't put the generator on until a long time after dark as we watched and listened.

We did hear some helicopters that sounded different. They had a quiet sound unlike the noisy Argentinian jobs that could be heard for miles. The sounds seemed to come from the Impassable Valley, but we couldn't see anything because it was pitch black and there was also clinging ground-fog. The same noise came from the Green Patch direction a little later. Our minds began to imagine all kinds of things.

Terry Peck arrived at Lorenzo, a house just outside Douglas, on his way he had found what he thought was an unexploded bomb. He was now travelling on a motorbike so he should get to Port San Carlos the next day.

The Argentinians asked the British to remove the hospital ship, *Uganda*, which they said was anchored in Grantham sound. The Ministry of Defence wouldn't comment on the position of any of the ships of the Task Force. However, a spokesman said that the *Uganda* was miles away.

Thursday 27 May

There was mixed news from the BBC. The *Atlantic Conveyor* hadn't sunk and the military were trying to salvage as much as possible from the stricken vessel. Unfortunately, nine crew members, including the captain, were missing. Although two Exocet missiles were apparently fired at the ship, only one hit it.

Two Argentinian helicopters searched the land either side of the creek once again. Back and forth, to and fro, hugging the ground and making plenty of noise. With that kind of noise, they were certainly giving plenty of warning to any British forward patrols.

Tony, Jack and I went down to see if we could get the Teal Inlet tractor out of the sea. We decided to use a different method because it was obvious from the other night that it wasn't going to come out with a straight pull.

The Estancia tractor, with double wheels on the back and a strong electric winch, was parked on the bank. We all took turns to dig a deep trench behind it. We then tied a strong piece of rope to a sturdy lump of timber and laid it in the trench horizontally. To stop the wood from rising, we pinned it in the bottom of the trench with fencing posts hammered at an angle, and the rope from the wood was attached to the back of the tractor.

We then attached a series of pulleys to the tractor winch, plus another piece to the Land Rover we had bought along. The moment of truth had arrived.

The first pull snapped the rope and the second did the same. We reconfigured the pulleys which lead to a successful pull, unfortunately the pulleys had been doubled up so that each pull little more than tightened the rope. However, each bit moved the tractor a fraction. The Land Rover was making some grating, scraping noises undertaking its part of the system due to some previous failing of a broken half shaft or differential and we wondered if it was going to stop working totally.

The Land Rover did manage to hold on and bit-by-bit, although sliding slightly, we inched the tractor out of the creek.

By this time the tide was really high and without a huge diversion it was impossible to get back to the house, so we drove as far as we could, but decided to walk the last few hundred yards.

Later in the afternoon, once the tide had gone down, I went to get the Land Rover. As I walked a helicopter beetled over the hill by the Argy position heading towards the Malo Hills. The Land Rover made a hell of a noise from the back axle as I drove it home, but it didn't falter.

Later Toni came with me to get the tractor and trailer, but as we got out of the House Paddock and into the open ground the Argy helicopter that I had seen earlier returned. It flew low up the creek and then lifted up, skimming over the house, but just as it got past it swung violently round and headed straight for us. We had seen these helicopters searching for a couple of days for something and couldn't help wondering how on edge these people were.

We carried on walking away from the house as the chopper flew by, because by then it was everyday stuff. We both saw it turn and at that height it didn't take much to guess the crew's intentions. 'It's coming after us,' said Toni in an alarmed voice. 'Just carry on walking,' I said, as calmly as possible, 'Imagine that it's not there.'

The distinctive noise of the Bell Huey helicopter got louder as it closed in on us and although I talked calmly, my heart was in my mouth. As it flew over quite slowly, it sidled out to the side and sitting in the back was an Argy soldier with his big machine gun trained on us. I tried not to falter and give him any encouragement to pull the trigger unless he was prepared to gun down two obvious civilians.

We could see the bore of the gun and the mechanism as well as the grimace of the man between his great big army coat and his peaked hat. He was so close – probably less than twenty feet. They must have realised we weren't military and turned away.

As the helicopter got further away our heartbeats regained a respectable pulse and we could no longer hear them thumping in our ears.

What would have happened if we had panicked and thrown ourselves down or started running? Wearing heavy winter coats as we both did, it would have been impossible to discern whether we were a man and a woman, two men or even two women. The Argentinians were obviously aware that the SAS and SBS were operating in the vicinity.

The BBC announced that the British were advancing from their bridgehead. They said an unofficial report suggested that the 2nd Parachute Regiment was advancing on Goose Green and the marines towards Stanley.

Once again we heard helicopters at 8pm, but it was too dark to see the craft.

Friday 28 May

The British fleet must be wearing down the Argentinians who were dug in around town by shelling their positions, because late last night there were flashes, bright and clear, all night with the accompanying bangs.

This morning it was not so bright. It was foggy and overcast once more. We heard Keith Whitney at Rincon talking on the 2 meter to Trudi at Brookfield. Trudi told Keith that the settlement where his sister lived, Goose Green, was back to normal. We were very impressed and surprised as to how Trudi knew this.

Although listening on the 2 meter was highly illegal, we were beginning to listen increasingly each day. The day's fog prevented prying eyes from the mountain although the aerial was ready to be hauled down at a moment's notice. We listened out for helicopters, but I hadn't heard one yet that could sneak up on us. How seriously the Argentinians would take it if they caught us using the radio was open to conjecture.

The taking of Goose Green was great news and after listening to the Argies dishing out a lot of punishment to the British fleet it was refreshing. Terry Peck then came on the 2 meter and categorically told us that Goose Green was in British hands.

Our continual vigilance paid off and fortunately for us with all the good news we hadn't become complacent, because down from the mountain side, in a very casual manner, came the English-speaking Lieutenant, unarmed, with his man.

He asked Tony if he would drive three of his men to town in his tractor because they were sick. Tony said no, but added he couldn't stop the Lieutenant taking the tractor. The officer said that he couldn't take it, because he had tried to take the Land Rover he had commandeered, but had got bogged no more than 50 metres from his camp.

Tony told the Lieutenant that although he felt sorry for the sick men, it was too dangerous for him to drive to town, because he had seen what the Harriers had done.

The Argentinian Officer argued that the Harriers would only attack important targets and that when they were attacked his men fired everything they had at the plane, but the pilot didn't waste his bullets firing back. He then went on to say how there might be a small number of British forces about, but they would be lying low.

'They won't come in large numbers,' he said, but with that, we all spontaneously laughed. The Lieutenant, who was now sipping a cup of coffee, tried a different tack and told us not to take any notice of the BBC, because if they were right he would be dead. Obviously an avid Radio Rye listener, he went on to tell us that half the British Navy had been sunk and how he didn't worry while he had his bath at Moody Brook as the Navy bombarded Stanley. I wondered how many others up on the hill enjoyed a bath.

Ailsa gave the Lieutenant some Alka Seltzer because he said he had a bad liver.

The two Argies set off for Mount Kent, giving the tractor a covetous glance as they departed. I don't think they had gone three hundred yards when two Harriers side by side shot round and over them. They were out of sight in the valley, but I am sure it gave them an adrenalin rush. Even if we could have seen them, we were too busy shouting and clapping to note their reaction. In retrospect it was a bit of an emotional frenzy.

Once the Argentinians had left, and the excitement of seeing the Harriers had died down, we switched on the radio to listen to the BBC. The news wasn't good. The marines had suffered casualties in a bombing raid with four dead and a number injured. A Harrier had also been shot down. The good news of the morning had nearly been cancelled out by the bulletin.

Tony, Jack and I went to the newly-completed shearing shed to make some more concrete blocks. We were starting the third mix and Tony was banging down the lid when we heard a plaintive sound from outside. There, looking rather sickly and miserable, were two Argentinian soldiers. They approached us apprehensively.

One Argy was thin and of medium height, dark complexion and a square head. He might have had both Spanish and an Indian heritage. The other guy was a short, squat, dark-skinned man, who was almost certainly of Indian decent. They didn't appear to have any weapons and all we could see was a small bag, which contained a cup full of rice and an onion, soaked in oil.

They looked very lost and forlorn. As we took them to the house the short chap was clearly very lame and the other man looked ill with fatigue.

Ailsa gave them some food and Margaret began to tend the lame soldier's feet. In the half-light Margaret scrubbed an apparently black grubby foot, which caused the lame fellow some discomfort. When Tony put the lights on, it was obvious that something was wrong.

Not only were his feet indigo black, in and around his toes in particular, but they were so badly blistered that in places, combined with the wet that he had endured for ages, his feet looked badly burnt. Margaret stopped scrubbing and bandaged them up in a very professional-looking way.

They must have thought we wouldn't harm them, or they were so hungry and exhausted they didn't care, because they tucked into the food like wild men.

Tony asked Don to tell the Argies that he and I would take them up to their friends on the mountain. They understood this, but were not at all keen. Whether they thought we were tricking them into going to the British, or they were too tired to go on, or to become involved in the fighting again we didn't discover, but they didn't want to budge.

We allowed them to stay in the shed by the house, which had a fire, and gave them a couple of buckets of peat fuel. We also gave them sleeping bags and then left them to get on with it, although we continued to feed and water them.

The BBC announced that Goose Green and Darwin had been retaken by the British. The Pope started touring the UK and has asked for peace in the South Atlantic.

Saturday 29 May

The two Argies were still with us. I stood holding the 2 meter aerial when one of them came to the door, so I just bid them a cheery 'hello'.

Two Harriers flew in from the north and fired rockets at the side of Mount Kent. A great expanse erupted in a mass of flames and explosions. It was hard to imagine such a large area being hit like that and it was definitely a case of seeing was believing. We had been watching the side of Mount Kent, but hadn't seen any Argies in that vicinity, but if there were enemy troops in the region I couldn't see how anyone could have survived such devastation.

We took turns at examining the area on Mount Kent, but we didn't see anyone come out of that zone. Later, we noticed a stream of black dots hurrying along the foot of it, heading towards the encampment on the mountain.

Our two Argentinians were now even more reluctant to venture out and cowered back in the shed like two whipped pups. Even when their own helicopters flew over, made distinct by a yellow square on the tail, they would deliberately hide. We encouraged them to flag down one of their helicopters, but it was impossible.

Using the 2 meter set, we contacted Brookfield and asked them to speak to the doctor in Stanley. They told the Argentinians that we had two of their soldiers that needed to be picked up.

A Bell Huey helicopter flew in and got them. The pilot made a very skilled landing close to the house, but surprisingly he was incredibly lame. When he stepped from the chopper he was dragging a leg to such an extent we wondered if it was false.

Our two Argies were united with their friends, but left with mixed feelings. The soldier with the bad foot looked pleased, but the other man looked distinctly worried. The latter probably wondering how things would go when the question was asked. 'What were you doing at the Estancia when you were supposed to be at Goose Green?'

We asked the pilot to bring us some bandages just in case other soldiers came in. He promised that he would, and later that day, hugging the ground, he returned with a number of dressings in a dirty, old, hessian bag.

A Harrier flew past the Estancia just after dinner.

The commanding officer of the 2nd Parachute Regiment Lieutenant Colonel Herbert Jones had been killed in the battle of Goose Green. Local rumours said that the Argentinians showed a white flag and as he went forward they opened fire. This turned out to be untrue, although there was meant to be an incident in the battle involving a white flag.

At night the Monopoly board came out and we spent the evening joking about Monopoly money and Argentinian pesos making cheap wallpaper. The game came to an end and we had a cup of something, banked the fire, put the cats out and went to bed.

Ailsa turned to Tony and said: 'I hope the British hurry up and get here.' With that they heard gunfire, and Tony instructed Ailsa to switch off the generator.

As the engine got to the last chug, gunfire of all kinds echoed all around us, the sky lit up as a number of flares went up. I couldn't believe it. I pushed Toni on to the floor and pulled the mattress off the bed and on top of us, although it would hardly have stopped anything.

We started putting clothes on. I shouted at Toni when she sat up to put her clothes on. I dragged the bed from the wall and we got behind it. It was scary because there was nothing much in a wood-framed house to stop a high velocity bullet apart from the brick chimney.

Everybody else had made it downstairs and were lying on the kitchen floor. There was a lull in the shooting and so, keeping as low as we could, we crawled through to the kitchen as well.

The shooting started again. Tony was hanging out of the back door shouting 'Who's there?' There was no reply. Flares continued to light up the sky and there was more gunfire. Ailsa phoned Teal Inlet in an attempt to get David Barton, a fluent Spanish speaker, just in case the Argies stormed in.

After what seemed like hours, but was probably only a few minutes, there came a heavy knock on the door. 'Who's there?' shouted Tony. 'British Army, open up,' came a very English voice.

Ailsa had banged Nyree's head on the table, and when she went outside a large soldier said 'sorry we made the baby cry love.'

Ailsa was very perturbed that this forward patrol should come down kick up a row and then disappear and she told them so.

What a fright we all got. We thought it was two patrols meeting up and shooting at one another with us in the middle, but it was far from that. This party of SAS had seen the Argy helicopter come to the Estancia twice from their observation post and they therefore thought there were Argentinians here. The noise had been to flush the Argies out.

Sunday 30 May

World Service reports that there are 1,200 Argentine troops captured at Goose Green. The local inhabitants have been locked in the community hall for a month. The Brazilian Embassy in London has told the British that Argentina would regard her hospital ships as hostile if they didn't leave the battle zone. Britain countered that she had informed the Argentine of the movements of these ships laid down under the laws of the Geneva Convention.

People's homes at Goose Green have been looted, damaged and soiled with human excrement. The type of people that have been on these Islands unlawfully are being shown to the world for what they are.

The Harriers call on our neighbours in the mountain with rockets of some kind. Combine this attack with a heavy frost and things are certainly rough for the Argy outpost.

Whilst listening to the British armed forces on their frequency we heard the Army thanking the Navy for their accurate bombardment. They told the Navy that they had destroyed some Pucarás, an ammunition dump and caused heavy casualties.

Harriers struck again, this time to the east of our Argies on the mountain. Things are really intensifying.

The BBC report 12 British casualties at Goose Green plus 31 wounded. Either the Argies didn't give much of a fight or the Brits were superior in their fighting qualities especially as the paras were attacking an entrenched and prepared defensive position.

Tony and I worked on the Teal Inlet tractor, draining the oil and diesel and cleaning it up generally. We gave it a tow and much to my surprise it went. I thought that after a couple of days and at least four tides over it, it would take more to get it going. Just after lunch we saw something on the Malo Hills and as we watched hundreds of troops appeared walking along with some articulated, track vehicles called BVs. Without the vehicles it looked like a scene from a western when the Indians appear on the hill in overwhelming numbers. There were a few helicopters supporting the advance as well.

As night drew in and dusk turned to dark, action began in the mountains to the southwest. Projectiles, their course clearly tracked by balls of fire, shot off the Bluff Cove Peak back into the ridges to the west. We could also see heavy machine gun fire with tracers going in the same direction. We couldn't really tell who was who, although we did find out later. One of the projectiles hit the ground and lit up in a ball of white flames and burnt for a number of seconds. There were numerous flashes lighting up the area from what seemed like everywhere. (Special Forces had got behind an Argentine patrol cutting them off from their lines and then attacked them.)

A helicopter started to buzz down in the valley and another one flew over the creek with a searchlight sweeping the ground like a white finger. It began to snow after a while.

The Scorpion and Scimitar light tanks of the Blues and Royals arrived.

At around 11pm an advance party from 3rd Parachute Regiment arrived and with them was Terry Peck. It was very emotional in a British way. Toni gave Terry a big hug.

We all pawed over maps and gave what information we could. It was really exciting to think that we were now behind British lines and contributing to the effort.

A para called Blue told us that the mountains would be cleared tomorrow. There was no doubt in his mind, and looking at him I was as confident as he was. They had to clear away the Argies and their OPs (observation post) on the mountains before they advanced any further.

We talked well into the night about all aspects of the war and especially some of the atrocities that the Argies had committed. Apparently the Argies that retreated through Douglas had shot down a helicopter at Port San Carlos and then shot the survivors as they swam ashore.

Monday 31 May

Bangs, we think, are mortars coming from the mountains to the south. Ailsa is rather hasty and premature, I feel, in making a 2 meter call to Stanley to say all is well at the Estancia.

Bangs started around 9am and Toni spotted soldiers up on the ridge to the west of Bluff Cove Peak.

We began to see the fall of the mortar shells as puffs of bluey white smoke and rubble seemed to walk up the valley towards the Argentine positions. Later in the day we saw British soldiers building a lookout up on top of Mount Kent. These men don't seem to mind who sees them.

Tony, Jack and I spent the morning clearing sheds, lining others and generally preparing for the arrival of the 3rd Parachute Regiment.

The paras started arriving just before 6pm. What a lot of men. The sheds were soon full and they were still arriving.

The BBC speaks of fighting around Mount Kent. We have now been officially liberated and what a great feeling.

Tony, Toni, Ailsa and I went out to see the tanks. A bloke showed me the insides and the controls and the very impressive night sights. The image was grainy and green but everything was visible. The sights for the gun were impressively simple. There was a circle for shooting planes and you just put the plane into the circle and fired away.

There were three different types of round for the main gun. These tanks had come overland without many mishaps over soft ground that would test a Land Rover. Made from aluminium they weigh considerably less than a conventional steel tank.

There are sleeping bodies everywhere. The sheds are full of sleeping squaddies. No one could imagine how tightly they were packed in unless you saw it. You couldn't step between them. Even outside troops had just thrown themselves down anywhere and gone to sleep.

The weather has got bitterly cold. Frost has been a nightly occurrence for the last three days. Soldiers cover themselves with sacking, tin, just anything to ward off the cold.

A Major came to use the loo and was surprised to find a number of his men dossing in all the vacant rooms. As more came to plead for floor space the civilians sorted their beds accordingly.

Tuesday 1 June

I got up, went outside and had a walk around. The more delicate members of the Parachute Regiment and the other support detachments queue for the toilet.

Toni and I start digging a trench a few yards from the door of the house. There is no doubt that we now represent a legitimate target. Blue, one of the para's forward patrol that had arrived a few nights ago with Terry, sent two chaps to help.

The Argies big guns in Stanley began to range in on Mount Kent. They seem to be quite content with firing blindly into the valley between Mount Kent and Estancia, in the vague hope that they might hit something. The consensus of opinion has these guns down as 155mm. These guns are bigger than the British 105mm and so have a greater range.

People from the North Camp – Rincon Grande, Green Patch, Brookfield, Long Island, Murrell, Port Louis and Johnsons Harbour – arrive with Land Rovers and tractors to help the British forces.

Some soldiers who were the Air Defence people showed me how the Blowpipe missile launcher works. You put the launcher on to your shoulder and then look through the sights, putting the cross onto the target. Where you hold the launcher there is a button for your thumb with which you are meant to guide the missile onto the target. The outfit that were here had already hit a Pucará at Port San Carlos. The launcher and missile wasn't very heavy, more cumbersome, however carrying it for miles would definitely be a different story. On the journey from Port San Carlos a tank had run over one and the guys had dismantled the missile for a souvenir.

The house was the epicentre of a lot of activity. Not only was the loo in constant action but people also started clamouring at the door for water. The doctors who had set up their surgery in the sitting room were tending a number of soldiers with troublesome feet. The march over rough and wet ground through ditches and creeks with heavy Bergens (big rucksacks) had taken its toll.

The BBC announced that an Argentine Hercules transport plane had been shot down.

The troops started leaving the Estancia and with the aid of many tractors, trailers, Land Rovers and willing hands from the surrounding settlements, moved up and forward onto Mount Estancia.

Helicopters started bringing forward supplies, mainly food and also some kitbags.

I got the Teal Inlet County tractor started and hitched up a trailer. I soon had a large load of paras and kit bags. Although the County has four big wheels and is 4x 4, the tyres are very narrow and with a very heavy load I had to work hard not to get bogged, but eventually just before the foot of the Estancia Mountain down she went. The paras jumped out and unloaded the bags and someone towed us out.

We were soon on our way but it was a slow trip and it became very slippery as we climbed the mountain. Eventually we couldn't go any further but there were only a few hundred yards to go. It was a very busy track with tractors and trailers, crawlers and Land Rovers going this way and that trying to find the best track.

The many trips that went on that afternoon and evening weren't without incident. Pat Whitney who had kept the lifeline of stores, supplies and mail going until the last few weeks, tipped his contingent of paras out of the Rincon trailer twice. Roddy McKay from Brookfield managed to shed a track from the crawler he was driving.

The harsh sticky smell of hexamine cookers began to seem normal as men brewed their tea or cooked a concoction of compo (field rations).'

I was called out to take a message by motorbike to the CO (Commamding Officer).' who was in a forward position on Mount Estancia. I took a fully kitted para with a weapon on the back. I took Toni's bike because it was really low geared and had a big knobbly tyre on the back.

We went up the mountain picking a track between the stone runs that wasn't too steep and that hadn't had the top sod removed by the countless vehicles. With the weight of the para and I, we needed every bit of grip we could find. It was early morning and I really had to concentrate to get the bike and its load up the mountain. This took my mind off the feeling of isolation and vulnerability.

At another time the picture of the two of us would have been comical with me in thigh boots big coat and a bobble hat and the soldier on the back towering over me, his size exaggerated by his helmet, webbing, rifle and boots.

There were signs that the bike was heating up, as the mud that was splattering up cooked on the engine and gave off a pungent smell. We had to get on to the top and pick our way through a para company that had already got their bashers set up and blending into the stones and rock. We stopped and asked for directions.

The CO (Commanding Officer) was on a formation of rock, which overlooked the East Falklands towards Stanley, which was in the distance. We couldn't get right to the position because a massive stone run spread in all directions. The para got off and trotted off into the outcrop and the bike's suspension heaved a sigh of relief.

It was at that moment that it dawned on me the meaning of being on the frontline. There was a veil of fog, which was slightly reassuring but it wouldn't stop a lucky shot from the artillery in Stanley. An Argy patrol could be using the fog for cover to infiltrate the 3rd Parachute Regiment lines.

The journey down was quicker although I managed to lose my bearings with all the newly formed tracks and options and especially at times when the visibility was very poor.

We had just sat down for a cup of coffee when news came in that someone had fallen in a stone run and fractured their pelvis. A driver was needed to take the tractor out with a trailer and get the casualty. I grabbed the nearest tractor and trailer and set off. Fortunately for him and me the injured para was not at the top of Mount Estancia. He was in the rocks just above the valley on the side of the mountain.

Driving a slow tractor gives you plenty of time to conjure up visions of trigger-happy over-zealous paras opening up on you as you arrive, or even Argy Special Forces patrolling onto the para frontline.

When we arrived at the position they brought the soldier out and put him in the trailer. The poor chap wasn't getting much sympathy with his mates who were in good heart, some even laughing. The victim had a strange smile on his face as though he saw the funny side of his accident. They explained that he had slipped into the stones when he went out to relieve himself. 'I'll take it slowly,' I said. 'Doesn't matter how you go, he won't know, he's on cloud nine mate' said one of the crowd who had literally thrown the patient into the trailer. The strange smile from the injured man was now clear – he was high on morphine.

The journey back was a bit slower, with care at all the buffalo ditches, the pass through the stream and back to the medical facilities at the house. This was a change to the medics' routine because ninety percent of their work was for problems with feet.

Wednesday 2 June

Trudi and Tony, oblivious to the laws of a minimum of eight hours sleep requirement, burst into an early dawn chorus with the noise they made departing. They got up, loaded their Land Rovers with rations and disappeared up Mount Estancia on a replenishment run with a number of other vehicles.

Meanwhile the Estancia becomes a hive of activity. Men are digging-in on every point of 360 degrees around the farm. Many of the trenches on the small cliffs by the creek had filled with water so other drier locations were sought.

The peat resources at the Estancia are rapidly dwindling as this fuel is industriously wheeled, carted and carried away to various fires which envelope the area surrounding the Estancia in a permanent blue haze.

Although the fires pinpoint the Estancia as accurately as any pathfinder flare, the effect on morale is quite apparent. 45-gallon drums with the tops cut out and the bottom punctured with holes make very good stoves and water in large containers could be heated for washing and shaving. Not quite as invigorating as a cold dip in a stream but when you're frozen anyway, how invigorating is that?

I took the tractor and trailer belonging to Johnson's Harbour up Mount Estancia with men and equipment. The mountainside is black with tracks by this time but because of the various stone runs that dissect most areas of the mountain some crossing points had to be used continuously. Although the Johnson's tractor was well shod Tony had to tow us up some of the steeper gradients. His tractor having double wheels on the back was a great asset.

Another trip on the bike came soon after this with a message up to a company in the mountains. The journey was a Sammy Miller special and even on my own this time, with so much of the mountain chewed up by the relentless traffic, it was not at all easy.

Everyone that had arrived with vehicles was needed in one way or another. A representative had come from every settlement in the North Camp. As I was off delivering the message a number of Land Rovers were fuelling up and heading for Teal Inlet to pick up medics and support personnel belonging to 3 Para. This journey turned into an endurance test with the Land Rovers not arriving back until the next day.

The journalists are having an internal war and accusations against one another are rife. A reporter who is miles back from the frontline at Teal Inlet is apparently gleaning information from the reports sent back from the front. The indignation is very noisy and one thinks in this frame of mind perhaps they should lead when 3 Para move forward to take Stanley.

After the war the book with most laughs directed at others spoke of staying at Estancia House. This is true. The house was packed with men even sleeping on the pantry floor. The reporters asked for a place to sleep and they were able to use the loft. Many reports portrayed the civilians as uninterested.

Reports reach us that Top Malo House was a burning wreck. A group of Argentines had been parachuted in behind British lines. The SAS were tasked to flush them out. The battle left seven dead and five wounded and the rest gave up. (There was a battle between the two sides, which left Top Malo in ruins but proved not to be that accurate in casualty terms but that is how we heard it at the Estancia.)

Keith Whitney from Rincon driving the farm 4x4 tractor with a full load of ammunition in company with Roddy McKay driving a Fordson crawler and another trailer full of ammunition had come under attack from the Argentines. The 155mm guns of Stanley had ranged in on the track that runs up between Mounts Kent and Estancia. Every so often they let go a few rounds. The vehicles were bringing ammunition back from the front where it was decided it wasn't needed after all. All of a sudden a hole appeared 50 yards in front of the tractors, another landed to the side almost immediately. Both men leapt from their tractors, Keith got such a fright that he left without stopping his and subsequently had to leap back on board and stop it.

Thursday 3 June

The pace never slackens. Toni arrives back from Teal Inlet at 6.30am. They had an eventful trip with the Scimitars and Scorpions of the Blues and Royals nearly opening up on them. The trip up was fairly uneventful in travelling terms but the return run was made slightly awkward with the guide that knew the track intimately deciding that a premature celebration was in order to salute the retaking of the Islands. Coming home in the dark with heavily laden vehicles and an inebriated guide was a different undertaking.

I made ready to take another bike trip with a soldier but plans changed due to thick fog blanketing the mountain.

As the fog cleared later in the day helicopters started to appear. Sea Kings brought in the 105mm artillery and placed them behind the eastern peak in a shallow valley. Conditions were still far short of perfect and the gunners used flares to attract the attention of the pilots.

For a group of men at war they were tidy. I took a few 45-gallon drums of rubbish up to the dump. While I was there a patrol came over the saddle between Mounts Kent and Estancia and guided by Terry Peck arrived a short while later. They had brought down fire on Argentine positions in and around Longdon. The group looked worn out but pleased with their endeavours.

I stood by for a casevac (casualty evacuation) as the BVs arrived in numbers. These are articulated, tracked vehicles that can go virtually anywhere, even across swamps and soft peat where a tractor couldn't go. These vehicles were to take over resupplying and they were ideal although they cut the ground up even more and the black tracks became even blacker and in every direction. The vehicles were centrally heated with radiators in the back. Although BVs are track vehicles they are steered by a wheel, which isn't very track like.

Bruce May from Johnson's loaded Milan Missiles and their launchers onto the Johnson's trailer and soon, with the Milan section, disappeared towards the valley. Meanwhile Claude Molkenbuhr from the Murrell Farm and Tony took 7.62 ammunition and the mortar section out. Tony's tractor had a transport box full of 7.62 and the trailer was full of mortar ammunition and the launchers.

A number of tanks moved out from the house and headed for the hills. The Blues and Royals said they were going forward to become mobile sentries because they had good night sights. The recovery tank stayed at the Estancia but was deployed one night when a tank rolled over a bank. Miraculously no one was injured.

The momentum forward has slowed right down with issues on the south flank. The marines had to take the Two Sisters before the paras could take Longdon because the former overlooked the latter. (This was only partially true.)

The British artillery roared in the day to answer the spasmodic fire of the Argentine 155mm guns.

It came over the radio network that a member of the marines had trodden on a mine. Poor sod.

The tanks returned because they are low on petrol. Petrol is very scarce and the BVs and tanks scoff it at a gluttonous rate. Some of the civilian Land Rovers take petrol.

Friday 4 June

Another day of indecision. Firstly, we were all made ready to get tents that were up in the valley. Plans changed and Andreas Short from Port Louis and I got ready to take a Sniper section up and towards the Murrell Bridge. Just as we were about to move out plans changed again.

The reporters seem to have recovered from their internal problems and are now keen to get forward and get a story. The four-wheel drive tractor and the crawler are still out in the valley where they were left after they were shelled by the Argentines because no one seemed to know where this ammunition was needed.

Ray Newman, the Caretaker of Government interests at Green Patch, the farm that had been bought by the government and split up into family sized units, left on a bike to show the Blues and Royals the track over the mountains to Fitzroy. The bike broke down on the way but he was able to carry on and complete the task. The tanks never cease to amaze me at how well they adapt to travelling over rough and soft ground. Arrangements were made over 2 meter to have someone meet the tanks and escort them into Fitzroy.

As this was all happening another convoy of Land Rovers went back to Teal Inlet for petrol and diesel. Communications had ceased from Rincon Grande including the phone so Connie May and Trudi McPhee drove up there to make sure all was well.

The news from Rincon is that the Special Forces had arrived at the French Wreck at Rincon to evict the Argies from their observation post.

We are all sitting down late in the afternoon having a much deserved cuppa when there was an almighty series of bangs. It sounded and felt as if a couple of thousand pound bombs had landed in the garden. Everyone leapt to their feet and looked out.

Finding anywhere in a building to operate from was scarce. Intelligence were lucky enough to find the dairy shed vacant. News coming from them reports Argies in an OP (observation post) on one of the mountains overlooking Fitzroy have been told to waste their ammunition, throw down their weapons and make for town.

Today a few of us went to investigate the shell holes by the tractors that Roddy and Keith had abandoned. One of the holes was only 30 yards from the nearest tractor and as deep and the same size as the kitchen. No wonder Roddy had said the blast had lifted the crawler up into the air. The paras reckoned that the peat absorbed a lot of the force thus saving Keith and Roddy from serious injury.

Later at the house, we got an air raid red and blokes were shouting and whistles were giving short blasts as we all tumbled out of the house and down the trenches that we had dug. Tony, Ailsa, Nyree, Jack, Kay, Toni and I. It was a deep and narrow hole, which accommodated us all but with little comfort.

All clear came with long blasts on the whistles. Green Patch eventually came on and they had had a bad scare with bombs striking the water half a mile from them. People watching at Port Louis saw the bombs hit the water. (Big holes were also found after the war in a paddock just outside Green Patch.) We think that these were the big bangs we had heard earlier.

With a sense of timing calculated to interrupt the World Service News there was another air raid warning red. Fear of bombs gave me the incentive to collect coat and boots in one movement and make for the trench. The more casual amongst us that refused to be bullied by the Argentine air force indifferently dressed and filed out to their shelters.

The bangs were spectacular to say the least and the ground shook, the sky lit up and my heart beat shot into the red on the tachometer.

This raid was at night and as we had been told the Argies couldn't mount an air raid at night they were obviously giving it a shot.

News the next day on the World Service had Argentina claiming that they had bombed Mount Kent. We didn't hear any planes and so it was assumed it was high altitude bombing with Canberras.

Soon after the explosions Tony left the shelter and maintained the pose of landowner walking up and down in a very casual manner. The feeling of security didn't melt the fear in the trench or the desire to leave the reassuring sanctuary of our hole in the ground.

Saturday 5 June

Up at bloody 5.30am. A buzzer is sounded in short bursts and voices are shouting out red alert. The majority of people dash to their holes. Some people are too tired and can't be bothered.

Possibly this alert was caused by a Hercules because by this time the British realised that these planes were breaking the exclusion zone nightly.

As soon as light permits helicopters of all shapes and sizes come forth with stores and ammunition slung in nets underneath. Wessex, Gazelles, Scouts and Sea Kings of the anti-submarine variety with the dome behind the rotor and the ones without. All these machines flying to and fro have their own particular noise. The Gazelles had a distinctive whine, which could be heard for miles. The Sea King had a fairly noisy action with a wheezing sound accompanying the engine noise. The Wessex had a more distinctive smell, which one would associate with paraffin heaters that are burning a cheap grade of paraffin.

After sampling the comforts of being doubled up in our slit trench, which was too thin to squat and not deep enough to stand up straight, Toni and I decided to carry out some alterations. Because the top was a comprehensive pile of mud, tin and wood we decided that the best method would be for someone to dig down in the hole with someone outside with a rope and bucket. I took the spade and Toni hauled the spoil out of the hole in the bucket on a rope. It was a slow and tiring business. This however resulted in us needing a ladder to get in and out from then on.

As Toni and I sweated over our trench improvements a para borrowed Toni's bike. He was an expert rider with experience of rough riding. A medic informs Toni during the day that the soldier has abandoned her bike because he fell off and then couldn't get it started. It was too late to recover it when we were told.

Vernon Steen, a mechanic with the Government Air Service and a Falkland Island Defence Force member took out a patrol to Mount Longdon. As Vernon left, Tony was on his way up to the old Argy camp to get some tents and food. The small room that we sleep in is now chocker block with people. Even the small amount of floor space has a sleeping body squeezed in.

Tony gets his 3kw diesel generator going. This fed a lot of army equipment and kept lights going in the dairy, which was the intelligence headquarters and next to there was the command post of Major Roger Paton of 3 Para.

The problem with this engine was the size of the fuel tank. This had to be refuelled every four hours. All the civilians went to bed at night but elements of the army wanted 24-hour power and so a para was given the task of filling the generator every three or four hours.

Sunday morning the engine ground to a halt. The para, probably half asleep, cold and exhausted, put petrol into the tank instead of diesel. Luckily there was no permanent damage and after draining the petrol out and putting diesel back in and bleeding the fuel lines and fuel pump, off she went.

Sunday 6 June

Vernon came back. Their patrol had brought down fire onto Land Rovers and trucks. These vehicles were thought to have been abandoned by the Argies when they became bogged but no one seemed to care as long as the enemy couldn't use them again.

Another patrol reported to have hit a command post with a 66mm anti-tank missile. A para sniper was also meant to have shot an Argentine on Longdon. The Argentines seem unable to fight back.

I went to find Toni's bike. A BV came along and offered me a lift. They had to go around a few positions but they would drop me off on the way back. The BVs aren't that comfortable but they are amazing on camp. They just drive along as if nothing will stop them. Up inclines and banks that looked too steep and always travelling on black slop that was the track and would have stopped anything else. The journey was in aid of water. Jerry cans were filled from a tap on the green, and sometimes the house, and then run up the mountain to the troops. Even though the military had been told countless times that the water on the hill was the same water that went to the house they seemed to only be reassured if they could see a tap. The only water that is treated in the Falklands, in any way, is the water in Stanley.

We dropped off the water and Arctic rations to company C. A sergeant shouted to a private, 'Take this scoff. Take it to my basher and don't touch it until I get there. Got it? Go.'

I must have been staring hard although I did get the gist that he wasn't being nasty. 'It's all right,' he said. 'If I didn't say that they would nick half the scoff before I got back.' Before I could give a half-hearted answer he was telling everyone in the BV about the virtues of eating the rolled oatmeal blocks. You have to dig a bloody deep hole he explained and then went on to say how straining keeps you warm.

I marvelled at the sense of fun these blokes had at the top of a cold, windswept Falkland Island mountain in the middle of winter, their homes just a hole scooped out between some stones with a flimsy bit of waterproof fabric over the top.

Our next stop was a gun battery. They were situated in a saddle halfway along the Estancia Mountain. The guns and supporting BVs were draped in camouflaged netting and sod walls had been built for bashers and protection. In the misty conditions of the mountains the camouflage was very effective with the gun muzzles sticking out ready to take coordinates and fire.

The BV got behind schedule so took me back to the Estancia. It was a totally unknown track to me but then driving a BV you didn't have to worry about ditches or soft stuff. As it turned out the keys for the bike were back at the Estancia because a para also went to get it but hadn't been able to start it and so came back with the key.

A para called Bob, who was always to be found directing the myriad of helicopters down and organising men to run in and unhook a sling and unload the cargo, eventually rescued the bike. He managed to slip away for a while and do the deed.

Looking at Toni's bike someone had obviously had a good fall because the handlebars and forks were severely twisted.

What a miserable day with driving rain all day. A para in the mountain finding that I was born and bred in the UK asked me what I saw in the Falklands. I said that the Falklands were all right and that this was winter but that if I had walked from San Carlos to the Estancia Mountain and then lived for a number of days under canvas I wouldn't be over impressed. This hard para agreed wholeheartedly.

The World Service has relegated the Falklands war to second place for the first time since it began. Israel has invaded Lebanon. We feel the pressure in the Falklands but conditions in Lebanon will be horrific and more civilians will be killed and injured than make up the total Falkland Island's population.

Another marine stood on a mine during a forward patrol around the Two Sisters.

Rumour has it that a British Sea Dart missile has shot down a small British helicopter of the Army Air Corp. All four men on board were killed.

Monday 7 June

There's an air raid warning red at 8am. I wish the Argies would be more considerate over their hours of attack – they must know that an attack at this time interferes with Radio Newsreel from the World Service of the BBC. My priorities are correct as I choose to stand against the clay of the trench with Toni, Jack and Kay. It's another false alarm or an attack that doesn't reach us and by now a number of people can't be bothered to seek shelter.

During the air raid, a number of people saw a trail like a missile going up and a bright explosion over Teal Inlet. They think it was an Argentine getting his just desserts.

The morning starts with fears for the safety of a patrol that hasn't made its contact time. Whatever their problems with communications they walk in, all safe and sound later in the day.

The Davidsons return from Brookfield after having a night's break there.

A big armoured vehicle arrives. This machine has a bucket on the front and an anchor that it fires off if it gets bogged. The anchor is attached to a winch and this supposedly lets the vehicle pull itself out. The debate about this ability goes along the lines of 'sure mate!'

This vehicle goes down onto the beach and runs over the sewage pipe. We are all waiting for Tony to throw a wobbly but he has quietly sat back, as wood, tin and other materials have disappeared to improve bashers and a fair amount of two years supply of peat has walked to the many fires. Fences have been trashed and the ground cut up by the many machines supporting the British effort, but Tony seems to remain quite composed.

The sewage pipe was unnecessary and the stink is grim. How could the driver have missed the pipe that was cocooned in concrete or thought that his machine wouldn't crush whatever it was? There is no time to get worked up about it.

Sally Blake, the manager's wife at Hill Cove, is on the RT (radio telephone) to report that she has seen a plane falling from the sky to the north of the settlement.

Israel is number one again on the BBC World Service.

A number of newspapers arrived today. I tore through them all searching for news but we were all disappointed because most of the news is old hat.

The soldiers are taking advantage of a clear bright day and sleeping bags and clothes flutter from the fences and buildings all around.

The British turn up with a Spanish-speaking officer and try the phone line. I don't know where they got the idea from because the line to Stanley has been inoperable since the beginning of May. They then tried on 2 meter. They had no joy so off they went.

Later a patrol managed to catch some Argies. The feeling was that the Argies were finished and all the Brits had to do was to walk into town.

Tuesday 8 June

The Argentine Air Force, who now obviously enjoy BBC Radio Newsreel, attack just after 7am so that it gives the survivors enough time to get back for the 8am broadcast.

The interpreter that was at the Estancia yesterday, Captain Rod Bell, called Stanley once more but this time during the one-hour medical schedule on 4.5. He asked the authorities for a 24-hour channel to make arrangements for the civilian safety in Stanley.

Terry Peck leaves the Estancia with a patrol just after 10am. A number of Land Rovers leave in the afternoon to bring the patrol back.

We spent most of the afternoon in the dugout because of continuous air raid reds. Major Patton got increasingly angry about taking cover and orders his men into their trenches. A number of paras complemented by a group of civilians have become nonchalant about the dangers as the many air raid reds come to nothing at the Estancia.

Over the mountains the warnings had been valid and at Port Pleasant just outside Fitzroy the Royal Fleet Auxiliary vessels *Sir Galahad* and *Sir Tristram* had received deadly attention from the Argentine air force. The frigate *Plymouth* was also hit during other action.

The Welsh Guards were on the Fleet Auxiliaries and they have taken heavy casualties with some estimates suggesting 50 killed and many more injured. The way people were talking it was an obvious disaster but also a set back to the taking of Stanley.

As time went by the BBC World Service reported the tragedy but wouldn't state the number of casualties so rumours began to seesaw from both the military and the civilians. Numbers were bandied about from as few as ten to as many as a hundred.

From all accounts it seems that someone was over confident. The taking of Goose Green and the advance from Port San Carlos to just outside Stanley had made it look too easy. Troops were crammed aboard these ships and kept on board for five hours, some watching videos rather than getting ashore and digging in.

The Argentines were still in some of the hills outside Stanley and you wouldn't need the sharpest eyesight to see two big ships in Port Pleasant.

Two Argentine planes were shot down in these raids but this was a small consolation.

The World Service reports that an unidentified four-engined plane attacked an American tanker, the Hercules . The tanker was addressed over a radio to head for an Argentine port within a time limit. The ship was 450 miles from the Falklands and refused to comply. Shortly afterwards it was attacked by what is thought to be a Hercules transport plane with the bomb being rolled out of the ramp at the back. The ship is now sailing for a Brazilian port. The Ministry of Defence said that none of its planes were involved. The Argentines say they haven't got a plane with that kind of range.

Tony goes and digs a huge shelter and then drags his fencing sleigh over the top as a roof. Although the shelter was a long way from army regulations it was comfortable with steps to help the occupants in and out and had blocks of soil within to make seats. It was palatial compared to other trenches but I had a feeling that if a large bomb got anywhere near, the sleigh would be joining people in the hole.

Tuesday 9 June

A large patrol crept up to the Argies on Mount Longdon but weren't allowed to fire upon the enemy. They were testing the alertness of the defenders.

The civilians in their Land Rovers supporting this exercise came under mortar fire and guns. What was believed to be a 150mm mortar round landed 25 yards from them. Some of the drivers ran for shelter but others just sat there. It must have been a cold, long night.

Reports have it that six of the eight Argentine planes that attacked were shot down in yesterday's attacks. Four Mirages downed by two Harriers, which sounds pretty incredible.

The artillery starts softening up the Argentines on Longdon and the Two Sisters. The shells leave with a sort of 'ting' noise followed by a whistle and a crump seconds later. They must be setting their sights for the next stage of the British advance. The paras were really keen to get stuck in. A member of the Milan section was saying 'I didn't carry this stuff all the way from San Carlos not to use it.' There was an echoed agreement from the others. The forward companies who had taken it in turns to return to the relative comfort of the Estancia talked of nothing else apart from killing the enemy. Some even spoke of leaving the Parachute Regiment after the war because a battle and legally killing was all they joined up for. I knew they had been psyched up for the battle but these were hard men and sitting in holes in the snow and rain hadn't helped them to consider the Argentine's finer points.

The Ministry of Defence clarified the story about the American tanker. It was called on its own frequency and told to head for an Argentine port or it would be attacked in fifteen minutes. It was subsequently attacked.

The weather isn't very extreme just a light breeze and a few clouds. Tony has taken the opportunity to kill some scrag sheep (old skinny things). He hung a number up for the troops and hid others up in the drafting race. I took the dogs for a run and sneakily fed them some scrags, trying to keep their location a secret.

We had a number of air raid warnings during the day. Scurrying into the shelter had become second nature. The regulars in our trench were Jack and Kay and us. Again nothing was seen or heard.

The news on the radio concerning Fitzroy is not encouraging. They say no news is good news but this time I am not so sure.

Thursday 10 June

Two Pucarás bombed C Company of the 3rd Parachute Regiment. Rumour control has it that it was napalm but this hasn't been confirmed. These planes must be operating from Stanley airport. The media has reported nothing about this attack. A couple of Harriers screamed over but a bit late to catch them. Back with C Company fortunately they didn't suffer any casualties but it shows that the fight is far from over.

Someone listening to 2 meter traffic from the Argies, report that there is still an OP (observation post) post on Wall Mountain. This post could easily be the one responsible for the air attacks on Fitzroy. It's a pity this information didn't come a few days earlier.

We suffered the indignity of two air raid red alerts and again it meant a lot of time spent underground, but better safe than sorry. We all scurried for our holes when an air raid red is shouted. We all dive for our various holes only for two Harriers to fly past.

Harriers came again in the afternoon. The sound and then the sight of them hugging the ground using the cover of the mountains up behind Bluff Cove Peak gives people added confidence with their presence. They carry on along the mountains on the south side hugging the contours; a second plane followed in the wake of the first.

The only surviving Chinook appeared in the afternoon weighed down each trip by a magnitude of equipment shoved in nets underneath. The Chinook looked well used and even had a door missing.

Not only the Chinook but also helicopters of all kinds ferried in ammunition, especially 105mm for the artillery. We are building up for something here and it must be the next assault. Significantly the press have had their circuits closed.

The World Service reports that a Vulcan bomber, which has been forced to land in Brazil, was being released but without the missiles it had been carrying which will remain in Brazil.

A lot of Land Rovers have made nightly excursions supporting patrols and suchlike. A number of these Land Rover convoys came under mortar fire from the Argentines. I heard one conversation where the civilians were saying how the Argentines were playing with the convoy with shells landing one side and then the other, and thinking to myself, 'no, the bastards are trying to kill you but haven't been able to.' The British mortar teams complained that they found it difficult to find suitable sites where their base plates didn't sink or move in the peat making it hard to accurately target the enemy and to me the Argentines were probably finding the same difficulties.

Major Roger Patton got all the civilians together and gave a pep talk about the dangers involved if and when the Land Rovers were needed. He explained that although 3 Para would protect them it didn't necessarily give us foolproof invulnerability. The Land Rovers would be used as a standby just in case visibility due to fog and mist made flying by helicopters impossible. The next sortie was right to the enemy's back door.

The evening's news had the Ministry of Defence refusing to release casualty figures in connection to the Fitzroy fiasco. They feel that such figures could help the Argentines calculate when British forces would be able to attack.

Friday 11 June

There were so many troops that many individuals were familiar faces and had become part of our lives. Most of the guys were in constant good spirits wherever they were, whether it was just a head thrust out from within a bivvy to hurl some banter at an oppo (friend) or down around the house grabbing a shave from a makeshift boiler. But now there was the serious job at hand after days of waiting. Now these friends, 3 Para, were moving forward to engage the enemy.

The Land Rover force was used to transport one of the companies up to the start. I took the long-wheel based Land Rover belonging to Johnson's Harbour. A long -wheel base Land Rover has got room for a number of men and their kit, the weight is still distributed over four wheels. The old hands took two or three paras and their kit. Six climbed into mine and I thought we would give it a go.

We didn't get off to an auspicious start with the Land Rover bogging in the first ditch outside the settlement, but once we were pulled out we didn't get stuck during the rest of the journey.

The Land Rovers swung from one side of the valley to the other as the drivers in the lead searched for the best track and everyone behind searched within this area. All the usual tracks were black and long past a usable condition for a Land Rover.

Looking up in the air two planes criss-crossed each other's slip stream. A hail of bullets shot in the air from elements of 3 Para. This reaction did worry the members of the convoy who were sitting ducks if these planes were Argentines. Obviously 3 Para were ready for a fight.

Death as an entity. Death, mutilation, destruction. All this was clarified by four bodies that lay west of the meat palinkey (two tall posts close to each other with another sturdy piece of wood joining the two at the top. This structure is used to help slaughter and then hang beef).' The Royal Marines' bodies were the result of two British patrols meeting each other in the dark. I am sure this kind of thing happens all the time in wars, but it's a fact of life in war that seems most unpalatable.

I am kept in reserve as most of the other Land Rovers creep further up the mountain, keeping just behind the summit and not visible from the Argy positions, waiting for the night and the order to move forward.

I return to the house to run fuel between the house and the Tarbarrel. On one occasion I got bogged in a buffalo ditch but was easily towed out by a BV.

As work goes on in the settlement, like despatching gear to troops and receiving ordinance from Teal Inlet, Argy shells start hitting the rise just in front of where the Land Rovers are stationed. Smoke rises and it is an anxious time for us down in the comparative safety of the house.

The weather has changed and so all the noises of war seem magnified. The planes, the artillery and the explosions.

Saturday 12 June

Helicopter pilots say that the Royal Marines have taken their objective, the Two Sisters. They say the fight was hard but they have taken many prisoners

Great tragedy. Today's doctor's hour, which was very late, speaks of civilian casualties in the local population. It is a bitter pill.

Sue Whitley, who taught art and domestic science for many years in the Stanley senior school, and Doreen Bonner have been killed. Mary Goodwin, the lady that I had lodged with when I first arrived in the Islands, along with the Superintendent of Education, John Fowler and his family, are in hospital after the house that they were sheltering in was struck by a shell. It was a stone house, which was considered safer than the wooden houses and other people had sought shelter there.

Late in the afternoon the Estancia House is occupied by a number of lame paras and the logistic staff. We all know the plan and so it is just a case of waiting.

It's a depressing day and the stillness exaggerates this feeling. The noises from the front stretch everyone's reserves.

3 Para were supposed to start their attack on Longdon at 8pm and the Marines on Two Sisters an hour later. We all went and stood on the steps and listened. Nothing. We are all hoping for a quick and bloodless action.

The first contact happened 9.07pm, local time, when a para trod on a mine. Poor sod. We all ran to the steps and looked up the valley.

Flares lit up the sky and the odd tracer could be seen. The guns situated in the mountains were pouring fire towards their targets with the crump at the receiving end.

3 Para that were in and around the Estancia have taken heavy casualties taking Longdon with nineteen killed and many injured. I hate to think how many Argentines have died.

It is now said that three hundred Argentines surrendered on the Two Sisters to the Royal Marines. The marines are finding it hard to cope with so many. One of the Argy officers has a map of all the gun positions and other useful information.

The Glamorgan has been hit but by what isn't quite clear, although rumour once more thinks it's a land-based Exocet.

Sunday 13 June

Once again the helicopters are working nonstop. A Sea King is out of action in front of the house, having sucked a plastic bag into its engine. A lot of cursing, accusations and counter claims are going on between the helicopter crew and the ground staff.

Just after 11am local time we had a red alert. They are annoying because they don't seem to affect us and if all that is being said is true the Argentines shouldn't be able to mount a significant attack. So after many days of red alerts and not a sight of an enemy jet there are a large number of people that don't bother taking cover.

This all changed and people dived for holes as two waves of three Skyhawks shot over the ridge between Kent and Estancia Mountains heading east to west.

If the planes didn't get you if you stayed out in the open, the ground fire would, as anyone and everyone fired whatever they had towards the planes. A tank that had arrived back with mechanical problems opened up with its 30mm cannon. The vibration or recoil of the gun was so strong that it shook dirt down into our trench and we were 100 metres away.

The more adventurous stood and watched as one of the Skyhawks dropped a parachute bomb on to what we thought was a gun battery just below Bluff Cove Peak. One plane turned as if it was going to come again but it dropped its drop tanks and left for home.

There were no casualties and a number of the bombs failed to explode. The attack had apparently been made against the headquarters of 5th Infantry Brigade. This was the first close sight of the famous Skyhawks, which had been the backbone of the Argentine air force.

Toni and I went for a walk after dinner. It was easy to get depressed listening to the para radio link and to be told periodically that someone else had died or been badly wounded.

We went across the creek and up the first gentle slopes of Mount Estancia. The weather was calm again. I took my camera and took a few shots of the Estancia house hoping to catch the black tracks that lead away to the many destinations and the many fox holes that made the Estancia look like the set for the *Watership Down* movie.

There was an Army Air Corp base in one of the undulations in the valley. We were several hundred yards away when they came running out of their tents and from under and around machines to dive into the various shelters situated on the outskirts of their camp. Toni and I decided to just lie down.

I lay in a slight fold in the hill, which gave some protection from bombs directed at the Army Air Corp and hopefully from the hail of indiscriminate fire that might come from the Estancia. Toni felt safer in sight of the house.

After a while the Army Air Corp chaps popped out of their holes and went back to the jobs they'd left. I walked down to Toni and simulated a bomb dropping by whistling. Instead of realising that I was fooling around she believed that a bomb was falling very close. She thought 'Here it comes, what should I do?' She glanced around but instead of a lethal 1000lb bomb she saw me.

We decided to hotfoot it back to the Estancia where we found the heads and weapons protruding from every hole.

Special Forces arrived at the Estancia. The SAS that had rudely disturbed our sleep were there. They told us the full story of that night. A naval officer, Roger Edwards, who is related to Toni because he is married to a cousin, was with them. His wife had told him to go and get the Falklands back. These troops were off to attack positions around the Murrell. We didn't see this group until they visited us again in Stanley and then two of their number were missing – wounded.

The BBC announced that the *Glamorgan* was hit and that nine men were killed. This is grave news but the ship hasn't been lost. If it was an Exocet the *Glamorgan* was fairly fortunate.

The Argentines have agreed to a safety zone for civilians. This is reassuring as everyone has friends and relations in town.

The 2 meter sets are now in full use in the North Camp. News from Long Island of a ship approaching. No one seems to know anything about it. I hope it's not the Argies trying a last ditch attack from behind.

'Its air raid red,' someone bellowed. Having always taken the threat seriously we hurled ourselves into our trench. As we hit the bottom, the order all clear was passed around.

A little later another air raid red had us reaching for coats, boots, hats, etc. Lami Dozo's (The commander of the Argentine airforce) bunch of merry men just didn't know when they were beaten. Lami Dozo's boys didn't turn up. Two Harriers arrived from the south over Mount Kent. The reaction from the troops hopefully isn't in the best British traditions. A hail of small arms fire, given away by the telltale tracers, rose from the ground to meet them. The planes, so rudely welcomed, shot up in the air. The tank crew obviously, the intelligence staff's favourites, recognised the Harrier as a friendly plane.

Things aren't great at the front. 3 Para are dug in on Mount Longdon and are being pounded by Argie guns sitting in the residential part of Stanley itself.

The Argentines have been seen reinforcing Tumbledown Mountain with helicopters from Stanley. Perhaps the Argies are going to fight back.

Hilarious news comes back. The Samson, the recovery tank with the Scorpions, tried to cross the Murrell Bridge. The tank and bridge now lies in the Murrell River. The Samson, loaded with extra ammunition and a heavier tank than the others in theatre, is supposedly upside down. The bridge was wooden, supported by two steel poles – these poles were rusted through. Luckily no one was hurt.

Many locals had explained to the tank crews about the conditions of the bridge on the Murrell and that it was only designed for tractors and trailers at most and had told them about the passes. There's one downstream and one above on the first bend. This local knowledge was totally ignored but then one has to realise that driving in the Falklands with concepts like passes is totally new to many in the British Army.

Monday 14 June

2 Para took Moody Brook last night and 3 Para secured Wireless Ridge. The Scottish Guards have taken Tumbledown.

Reports coming in over the Para's radio network have the Argies pouring back into town. 2 Para has been told to hold their positions but from the confusion they have said their radios are not working. A good idea as they vie to be the first into Stanley

An Argy prisoner is in the old shearing shed. Poor sod. He looks about fifteen. Apparently he was found hiding among the dead. He is a pathetic sight. One of the locals who can speak Spanish is interpreting. He thinks the paras are going to eat him.

2 Para are 400 yards from Government House. Faulty radio or not, they are now standing firm.

A number of Argies are seen to throw down their arms and surrender. At 12.30pm local time 4.5mgs, the frequency used around the Islands for communications, comes to life with the Navy talking to the Argentines.

They wanted a delegation to meet at Moody Brook, the old Marine Barracks, but British Artillery had demolished this building and apparently it was still burning fiercely. The Argies suggested meeting on the hospital ship but it was pointed out that this was contrary to the Geneva Convention. It's eventually agreed that a British helicopter will fly in at 4pm to the football field in Stanley.

Now something happened which has never been verified and I never heard of it again.

The radio net was still speaking to Stanley. There is an Argy C130 near the Islands and they wanted permission for it to land at Stanley. This was refused. They said that Harriers would escort it to Goose Green. What happened to it?

The British and Argentine Generals met at the Secretariat and signed a document, which surrendered all Argentine forces to the Brits. So it's now all over.

One of the locals, who had been forward with 3 Para in his Land Rover, immediately drove into town. I was amazed that someone could think so little of their own safety.

The next day was a torturous abuse of time. Toni who had been worrying about her folks was frustrated because there seemed no way of getting in to Stanley.

Don and I walked up into the vacated British Artillery positions up on Mount Estancia. It only seems yesterday when I was up in a BV watching the barrels recoil into the camouflage netting. Now the netting was mostly gone, a few tattered remnants fluttering idly in the breeze.

Brass shell cases lay untidily in drunken heaps splayed out from the once all-action of the gun positions, hurriedly cast out of the way as they supported the assault on Longdon.

Don and I began to work through the position. There were one or two live rounds at a couple of the positions. There were also slings used by the helicopters to bring the ammunition.

Some of the dugouts were works of art, built from sods dug from near and far. A residence which looked as though it could have been occupied for months rather than days. Among these sod habitats I came across an anti-tank missile, one of the type you pull out and fire and then throw away. Someone had felt that the move forward was far enough without this extra weight.

Now it's all over, my mind was thinking of the number of rounds, weight, type etc. Where exactly was the fire falling? Funnily I also thought of the Argentines. Not so much the arrogant generals who have deafened us with the pledge of national dishonour and fighting to the last man, the last drop of blood, but the ordinary Argentine soldier, a person of a country called upon to fight for his country. Something men from all over the world do.

We walked back to the Estancia. The ground around carrying the scars of war, but on the whole deserted.

We were all ready to go to town but it didn't look possible. Helicopters were too busy, and over land was too fraught with dangers such as minefields and associated problems. 3 Para were tying up the loose ends.

Two days after the surrender it was suddenly possible that a journey to town was imminent by chopper. To our small circle that had lived in one another's pockets for a couple of months we were now eager to pick up the pieces. The helicopter arrived at very short notice. A chance became actuality as we stormed up from the house, just essentials crammed into a bag.

The Wessex took off and swung in the direction of town. I had my camera at the ready and banged away.

We flew up the valley where we had watched the Argies dig in, later get attacked by Harriers and finally chased out by 3 Para's mortars. We then flew along the side of Mount Kent over the Argentine Chinook and Puma that the Harriers destroyed many days ago. Holes began to get more frequent the nearer we got to town. Neat patterns along the ridges, the odd ones in the peaty valleys.

Smoke was belching up from around Moody Brook, or what little now remained. The old building that was near by and had been condemned and nicknamed Belsen Block still stood snubbing its critics having withstood at least one direct hit.

The winch man beckoned me forward and opened the door, he held on to my coat as I hung out taking pictures.

Stanley from the air was so different from pre-war conception. Ships galore in Stanley Harbour, Port William and between McBride's Head and Cape Pembroke.

We landed behind Race Course Road and saw some of 3 Para we'd met at the Estancia. Argy helicopters, the ones that had flown about in large numbers, which appeared in ever-decreasing numbers, littered the racecourse. There looked to be nearly twenty.

We shouted welcomes and regards. We then flew to Stanley football pitch west of the hospital and the Secretariat where the surrender was signed.

An Argy helicopter with red crosses was in a field, which was an area fenced off because of suspected mines.

Toni and I grabbed our bags, yelled our sincerest thanks and made for her mother and father's.

It's hard to describe the indiscriminate handshakes, hugging and dare I say it – kissing of Toni's relations and others.

The Pettersson's house was jam-packed with red caps but it didn't really matter –

the Argies had been booted out. Apparently the Sergeant Major of the MP (military police) knew Heather when he was in the Marine Party in the Falklands many years ago.

There were problems in town. A tummy bug nicknamed 'Galterie's revenge' was rife. It could strike you down time and time again. The water was non-existent for many days because the filtration plant had been damaged along with the main pipe heading into Stanley. The water that you could get had to be boiled thoroughly.

Town was riddled with Argy trenches. Because of the absence of any sanitary arrangements for these troops Argy shit was everywhere and the smell that goes with it was clawing at your nose.

Not only were the streets covered in shit but also the houses that had been lived in, had shit everywhere – in beds, fridges and ovens. The post office boxes from which town people once collected their mail had had a late Argy delivery of crap.

The British troops were still sorting out the Argy troops. Long lines of these soldiers stood about wrapped up in their coats and they were a pathetic sight.

Piles of weapons were at several locations including pistols, rifles, knives, bayonets and machine guns. Civilians were sorting through some of these piles without any concern from the British soldiers.

It wasn't only the arms that were being examined by troops and civilians alike. Many hats, coats, trousers and boots began to appear.

One of the things I distinctly remember was the number of Argy containers which had been opened and found to contain food, clothes and booze. One of the containers had macaroni pouring from it. A big strong black and white horse had been wandering around town much to everyone's surprise. This animal was later found dead. It lay by the side of the road in front of Government House. Most people thought a vehicle had knocked it down but others suggested that it had died from eating too much macaroni. It had swollen to a grotesque size after its death.

A helicopter abandoned by the Argies lay beside the gorse where most of the British newspapers had pictured the Royal Marines face down on April 2 up by the War Memorial at the west end of town.

The west end of town was full of the two parachute battalions. Toni and I walked up to see if they wanted anything. We passed the house where members of the Falklands' small community fell. The house was peppered with shrapnel holes. I wondered how the others in the house had survived.

We also witnessed one of the 155mm guns that had been shelling the valley above the Estancia. This gun had been firing from Davis Street. All the bigger Argentine artillery pieces had been firing from among the houses and so had proved difficult to neutralise.

One night an incident occurred outside the Globe Hotel and Argentinians ran riot managing to burn down the Globe Store. Rumours have it that drunken locals along with a few Brit servicemen became abusive to a group of Argies who were waiting to be disembarked onto ships in the harbour.

-Ends-

Things change over time and the feeling of being invaded by a foreign country will never leave most of us that witnessed the Argentine's occupation.

One of the memories that I didn't include in my diary was Tony talking about feeding the next visiting Argentine soldier to the pig and me not totally sure that he was joking, and trying to highlight the dangers of doing such a thing with the group of enemy soldiers not that far away. I tried to impress on Tony that these guys, especially if they were watching their mates through binoculars, might need a little convincing that it was all a bit of a misunderstanding.

Something else that is very clear to me, but no mention again in my diary, was the BV crews filling jerry cans with water from the tap on the green which interrupted the flow at the house. They would load up these cans and distribute them to the soldiers in the mountains.

A vivid memory that I didn't record was being at Rincon and the Pucarás flying straight at the top settlement that was built on a hill. They pulled up high into the air and raced off to do this time and time again. There is a possibility that it was just a good place to buzz but I wondered later if they mistook the inhabitants here for the Pitalugas who lived opposite across Salvador Waters at Salvador. Rob had been politically active but of course this is all conjecture.

The two things that take me back to the war is the smell of the hexamine blocks for cooking and the Bell Huey helicopter with its single main blade that gave it a unique noise and dove-tails into how I remember the Vietnam conflict.

I thought then, as I do nearly 30 years later, that we civilians helping the paras in the push forward were very lucky that no one was killed or injured.

Finally after going through my diary which I wrote at the time there are a number of inaccuracies but I have changed very little.

20. POST-WAR REPAIR AND RECOVERY

Giles Mercer

I decided with a heavy heart to come to town and eventually got a job with the Public Works Department (PWD) working as a carpenter/handyman. At the same time Giles Mercer, a big, loud and aggressive (although not in a fightable way) American joined the team.

Giles was a workaholic and had a sense of urgency in repairing property to get people back into their homes. Giles would get a list of jobs, finish them, and then be pestering our foreman for the next. This kind of attitude was rare in the government departments of that time. Of course, this didn't make Giles popular with his boss because he was always hounding him, or with many of his workmates, who were quite contented with a slower, easier pace of life.

Giles and I had a little history and at that stage I thought he was too 'in your face'. I knew his wife, Christel, really well because she was a settlement teacher at Fitzroy and had attended the seminar at Darwin and then, like you do, we met at different functions here and there over the years. At one of these meetings Giles was offering the opinion that the Brits should keep out of Ireland. Where upon I thought that this was a strange opinion coming from an American whose country gets involved all over the world and – not too far in the distant past – Vietnam, which is nowhere near America. We had a frank exchange of views.

To cut a long story short I found out that I quite liked Giles and he found out that he could tolerate me and so we worked together repairing people's houses and getting them habitable. We spent months repairing shrapnel damage. We replaced whole windows and individual panes of glass, corrugated iron on roofs and flat iron on the sides of houses.

Replacing tin on the roofs could be trying because we would take old damaged sheets up and try and replace them with new, only to find out the corrugations were different. When you were driving the springhead nails through two thicknesses that didn't match, you had to give them a hard swipe with the hammer and occasionally you would hit a finger. If you did roofing work solidly for a week your fingers could get really sore. It is also interesting to note that the old tin that we removed was a lot thicker than the tin we were using to replace and repair. The new tin could easily be bent, by walking over it, unlike the old sheets.

The Government Central Store had never been busier and materials seemed to come in and out to the job in a seamless motion. The job of cutting glass wasn't a skill that anyone in the carpenters' shop seemed to have but we needed hundreds of panes of glass. After a few cutting disasters we sought out someone that could. Enter the ex-camp teacher and musician, The Fighting Pigs' own Gerard 'Fred' Robson who seemed to have a reasonable cutter and the technique to cut endless glass to fit the windows of numerous properties.

One day early on in our careers as government handymen, Giles and I were sent up to Government House to repair the greenhouse. We had only been assessing the job for a couple of minutes when Giles tore into some foul language. 'F*** this', 'F*** that', which wasn't that unusual, but the thrust of this outburst was the fact that people were still not back in their houses and here we were fixing the Governor's greenhouse.

'I'm off to see the Gov.,' said Giles and stomped off. I hid behind the wall peeping around occasionally to see if I could hear Giles cursing. I was imagining the 'Gov', setting his guard on to Giles or calling the police and Giles storming up and down the drive shouting and bellowing about injustice with soldiers and police hanging from him.

Giles eventually returned and we packed up our kit and went back to the workshop. Sir Rex, in his typical way, agreed with Giles's assessment and put the glass in his greenhouse on to a low priority. Giles and I never went back so someone else must have eventually replaced the glass.

Giles was not a perfectionist and it is fair to say that he was a little rough and ready but he probably did more than anyone else to get people back into their homes after the conflict.

I got to enjoy Giles's company but I could understand why people in authority found his abrasive manner a little overpowering.

Working at the Rose Hotel

I left PWD and went to work in the Rose Hotel, the pub owned by Toni's father and aunt.

In the days when the Stanley Airport was being repaired and there were thousands of troops billeted in and around the towns the pubs were manic. Every night they would be heaving, with money going one way and booze the other. It was rough with a capital 'R' and two 'FF's – RUFF.

There was rivalry between the three services – Army, Navy and Air Force – and then rivalry between different groups within the same service. There were the odd individuals that thought that they didn't have to comply with the laws of the land. It was probably just a feeling that they worked hard in difficult conditions and so they should be allowed to drink themselves into oblivion.

Velma, Toni's aunt, lived in the pub and used to get involved at chuck-out time. Tony was rarely seen, although he did have a full-time job and didn't live on the premises. Velma was the setter of standards and they were quite high. No gambling, no singing and certainly no getting completely trollied. Secretly, I think Velma would have liked to have had no drinking but then that would defeat the object of having a pub. It is true to say that after the war it was hard to control the hard-drinking military and locals alike. The one trump card was George, Velma's husband, who although he had another job at the

Power Station, did many hours behind the bar and supporting the general workings of the establishment.

The Rose heaved with people every night, with people spilling out onto the road. On occasions there were as many people out in the road as there were in the bar. The attrition on glasses was unbelievable, because as large parties of people decided to move on they would just take their drinks with them tossing the glass aside once they were empty.

It is hard to explain the events that happened on a regular basis as troops worked and played hard along with some Falkland Islanders and the people that tried to keep all this excess from getting out of hand.

One night there was serious trouble in the bar and the military police were called. As the police were manhandling some muscular engineers out of the door, one fired a large, full can of McEwans Export over one of the policeman's heads at me. It came at some speed and luckily missed but hit a swinging light and wiped it out. The policeman somehow didn't see the incident. Thank goodness that the can hit the light and not my head because it could have done a lot of damage.

On another evening there was a scuffle in one of the corners and I went to sort it out. I asked the person I thought was causing the problem to leave and as I turned he tried to bottle me. Again, fate was on my side, and a local chap called Phillip Rozee caught his arm so that the bottle never reached me. It was rather a close call. What luck, but many of the near misses were down to staying alert and having quick reflexes. I found that situations, like 20 or more blokes singing 'get them down you Zulu warriors', didn't like their fun spoilt by some tu'penny ha'penny barman.

I would use all the skills at my disposal to try and stop the problems at the first opportunity. It was guaranteed that if the Navy started singing at one part of the bar, the Army would start somewhere else in the bar and then the Air Force would chip in as well. Add to this the rivalry within the three main services. It might start off in a good-natured way but, as the booze flowed, one thing led to another and there was trouble.

I would try and explain the reason for the policy of no singing and usually in the early evening I had my successes but once the clientele were blotto, reason disappeared. If all failed I called Velma and, as a back-up, the military police.

It was remarkable how many patrons knew genuine Falklands' veterans and because of this association they thought they should be allowed to drink what they liked, when they liked and do whatever they liked. On investigation, most of these guys had fairly tenuous links with the actual campaign. The worst of this type of guy usually admitted that they only knew a veteran through a friend of a friend!

Most of the genuine veterans that I met were quiet and unassuming and wanted to know where the Falklands would go after all this hell and upheaval. All the genuine vets that I met after the war were in the Navy.

Velma was a large lady by anyone's standards and she would appear at kick-out time. Strangely the squaddies used to love getting thrown out by her and you would see them nudging one another and saying 'watch that fat bird kick me out'. Velma wasn't backward in responding to their requests.

On one evening two chaps foolishly mooned at Velma by the door. This was like a red rag to a bull, an affront on all Velma's sensibilities and she booted one of them out into the road.

The soldiers' commanding officer, on hearing about this base behaviour, brought the individuals back to the Rose to apologise to Velma. Instead of taking it in good grace and perhaps finding some stance on not overdoing it in future, Velma was very forthright and she said, 'I should bloody well think so and if I could have got both feet off the ground at the same time, I would have kicked both of you out through the door.'

Some individuals did get the better of staff members. At another kick out, as the throngs were persuaded to leave, the thinning crowds revealed a local chap horizontal behind one of the tables catching up on some sleep. He didn't snooze for long when Velma spotted him and woke him from his slumbers.

After each evening's excesses we would clean up, starting by mopping out the bar and cleaning the loos. On one night I went to sort out the loos and they were in a horrendous state – two pairs of shitty underpants adorned the toilet. It was too much for me. I was feeling totally disgusted, but in went George in a very matter of fact manner with a bucket and peat tongs and removed the offending articles of clothing, walked out through the front door and flicked them nonchalantly into the ash drum.

What went through my mind is how well do you have to know someone before you ask for their underpants? Obviously one guy got caught short and soiled himself and then after a bit of mopping down knew that he needed more material. Did he hide in the loo peering out until he saw someone he knew well and then asked for their underpants so that he could finish mopping himself down?

Another time a sailor walked in and went off to the loo and punched a window out and then came and admitted he had done it. I am not sure, but perhaps this is pent up energy.

It was hard, stressful work but Velma and Tony made some serious money every week. The atmosphere was smoky, the punters often restless and the pay not too bad. I don't think I would want to be a publican, even though at that time it was nearly a licence to print money, but boy you worked for it and not only in the evening but the next day restocking the bar ready for the subsequent onslaught.

The *Penguin*

Shoe-horned into this busy time, was the job of raising the *Penguin*, Dave Eynons boat, which the Argentines had sunk down at the Canache. We had got to know some engineer divers who could get their hands on an assault boat and, more importantly, a high volume submersible water pump. After at least one false start, we all met up at the *Penguin*. The harbour stank, in fact everywhere and everything was dirty. There was human excrement everywhere.

At low tide, part of the *Penguin* was above water. Dave was unable to dive, so muggins pulled on a suit and nailed two lead patches, smothered with red oxide paint, onto the side of the *Penguin's* hull.

I know it was a mental issue, but I felt as if I was diving in a sewer and although I kept my mouth firmly clamped on to the demand valve, I could still taste the fetid water.

I got out and quickly changed into some dry clothes on the deck of the *Penguin.* It was in the middle of winter on a freezing cold day when I changed out of the diving suit and back into my clothes, but it hardly seems worth mentioning after my wallow in Stanley Harbour.

The engineer divers soon had the pump lifting the water out of the *Penguin* and as the tide started to come in and the water came out of the boats hull, she rose and sat on top of the water.

As I was still spitting and hawking and trying to cleanse my mouth, the engineers put their assault boat alongside and off we went up the harbour as we made our way to the Falkland Islands Company's slipway.

Rincon Cottage

During my time at the Rose, Toni and I moved out of her mother and father's house and went to live in sin on Davis Street at the top of town.

Rincon Cottage was, as the name suggests, a house belonging to the Turners at Rincon. The house used to be occupied by Harry and Doreen Bonner and their daughter. They had moved from this wooden and tin house, on the outskirts of town where Argentine gun batteries had been set up close by, to a stone house, which was thought to give better protection. Unfortunately, a British shell hit the house that they had moved to and Doreen and Sue Whitley were killed.

Harry had been a settlement teacher at Walker Creek and he was a quiet, unassuming, middle-aged guy. Sadly he didn't live very long after the conflict. Their daughter, who was already bedbound, was sent away from the Islands to specialist carers in the UK after her mother died.

Diana offered us the chance to live in the house and we jumped at the opportunity.

Working with Les Lee

My next job was with Les Lee. He had been a small-time businessman who fixed windows or doors for a few quid with a chat, tea and a biscuit thrown in.

One of the contracts Les got and one of my first jobs was replacing a number of peat sheds that had been destroyed during the fighting as the Brits came into Stanley. In Stanley, most houses had a peat shed where their year's supply of peat was stored.

The Brits did some of this damage as they moved in but most was done by vengeful Argentines who wanted to be vindictive after their defeat.

There is no way that the original sheds would have been anything like the buildings that we erected. Not that I have carried out a study but many that I had witnessed were made out of any old flotsam and jetsam with old corrugated iron nailed to it.

Anyway, here we were framing up these sheds to a standard that would have graced a house. Les was a perfectionist and so every corner was measured for the perfect right angle, the horizontals double-checked with the spirit level. Les was on the first build and then his son-in-law and I built the rest. I don't think any of the peat sheds we built are being used for their intended purpose but if they were clad with something they would make great garden sheds and if they were taken down carefully there would be wood for another major project.

After the war there were some industries that thrived, especially the ones selling souvenirs. The Pink Shop, being one of these enterprises, decided to extend and widen the pathway leading to the front door of their shop.

Les Lee, who was a friend of the owners, was awarded the job and we arrived with our spades to start the digging out process. Funnily enough, and it sounds hard to believe even now, the company didn't own a wheelbarrow. What we did was to fill a big blue bin with what we dug out of the front and carry it to the back of the premises. The blue bins we used came to the Islands with cement in them and they had a handle each side to help move them around. These handles were a godsend, but even so with a heavy load of earth the bins were awkward and difficult for two strong men. We manfully stuck to our task but we did moan a little bit that having some basic tools wouldn't go amiss.

We also mixed the cement by hand to extend the pathway. I suppose that wasn't so surprising but it was certainly more than a cubic metre of concrete.

Over the next few years Les grew from the odd job man to a small businessman who employed several men, full time, taking on some medium-sized projects.

We got a lot of work at the large lap-board house of Rose Stewart's. We had to scrape all the woodwork ready for a coat of paint and repair some of the windows and frames on the first floor. Once again, we didn't have scaffolds or ladders we made wooden frames with boards running between the horizontals. They weren't perhaps as mobile as proper scaffolding but no one fell and was badly hurt.

Wally Macbeth and the foxes

It was at this time that work seemed to be increasing daily and so Les started employing more men to keep up with the work.

One of the guys was Wally Macbeth who had come to the Falklands many years ago from Inverness and had decided to stay. These kinds of jobs can get pretty boring and it's sometimes your workmates that can make it bearable with a bit of banter or, in Wally's case, a bloody good yarn. Wally had had a most interesting life and had bought the Island of Sedge and before there was a proper house, the family (including two girls and a boy) went to live in what was virtually a hut.

So a house was one of the first jobs that Wally had to undertake. He told me how they had carried the stone for the house foundation up from the beach in a canvas shopping bag, which to me put him in the proper category of pioneer.

One of his greatest feats was to eradicate the foxes on the Island, which he felt he had to do to make a success of Sedge as a sheep farm. He had us all listening to his every word as he described how he studied the foxes and learnt how clever and cunning they were in securing food. One day he sat while a pair of foxes took on a jackass (Magellanic) penguin. A jackass penguin lives in a hole and so Wally went on to say how one fox would go to the entrance of the burrow and attract the attention of the jackass while the other began to dig down to where the eggs or young were behind it.

'Yes,' sais Wally, 'I was there for hours watching those crafty buggers.' I was intrigued and asked, 'so what happened next Wally?' 'Oh I got fed up watching and shot them,' he said. It was an anti-climax, but I had to admire his tenacity in killing off these introduced animals. A guy called Hamilton introduced the fox along with some other exotic creatures into the Islands in the early 1900s. The fox certainly did better than many of the other species, but of course has been a pain in the areas it inhabits which rear sheep.

Wally remembered the last fox on the Island. He was sitting in the house in his chair when it walked unwisely across the house green, and Wally tore out and shot it. He remembered it vividly he says, because he also shot a hole in one of his water containers which was only an old tin but out on Sedge things like that were irreplaceable.

Renovating Pill House

Back on the work front, the renovation and expansion of Pill House was another project Les took on. By that time Giles had joined us from PWD. Pill House was a stone house on Davis Street. Giles and Les were like chalk and cheese. Giles an impatient individual who would tear into a job and some would consider him a bit rough and ready; and Les who liked to think things through before he started. They were to clash more and more as time went on but in the early days their working relationship was manageable

The job at Pill House was huge and that was to totally gut it – no problem – and then rebuild it with a taller upstairs, i.e. roof extension, higher walls etc.

So we started to rip the insides out and Giles was in his element because it was like legalised vandalism, kicking down walls and doors. Unfortunately, we had two rules that Les would not compromise on which slowed the whole process. Everything that wasn't needed had to be burnt in a 45-gallon drum (205 litres) and we were meant to take out all nails and straighten them if they were not rusty etc. It took us far longer to burn the rubbish than it did to accumulate it, even with bending Les's instructions past an acceptable limit.

Les had come through a time in the Falklands when things were tough and there wasn't much money, and labour costs were very small.

Giles started to get really ratty about the de-nailing, as it was not any fun compared to the demolition work. Burning so much material in a drum was frustratingly slow with sheets of hardboard and the like. As my diplomatic skills were better than Giles's – as in Kissinger to Attila the Hun, and that is only because Giles was so bad – I decided to have a chat with Les. We got on really well.

I explained to Les that pulling out all the nails and straightening them wasn't cost effective because it was cheaper to buy new nails than to pay us to extract and straighten old ones. Les, although one of the easiest going chaps you could meet, dug his toes in and said that he saw it as a health and safety thing because if the wood is lying around, with nails in, you could tread on one. And then there was also his aversion to waste.

The drum thing makes sense in a windy environment like the Falklands where it can turn from flat calm to howling gale in a very short period of time.

So on we went, Giles complaining, saving a selection of the better nails but burning some as well. We did have a number of drums that spilled over a bit but we were on top of it all the time making sure there were no accidents.

So that was the gutting out and now it was the rebuild and Giles was off doing other stuff so Les employed Arthur Gould who was basically a good but unqualified mason. He was going to lay a concrete floor in Pill House.

The plastic membrane was laid out on the floor and the material of sand, cement and aggregate was in the yard plus a cement mixer. Les had employed a young boy to load the mixer and my job was to wheel the barrow full of cement to Arthur in the house. This boy that Les had found hadn't got a clue about shovelling or about work and effort. He was superficially willing, but hopeless. I tried to show him how to start at the bottom of a pile of aggregate with the shovel. Even when he grasped that, he was too feeble to lift a decent shovelful into the mixer. We tried for the first half an hour and then it was balls to this. So I shovelled the stuff into the mixer, pushed the barrow to and fro and this young lad watched me. I was a bit pissed off but I just got on with it. I didn't say anything to Les although I did say to Arthur how it was, after he complimented the consistency of the mix. Compliments from Arthur were fairly rare, so it seemed a shame to waste them. I was completely exhausted that night and bloody stiff the next day. I think Les employed the young lad a few more times but I think he soon realised he had to find a lighter job to earn a living.

We did a lot at Pill House but I think raising the roof was eventually left to somebody else.

More renovations

We also did renovation work and one of those places was opposite the Rose Bar.

Now, the side room of the Rose was where Les and his senior management team used to meet and talk about peat cutting, horse yarns, goose and logger duck egging and life years ago at Port Howard. We occasionally talked about work. The management team, which sometimes comprised of everyone that worked for Les, always found it difficult to keep track of time and on some occasions there were unintentional extended lunch breaks as Les recounted such yarns as the time a horse called Stranger bolted with some fencing material that he was carrying to some far flung part of Port Howard.

The work on the house across the road from the Rose Bar didn't help our work ethics but it was hard to break this enjoyable habit. I think the downside of this arrangement dawned on me on a day that I had been working somewhere else, and returned to this site early one afternoon. It was a hot, calmish day. As I walked down the hill I could see one of our number stretched out on the flat roof. With the heat and a few beers, the outcome was less than satisfactory because one of our painters had fallen asleep and lay there for all to see. Not the best advert for future employment.

One of the things I learnt was about the material used in building many of the houses. The timber framing could be made of wood from several sources. Some of the stronger stuff was old ships' timbers, working down to bits of packing cases for noggins.

Mother visits

Mother came down to visit while Toni and I were living in sin at Rincon Cottage on Davis Street. I had told Toni how perfect my mother was and that she didn't swear, fart or criticise etc. As a consequence, Toni felt a little bit apprehensive.

Mother travelled down to the Ascension Island in the middle of the South Atlantic on a plane and then boarded the *St Edmund*, an ex-cross channel ferry that had been employed to run passengers down to the Falklands.

Toni and I waited on the public jetty as the passengers were brought ashore in tenders. Mother didn't look washed out after her trip on the South Atlantic in fact she looked invigorated and ready to enjoy what we had on offer in the Falklands.

So Mother came to live with us on Davis Street in our three-bedroomed house. The house was fairly small, split in two by a passage up the centre from north to south. At the end of the passage was a bathroom and loo. On the west side of the house were the three bedrooms. Ours was north and closest to the road and mothers was the middle. The third, and closest to the back yard, was used as storage as it was very cold. On the other side of the passage was the kitchen, opposite Mother's, and a sitting room opposite us.

Diving

As it happened I was taking a break from Les and had some diving work, once more with Dave, at Mare Harbour. We were doing a seismic survey prior to the development of the site into the port for the military in the Falklands. I left for Mare Harbour three days later on the local vessel the *Forrest* and motored down to East Cove on this small but seaworthy vessel.

We loaded the *Forrest* from the government jetty with all the things we would need for an extended stay away from Stanley. We loaded things from the shore to the vessel by hand then readied ourselves for the trip. There was something missing however. The cook couldn't be found and we were delayed a while until he was located, completely trollied, in someone's house at the top of town. He didn't seem that willing or keen to make the voyage at first but once on board we cast off and left.

The cook's nickname was Fluff but the name given to him at birth was Robert. Robert Kiddle was sobering up after a tough run ashore and was definitely suffering from a hangover but he was still able to tell me his life's story.

It was very graphic and very involved and quite sad in places as he ran me through the ups and downs of his innings thus far. After about an hour or so I was begging him not to tell me any more but to no avail. He was determined to tell me every last detail, whether I liked it or not.

Eventually the captain came and got him to do a bit of work and he took the helm, but the emotional damage to me had already been done.

It wasn't at all rough although there was a bit of a swell running so I made myself a cup of coffee, read a book and looked at the many sea birds going about their lives in the coastal waters. It was a way of consuming time as we made our way to East Cove. Suddenly the ship started going around in tight circles. We must have done half a dozen before the captain, Nutt Goodwin, could rush from his cabin behind the wheelhouse and stop it.

It wasn't Fluff going off on another chapter of his life. The ship had actually, unbeknown to Fluff, been on auto pilot and it didn't matter what Fluff did with the wheel. For some reason the autopilot had malfunctioned. I think Nutt switched it off and back on again which did the trick and there were no more dramas from there to arriving at Mare Harbour where we found the *Merchant Providence*, a cargo ship, attached to the shoreline. She was the jetty head and also provided accommodation and canteen facilities.

We found a small sheltered cove and dropped anchor.

The next day the engineer leading the seismic survey turned up with his helper and Dave arrived and so we were ready to start work.

The first meal on the *Forrest* was an interesting affair as we were all crammed around the galley table shoulder to shoulder. The seismic engineer, during the meal's preliminaries, noticed that the tomatoes were at his end of the table and that one of the ship's hands, Eric, who was at the other hadn't got any and thought he had missed out. He innocently asked if Eric would like some. Eric, without any warning made it perfectly clear about his dislike for tomatoes. 'I don't like fucking tomatoes. I don't even like the fucking juice.' There were a few other incidents during the meal, which highlighted a gulf between our well-mannered engineer and the rest of us.

The next day we dined in two sittings.

Eric was always up for those simple laughs. The galley and the mess were connected by a serving hatch and on the day in question we had the charts of Mare Harbour and East Cove spread across the galley table planning the work schedule for the next few days. The hatch flew open and Eric in his wheezy Scottish voice enquired, 'does ya want a cuppa coffee?'

'Oh yes that would be nice Eric, Thank you,' says we. Only for Eric to say, 'Well get it your fucking selves', followed by some demented laughter.

The diving gear had moved on from Dave's gigantic wet suit and I now had a dry suit, which was great but you needed some warm clothes, which weren't too bulky to go underneath. It was the same sort of rubber as an inner tube, with a thin rubber neck and cuff seals. I had an all-in-one woolly suit that I wore but it was slightly misshapen and hung down from my backside. Eric was quick to point out the similarity between a cartoon character and me. 'Ha, ha, ha, ha, it's Bugs fucking Bunny!'

The cook had recovered from his hangover and the food was pretty good. One of Robert's specials was pilchard pie, which sounds pretty disgusting but in all honesty was very good. In fact, most of the time Robert was a hardworking, conscientious guy but the problem was keeping him off the booze. All the booze on the boat was kept in the hold so it was strictly controlled.

However, all this control went belly-up when someone sent Robert a flask of gin in the mail. Fluff's behaviour got slightly erratic; he then threw a mega wobbly and resigned with immediate effect. The downside to all this control was that the cook had the keys to the hold so the gin led to Fluff snaffling the total booze provision before chucking in. Not a totally charitable act.

The crew of the *Forrest* were not used to being out of Stanley for weeks on end and began to get restless. Eric was kicking up about having to plant gardens until the captain said what everybody was thinking, that he did not believe there were gardens at the Victory Bar. The atmosphere could be cut with a knife at times but we persevered.

The ship would anchor at a precise spot, the cables would be laid and then Dave and I would go down and check all the sound equipment like the cable, hydrophones etc. Most of the dives were not that deep, but the ones in the main channel were more than 60 feet. At least I was out of Dave's wet suit, but the dry suit did not have an air bottle to stop the suit squeezing you as you went deeper and the air contracted. On the deeper dives I got some impressive bruises on my chest.

The ship always moved first thing in the morning but the rest of the show took for ages coming to life, so I did not get out of bed until we had arrived at our destination. One day we were going across the bay when the engine just stopped for no apparent reason and there we were drifting about in a small cove without any power. The ship's engineer was hard of hearing and thought he had been told to stop the main engine. A loud discussion ensued with the captain hanging over the bridge, shouting at the engineer who was at the top of the steps leading out of the engine room. The engineer was eventually persuaded to go back below and start her up again.

Another morning we were going somewhere full speed ahead when there was a funny zipping noise followed by an almighty bang and the ship swung right over and around. Another 'hearing issue' had had someone letting the anchor go as we were travelling at eight knots. More shouting, in fact I did hear the captain comparing his crew to the TV advert about tea, performed by a group of chimps.

The amount of stuff that the contractors building Mount Pleasant Airport (MPA) had accrued on the shore was impressive. There were rows of brand new plant, containers and other equipment lining the shore. A couple of D9 bulldozers had already made a huge hard standing and a road leading out towards what was to become MPA. We all went ashore one day while the engineer was compiling the data, we took pictures of one another standing in huge digger buckets or some other gigantic piece of plant. Rows of Wyseplan portable accommodation were also ready to be set up for housing the workers who were to build the airport.

At certain times we would eat on the *Merchant Providence.* On the *Forrest,* even when Fluff was in drinking mode, the food was basic but wholesome – if you did not like the food you either forced it down or did not eat. On the *Merchant Providence* there was so many choices, every cereal you could think of, fruit juices, at least three alternative cooked breakfasts. It is no reflection at all on the *Forrest* and its facilities but the comparison was like a good bed and breakfast and the Ritz. Funnily enough, months later there was some union member, John Mather, complaining about their food and choices and the monotony of the menu. Two things went through my mind. Firstly that most of these guys were just ordinary people doing a difficult and demanding job in the Falklands and I wondered how varied their menus would be in their own homes; and secondly I wonder how they would have fared with us out on the *Forrest.*

Peter Clement worked with us as a diver support person helping us into our diving gear, passing equipment in and out of the water and helping us in and out as well.

Nearing the end of the work, Dave got a cold and so I did more dives and eventually my sinuses rebelled and so I also had to stop. Peter could swim so Dave thought, with a quick crash course, Peter could do some of the shallow stuff while he and I recuperated. There was one complication, Pete had a magnificent beard and tash and so sealing the mask was going to be a problem.

Come the day of Pete's first dive and we probably scared the life out of him by being over attentive. But in he went and was bobbing up and down in the water on the surface, venting air from his suit and then it was time to go down. As he went down you could see the mask filling up nearly as quickly as the speed that he went under. Up he shot, mask off, splutter, cough, and curse.

Dave persuaded Pete to cut a little of his facial hair off, to try and get a better seal. Back in went Pete but as he went under, although not at the same speed the mask filled up with water, and that, as they say, was that.

At some stage in the proceedings, it must have been summer and we were sitting in a bay over on the west side of East Cove with a lot of time on our hands. A family of geese went by, two parents and six goslings. The goslings were fully feathered and just at the right age to eat. The dinghy was launched and for the next half an hour we chased down the goslings, some nice fresh meat for the larder. The seismic engineer and his mate had never seen anything like it and were quite appalled but the next night the goslings provided us all with a nice change of diet, with vegetables and the trimmings that we had at our disposal.

Eventually the job was done and we headed back to Stanley. The *Forrest* had been a comfortable home, if somewhat cramped at times. For all the days we were on site we probably had two complete days where it was too rough and we had to sit out a storm, as the vessel tugged and tried and tested the anchor chain hour upon hour. It was mainly the wind that stopped the work and for the divers once in the water it didn't really matter whether it rained, snowed or blew.

Toni and Mother

It was time to get back to Stanley and see how Toni was bonding with Mother. It was a bonus to be greeted back by both and they seemed in good fettle. Mother has always had the ability to say unfortunate things without thinking them through. She had said to Toni something along the lines of, 'You're a dumpy wee thing, it's a shame really,' followed by, 'Both my girls could have been models you know.' I think most women would have had something to say, but Toni managed to take it without retaliation. It was during this time that my sister Caris wrote, telling us that she was pregnant. Of course, this created a lot of excitement and Mother started to plan the event from 8,000 miles away.

We seemed to be talking about another world as we walked up to the Cable and Wireless Offices to speak on the phone to the UK. You could make this call from your home but it was clearer direct from the Cable and Wireless's offices.

As we were walking home, and we were all chatting about our call, Mother asked, 'What is for supper tonight?' Toni replied, 'I thought we would finish the cazuela.'

'You can't feed him that,' said Mother, 'There is not enough protein left in it.' Toni replied that she had been feeding me for about two years and I had not died of starvation yet so she thought it would be fine. Mother then went on to tell us that the thing that most annoyed her about her mother-in-law when she first started living with Pa was that she told Kate that she was not feeding him properly!

A cazuela is a sort of boiled spicy stew/soup, made with chicken and vegetables in a big pot. You can keep them going forever by just adding to the pot. What we were doing was just finishing it off as a rich soup. In South America, where this dish originates, it is reputed to have everything thrown in from a hen including the head, legs and feet.

Toni also had her way of printing her will on Mother in a subtle but real way. Mother is a cat lover but not to the highest of levels. One day Geoffrey, our blue cat, managed to get through into the house even though he knew that his domain was strictly the kitchen. Seeing Mother's bedroom door open, he went in and jumped up onto the bed and made himself comfortable between the pillow and the top sheet. Mother came in and stripped the bed because the cat had been in it. Mother told Toni about Geoffrey and they chatted about how Mother couldn't possibly sleep in her bed after a cat had been in it. I think Toni thought this a bit over the top. Toni used to bring a cup of tea to Mother in bed before heading off to work in the morning, and just by chance did not shut the kitchen door properly.

Who knows what goes through animals' minds, but of all the rooms and warm places, Geoffrey chose Kate and her bed. Geoffrey was on a winner because all he had to do was to wait until Mother was doing something and off he would sneak to her room and make a gap between the turned back top sheet and the pillow and go to sleep. This war of attrition went on with cat on bed, bed being stripped and made back up with fresh sheets and pillowcases until Mother just decided that it was not worth the effort.

Mother had travelled to many hot countries over the years including many extended stays in Crete, and so when we warned her about the strength of the Falklands' sun I don't think she believed us and in fact told us that she would not have any difficulty and why should she worry about the sun in the Falklands. At the day of the Stanley races, Mother was outside most of the day enjoying the horse racing that Toni was participating in. It was a bright day with a slight breeze, which made it feel cool. That night mum's face was like a tomato and lit up the house. The clear unpolluted atmosphere allowed the full force of the sun to cook another unwary guest.

Bomb disposal and cutting peat

For Toni and I, this was a time of plenty with both of us having a proper job and a wage each. Toni worked at the Agricultural Research Centre and me at various places.

In those days, each house had a peat bank out on the common somewhere. I went and found the peat officer, Mickey Clark, who allocated me a bank, which was on two levels down the Eliza Cove road. I was told it was the Waverly House bank but I didn't ask where the Rincon Cottage bank was. Two levels meant that it was deep enough to cut twice so that the first cutting was further back than the second. In this way you could get enough peat from a shorter bank. It was a good bank to cut but a bastard to get your peat home from because it was so soft and it was easy to get bogged.

I used to go down in the evenings after work and at the weekends. If it was after work, I wouldn't cut less than 10 yards and always try for 15. I used to take Bozo down for some exercise and he wouldn't go very far whilst I cut my quota.

This was not long after the war and a lot of cleaning up had gone on but there was still plenty of debris everywhere. The bomb disposal teams were still blowing stuff up daily and during the announcements on the radio they would warn the populous of big bangs when they were clearing something big. The whole town would shake with the big ones. People were reporting ordinance quicker than it could be dealt with. I found a hand grenade down by my bank and the commanding officer came out and put a bit of string on it to pull it out of the grass and then he took it with him. We had had a couple of commanding officer majors step on mines and we were talking about it and he was telling me how he was extra careful because of this fact. Unfortunately, within a couple of weeks he had also stepped on a mine. It really did bring it home that the Falklands were still a very dangerous place to live.

So night after night, if the weather was fit, with weekends included I cut my way along the bank. About a week in I was driving my spade in and clank! I hit something solid, something metal. I immediately thought it was a bomb or something dangerous and ran away from it, coming back to get in the Land Rover and drive down to the EOD (Explosive Ordinance Disposal). Back they came and I showed them the spot from a distance and then went even further afield when they started prodding around. It turned out to be an old domestic galvanised hot water tank and other junk. With all the ordinance that had been sprayed around this area I wasn't taking any chances. Mind you if a bomb didn't go off after being dropped out of an aircraft you would think it would take something exceptional to make it explode.

There were people taking chances though. Land Rovers had been commandeered by our Argentine visitors and so after the war people began rounding up their possessions but also looking out for some war bounty. One Land Rover was in the middle of a minefield and the EOD eventually got round to clearing a path out to this vehicle only to find that someone had pinched the gearbox.

The weather could be a bit changeable in October, when most people began to think about cutting peat, and Toni and I occasionally made silly bets to pass the time away. One of the two that I remember were firstly when Toni bet me it would rain just because I had decided to go peat cutting the next morning. I said it wouldn't so Toni bet me that she would buy a set of crockery for the house if she was wrong but I would be paying if she were right. The evening seemed opened skied, without any ominous clouds and I thought it was unlikely to rain hard enough to keep me from this task.

Bloody typical! I didn't even need the alarm clock to wake me. The rain was hammering on the bedroom window that hard I had been awake for a while. So down I went to the West Store and bought the crockery set that Toni had in mind. It was a creamy colour with grasses as the pattern. It was the run of the mill stuff for the early eighties. If you studied it the pattern was darker on some of the items and also the glaze cracked on most of it over the years. Having said that it gave us good service to the extent that there might still be the odd plate at the bottom of the pile, which we use when there's a house full.

The second bet I am ashamed to say was less than fair, but what better way to ensure that you don't have to pay out for another household item when you don't need to. I had built a gate to fit into the gap at the top of the yard. It wasn't a conventional gate with hinges but a piece that slotted into position and could be lifted out when needed. Toni came along and bet me that the piece I was constructing wouldn't fit the hole. Instead of admitting that I had already measured it I took the bet and shortly afterwards Toni was trotting down to the shops to buy a double quilt for the bed. In the case of bets, we were equal but in financial terms Toni won hands down.

At the end of the summer it was time to cart the peat home and throw it into the peat shed.

Bozo in trouble

There was a lot of local news about different people coming to the Islands and one such person was a Major Quinn, a bomb disposal officer. He had just been praised for his bravery for defusing a 500lb German bomb from the Second World War on the Thames Embankment.

One day I was carting peat with Bozo and I had to lay some plates to get the Land Rover and trailer full of peat over a small ditch and took my eye off him. I was just getting back into the Land Rover and looked up to see Bozo nipping one of a group of soldiers. It wasn't like a full-frontal savaging, he would sneak in and nip the back of your legs. I am not making any excuses – it was wrong – but the officer who had been bitten had got a huge surprise as much as anything else and he was very upset.

I told him who I was and he told me whom he was but in the heat of the moment I didn't make any connection to who I was talking to. I soon found out when Major Quinn the Bomb Disposal Officer wrote me a letter telling me that he was going to insist that Bozo was put down.

Obviously, Toni was very upset having raised Bozo on a bottle when his mother had fallen ill. He should have been as tame as any pet for this very reason, and to the family he was, but for anyone else he did have a huge attitude problem.

I decided to write a grovelling letter, which amongst other things, highlighted the fact that Bozo was of working stock and a group of men in khaki had appeared to him to be just like another group of animals, like a flock of sheep or a herd of cattle that had to be worked.

I am not sure if he rediscovered the bravery that had stood him in great stead while defusing the bomb on the Thames or that he accepted some of the arguments put forward, or just took pity on us all, because he didn't pursue his demands to have Bozo put down. I think in a UK environment Bozo might have had to go because this wasn't his only misdemeanour.

When Granny Johnson was still with us and Bozo was young she would come and visit the Peterssons at 10 Ross Road. Granny was a no-nonsense woman that had been raised in the camp and knew a thing or two about dogs and the like. On one of her visits Bozo met her at the gate. On the grounds of safety first, Granny hit Bozo over the head with her handbag and Bozo made a run for it. The first round went to Granny J.

You used to come in through a gate in the alleyway that was behind the Police Cottages and beside Joan Bounds' shop, go down a couple of steps and then along a bit, take a right-angled turn and go down a number of steps into the courtyard and then a few steps up to the back door and in.

On Granny J's next visit Bozo made himself scarce, only arriving as one leg was in the house but with the other, acting as a tasty morsel, still to join the first.

As far as I know the score stayed at one all.

Even in the Falklands I think it was our departure to camp that saved Bozo, with plenty of work and wide-open spaces.

Even at Sussex he did let himself down once more but it wasn't really his fault. We used to have a patrol once a month, year in and year out, in the first ten years. We would always be welcoming, but we would always say to these visitors that these dogs aren't pets they are working dogs and not used to people. We would also tell them about Bozo.

This was okay for everyone apart from this one lad who reckoned that he had a way with dogs. He said he could mesmerise them and somehow control them with positive thought, so instead of being a warning it was like a challenge. Unbeknown to us the patrol went to set up camp and this one individual sought out Bozo. I'm not sure if his powers were having an off day but he was soon at the house with bite marks on his face. He told us that he went down and grabbed Bozo by the cheeks of his face and, low and behold, he bit him.

Even Bozo had his Waterloos, however, and when in Stanley a cocky army vet told us that he would be pilling Bozo with Droncit, something we usually did. I left the house thinking he can get on with it then. I came back later thinking that Heather or Toni would have taken over and pilled Bozo. Not a bit of it. The vet had just walked up to Bozo pushed his lips between his teeth so that he couldn't bite, shoved the pill down his throat in one fluid motion and the job was done.

All dogs are dosed in the Falklands with Droncit because of hydatid disease, which is a serious disease with a life cycle that can include humans. Usually the cycle begins when a sheep is infected by the tapeworm eggs in dog faeces, when it eats the grass near the faeces. The sheep can then develop cysts in its lungs, liver etc. If a dog has access to this offal from an infected sheep, it in turn becomes infected and the whole cycle starts again. A human can also become infected by inadvertently picking up the tapeworm eggs around the dog faeces and develop cysts that require major surgery to remove. The dosing of dogs with Droncit, which kills the tapeworm, breaks the cycle, as does ensuring that the dogs do not have access to offal. The Islands have virtually eradicated this disease now, with a strict regime of dog dosing and control. There have been no cases of human infection for years, although there is still the occasional hydatid cyst found in sheep passing through the abattoir.

The FIDF

I joined the FIDF (Falkland Islands Defence Force) after the conflict and for all the time that I lived in town I would go down for an evening of instruction at the old Drill Hall on Johns Street. I thoroughly enjoyed most of the training, but it didn't take me long to realise that I would make a crap squaddie.

It wasn't marching that I couldn't master, even the saluting, the left or right turn, or even the about turns and the weapons drill. It was the way the words were delivered which to me was unintelligible. It was like a gruff Pingu – a series of noises which I found difficult to decipher.

Today the commands at the main FIDF parades seem to be far clearer.

I don't think it is over critical to suggest that the FIDF have moved to another level since the days when I took part. We were highly motivated, there is no doubt about that. We had just had unwanted visitors on mass on the Islands, however we didn't have the sophistication or the tools that have since arrived, through highly qualified instructors and an injection of cash.

The weaponry that we had were cumbersome 7.62s, which could have downed an elephant, but added to the ammunition and the other paraphernalia you had to carry it was a man's game and a strong man at that.

It was a boy's night out as much as anything and after our training we would retire to the Rose Bar and drink a few McEwan's or Harps and at closing time head home.

We often went on exercises with the British forces that seemed to tolerate us part timers joining in.

On one such jaunt we flew to Elephant Beach in a Chinook. It landed in fine 'Cowboy Bob' fashion, which was so common just after the war. The Chinook would fly into the landing position at a tight angle with the front up and the back down and anyone that wasn't tightly strapped in would have just shot out of the back and onto the ground.

We waited until the Chinook moved, from chopping all those that ventured out of the back into dice position, to the horizontal where we disembarked. The Chinook then took off vertically and then dipped its front down slightly and was off.

We had to man a hill overlooking a vast flat and told to make camp. We were also told that during our time there the other side would attack us. We went about our business of brewing tea and cooking compo on our hexamine cookers and placing our tents and sleeping bags.

The old hands told us about previous exercises that had been really bad for one reason or another and the usual tales of different calamities. This kept us all entertained until the early hours until we all drifted off to our sleeping bags, apart from the sentries.

Before dawn we were all out and standing to repel the pending attack. Nothing happened. In fact, it wasn't until midmorning when some black dots arrived on the scene at what looked like miles away.

On mass we assembled the reception committee and were under orders not to open fire until the enemy were close. In the Falklands, in the terrain we are talking about, 'there is nowhere to hide.' Not a rock, tree or bush, just an expanse of honey-coloured grass.

In real life it would have been a turkey shoot or a re-enactment of the Somme. All of us on the top of this rise, lying down, poured our pretend fire into the approaching men. Eventually we were overrun and unfortunately I became a prisoner. The casualties were able to jump up and decant to another location but the prisoners had a hessian bag pulled over their heads, hands tied and forced to kneel down and finally lie in the wet camp. So I am there thinking what fun it is to serve in the FIDF when the bag is pulled up to uncover my mouth, a Rolo is pushed in and a voice says, 'Just to show that I'm not mean with my Rolos' and with that the bag is pulled back into place.

After my spell at Fox Bay I went back to the evening FIDF training, but I knew it was only a temporary thing because we were off to our farm permanently. A couple of us were tasked to appear before the commanding officer and so we assembled outside his door. We seemed to wait for ages and then eventually I had my audience with the major.

I was marched in. He asked me why I hadn't been attending FIDF over the last few months, to which I replied that I had been working for my employer at Fox Bay East. Instead of saying that he didn't know, no one knew or okay but do you hope to attend more regularly now? He carried on with his reprimand and suggested that I should somehow have used my initiative to get in. Like a good trouper I kept my mouth tightly shut, but I couldn't stop my mind from one or two negative and insulting thoughts.

Rebuilding Fox Bay East

At some stage Les got the contract to rebuild Fox Bay East settlement and repair all the war damage inflicted by the Argentine occupation and the British attempts to remove them and make their time there as uncomfortable as possible.

I don't know why but Les decided to send Giles out as the forward worker to meet with everyone and make a start. Perhaps it was because by that time Les was struggling with all the things that Giles stood for. Giles, even though we were by this time best of friends, wouldn't have been my first choice to be our special envoy. It even occurred to me that perhaps Les didn't want the job.

So Giles went out to Fox Bay East as the rest of the gang finished off painting the Upland Goose Hotel, another biggish job for Les and his gang, although not a fraction of the job at Fox Bay East.

Giles could be awful. Before the rest of us arrived he got invited over to the military camp at Doctors Creek to see a Combined Services Entertainment (CSE) show with a local family. It was a long walk without transport so Giles accepted the invitation. They got to the mess to find rows of seats laid out and a number of people already there. They found a row and sat down. Mum, the two children and Giles. The mum saw some military friends at the other side of the room and went over to chat with them leaving the children behind with Giles.

These children had a reputation as having exceptionally 'high spirits', and some suggested on the verge of being out of control. So these kids were being a little bit boisterous, running up and down, clambering over Giles and going on a junior rampage.

It wasn't long before the lights went out and the show started, leaving the mother marooned with her friends and her children using Giles as a climbing frame as well as generating a little noise. All of a sudden it went quiet, and all that could be heard was the show. The two children were sitting like statues. No whispering, no fidgeting and these two were transformed into perfectly behaved kids. The CSE shows were pretty predictable and aimed fairly and squarely at the squaddies, with a compere, a troupe of saucy dancers cavorting around in black underwear, a singer or a band and sometimes a comedian. Most of the shows were reasonable although occasionally you would get a dud, but in the Falklands live shows of this type were unheard of until after the conflict.

Anyway, the mum was delighted with her brood's behaviour and congratulated Giles, commenting on how he was a natural with children. Giles didn't say anything and I doubt if the children did until days later. It is quite possible that Giles had made some dire threat to their wellbeing. Not a tactic I have read in any parenting book but very effective if true.

The rest of the gang eventually flew out to join Giles and to start the rebuilding of Fox Bay East in earnest.

Living at Fox Bay East

Toni and I flew out of Stanley to join Giles. Toni decided to take our cat Geoffrey. Toni has always been an appalling flyer and I expected her to crack open a sick bag at about the Estancia, which she did. What I didn't expect was the cat to crap itself in fright on take off. So I did have a slight advantage over the other passengers, but the combined stink from the back of the plane had us all gagging. My day wasn't going that well on the flight, although I wasn't sick, but helping to wash the cat down on arrival was a request beyond the call of duty.

Toni and I had decided to buy a farm so we thought the best way to generate money was if we both went to Fox Bay East. Toni as cook, but she could do other work such as painting when she wasn't cooking. I was the foreman with special responsibilities of stopping Giles upsetting the residents of the two Fox Bays. There were some big egos in the gang as well and some of them didn't have the work ethic of Giles – which was to work flat out from dawn to dusk – and this also led to clashes.

In all seriousness it was difficult to keep everyone happy when we lived in such basic conditions. There wasn't a day-to-day opportunity for down time, to relax and to do something other than work. We had a dartboard and Les had a guitar when he was out. Our lives revolved around work, listening to the radio, playing darts and drinking alcohol.

Radio had been transformed by the arrival of British Forces Broadcasting Service (BFBS) after the conflict and the combined efforts of the local radio and the forces radio staff. Instead of a few hours a night out in camp there was 24-hour coverage. It was pretty samey with the BFBS playing the top 40 to death and the local presenters also murdering them and the country favourite of the day.

The ex-manager of Fox Bay East and his wife had decided to set up a wool mill and were building up the infrastructure to make it happen. Richard Cockwell and a gap student were working on a skin shed, which they were trying to take down. The first job was removing the tin and it was happening slower than the arrival of the next ice age.

As they were laboriously undoing every bolt, we were busily making a start on repairing the damaged houses. We were replacing shrapnel-damaged tin with new, replacing the inside by relining with hardboard, re-plumbing stoves, bathrooms etc. In fact, our job was to refurbish most things to make the houses habitable once again.

That weekend we were given a lift round to Fox Bay West, which was on the other side of the bay, where there was a club. We worked hard but when we got the opportunity we played hard as well. Richard's man was also over at the club. I am not sure what really happened, apart from drink loosens tongues, but someone suggested that the work on the skin shed was painfully slow and that he should forget about saving the nuts and just split them with a hammer and chisel and buy new ones. The guy was very tolerant as we drunkenly ripped into the mills employment inadequacies.

We all came to, the next day, feeling more than a little grim. No feelings of self-righteousness about what to do or how to do it. We were saved a long walk home by the coastal vessel, *the Monsunen* that just happened to be working at Fox Bay West and heading to Fox Bay East next. At just after midday the boat that had been standing off the jetty turned towards the opposite shore and headed to Fox Bay East. Pale, forlorn, shadows of our former selves, someone noticed that all the tin had been removed from the skin shed.

Arthur Gould

Arthur Gould was a perfectionist and a skilled mason although unqualified. He always had a cigarette jammed in his mouth and was for ever winking and blinking where the smoke got into his eyes. He also had a passion for whiskey. I asked him what brand or make of whiskey he preferred and he was quick to point out that he really didn't care after about six as long as they kept coming.

Remarkably Arthur would drink half a bottle of whiskey every night and a whole one on Saturdays and take Sunday off and go for a stroll.

The stores stocking regime at Fox Bay East wasn't designed to cope with this kind of whiskey consumption so after a few weeks it had ran out. Thinking this might help Arthur to reflect on the stated safe units of alcohol for a man of his age and his long-term health targets, I wasn't that bothered. Arthur was bothered though and fell back on to his contingency plan, which was to make a start on the rum which he found weak in comparison so had to drink more.

Arthur's main job was to build the chimneys but the weather wasn't fit a lot of the time to perch on a rooftop. I would then task him with less specialised jobs like painting which he undertook reluctantly, I think because he thought it was below him with all the skills he undoubtedly had.

One day as Giles and another, lined out two rooms with hardboard, including the ceiling, Arthur had painted one small cupboard. It was perfection itself but it wasn't really a day's work… especially for Giles.

The humour was pretty foul, with Giles accusing Arthur of shirking and Arthur countering by accusing Giles of being rough and ready. Giles called Arthur a lazy, drunken, Welsh git and Arthur told Giles he was a big-mouthed, rough American. I did my best to deflect the abuse but I had my work cut out.

Les hadn't been out for a while and when I spoke to him on 4.5 radio telephone I suggested that this was a good time to come out with his guitar and take the edge off some of the tension.

Out comes Les with his guitar and a treat for Arthur – a bottle of red label Johnnie Walker whiskey to keep his mason sweet.

After work that night we had a few beers and Arthur a few whiskeys. Les played the guitar and all was well. As the first half of the Johnnie Walker went down, Les was the best bloke that Arthur had ever worked for. Good payer, undemanding, thoughtful. In fact, it was sickly to hear all the praise.

While consuming the second half of the bottle, Arthur evened it all up because poor old Les, who had brought him the bottle, financially and physically, was a useless, bow-legged, old twat that couldn't run a bath and on the last sip Arthur resigned and went to bed.

Arthur left us the next day.

The doctor's house

All that work as peace maker, all that frontline effort stopping Giles ripping his head off, and our only bricklayer had given up and buggered off back to Stanley. Arthur thought that he was indispensable and so did Les and I, but out of the woodwork came a young guy called Dave Harrison who had been a hod carrier and thought he could build chimneys. And it turned out that he could and to a high standard.

Some of these old chimneys that we were replacing were ripe and this was hardly through the actions of the Argentines and British. However, it seemed a bit silly to sort everything else out and then have the chimneys falling through the roofs.

On one house we picked the bricks off one by one from the stack by hand. We kept on going like this until we were at the ceiling between the upstairs and downstairs. Les stopped us there but it seemed that we could have easily continued. I don't know if the chimney is still there but we built back up on the bricks that were there.

The Falkland Island Company had got a cheap cladding into the Islands called Agrilux which was ridged plastic sheeting, about ten-feet long and three-feet wide, that was very brittle. It was designed to make even a reasonable house look like a shed. This stuff was a nightmare to work with even when moving it from its piles to the job at hand.

We had great fun covering the old doctor's house, which had been empty for years. There was nothing to do back at our house so we would work long hours using a lead light to carry on well into the night. We were paid £3 an hour, which in the 1980's was good money and so we did many hours and we got the job done.

Any wind was a nightmare with the Agrilux product. One night the wind managed to work the sheets out of the pile which had been weighed down with heavy rocks. The sheets scythed through the air ready to decapitate someone. They didn't last too long when they were blown along the ground, as they would just break up into smaller and smaller bits. On this night Giles and I did try and rescue the sheets but it was pretty hairy with bits flying everywhere. I did manage to rescue a piece intact only for the wind to catch it as I was struggling it back and I just ended up with a bit clasped to my body.

The doctor's house was fairly tall and so we had an ancient wooden ladder – an accident waiting to happen. It was two wooden scantlings side by side with wooden rungs nailed on. Attached to this were two lighter scantlings attached to the bigger ones by nails that also had rungs and extended it by another six feet or more. Such was its antiquity that it looked as if a few feet had been broken from the top.

I brought the ladders dilapidated condition to Les's attention. I explained that in my opinion it was dangerous and perhaps with a lot of high work he could buy us something that was a little safer. Les saw the ladder in a different light and told us this tale about an equally mature ladder that they once had at Port Howard (Les's spiritual home where he first 'turned to' at work) and this ladder went on for another 30 years.

With Les's sermon on ropey ladders and their life expectancy ringing in our ears we went back to work. A few days later in the middle of the afternoon Giles was at the top of the ladder and I was near the bottom, struggling with a sheet of Agrilux. There was an almighty CRACK and quicker than you can say 'O dear, what was that?' Giles was hanging by his bib and brace by the remaining piece of the ladder. 'Are you all right?' I said to Giles as his shoulders and head were in a large puddle. 'Just leave me here to soak up the wet man,' he said solemnly.

The merry banter over I untangled him with great difficulty. Giles weighed 18 stone if he was an ounce. I had to lift this dead weight so that I could get the strap of his bib and brace off what remained of the ladder. I am not sure if it was because he was cold and wet and needed to warm up, but Giles flipped right out. He smashed the ladder into small fragments and because I could see what was needed to dry him out I fired up the burning drum and then we burned every bit until there was nothing left.

The settlement was virtually empty of people compared to how it was before the conflict and as we went around sorting properties there were claims made on various articles. We weren't sure what belonged to whom because no one in the gang had lived or worked at Fox Bay in the past and so we took each request at face value.

Someone made a claim on the substantial wooden table that was in the doctor's house. It was a real heavy-duty, wooden table and weighed an absolute ton. We cleared a path to get the thing out through the porch and then we heaved and pushed and worked hard to move the table. I don't know how long it had been on loan in the doctor's house but the porch was definitely built after the event. Giles was a powerful man and I wasn't a complete weakling and with the effort of trying to get it out, we had it totally jammed in the porch and we couldn't move it either way. Giles had been booting it with all his might to force it along, with me pushing for all I was worth and now it was frustratingly wedged tight. Of course, this made Giles worse than angry and then the red mist descended. Giles tore off and came back with a saw and took off a leg of the table. That did the trick and out came the table Giles heaving it onto the cobbles and then he raced back in and tore out with the leg and heaved it into the night shouting, 'Here's your fucking table and here's the goddamn leg.'

I did feel guilty, but I was only the foreman and given fair warning I was able to wield some influence over the gang, but the spontaneous stuff I didn't stand a chance. I can't remember what happened to the table apart from it was never claimed while I was there.

Unwanted visitors

Fox Bay was another large farm that was split up into family-sized parts and sold off to local farmers. We lived in one of the houses that had been earmarked for a family buying a sub division of Fox Bay. It was a difficult situation in as much as we lived in the house but the pending owners wanted to show friends the house and run them through their future plans, thereby making our makeshift home seem like public property at times. It didn't bother me but others felt that the owners to be, could have been a little more sensitive.

This had gone on even when Giles was out as our special envoy, winning over hearts and minds. Giles of course quickly developed a counter tactic, which was when he saw the people coming he would lock the door and then hide in one of the other buildings. It became a game that the other party didn't enjoy playing.

It all came to an end one day when we were having smoko (morning tea break) and Giles was still on the way. The lady in waiting turned up and marched in. We were inviting them to join us for a drink and a bun when there was a shout of 'SAS attack' and the door burst in, coming right off its hinges ending up on the floor. A noisy entrance was typical Giles but he somehow over did it and the effect couldn't have been more badly timed. Even Giles looked a little sheepish as he stood on the door, which was lying in the kitchen.

Rogue sheep

There was a big pet sheep at Fox Bay East that resided on the green. I have seen bigger but this sheep had attitude, probably because some rotter had teased it. One day we were painting the outside of a house when a lad came running past as if he was a commando. Up to a building and flattening out as he following the outside to the corner and then carefully looking around to make sure all was clear before running flat tack to the next building and the same again until he reached the school. We just thought with all the troops and talk of the war he was taking part in his imagination. Anyway, this lad took these soldiery duties seriously. On the way to school and back he would hug the cover and dash across the open ground.

We were to find out that there was more to this behaviour than we had thought because one day when the boy's guard was down and he was in the open a sheep came flying around the corner and after him. He ran like the wind and just managed to find the sanctuary of someone's yard and pulled the gate shut just as the sheep arrived, his chest heaving and his body sagging after this exertion.

The gate belonged to a rather unsympathetic individual who promptly opened the gate and shoved the boy out. 'You teased the poor thing so it serves you right if it knocks you down.' I think the sheep had moved on before the lad's fingers could be prised off the garden gate but after this episode the sheep vanished. The ex-farm manager, Richard Cockwell, said he had taken it out to camp.

Before the sheep had disappeared however another amusing set of events happened. We were in the process of buying a farm and so Toni had acquired a bitch pup from Errol Goss who was working at Fox Bay West. She was not fully grown but large enough for Toni to start getting her interested in different things, including sheep. Toni would take her bitch out and teach her some basic commands and to begin building up a bond between them. All this would go promisingly well unless the aforementioned sheep came on the scene and then all hell would break out. The sheep would make a dash for it and the dog would soon be chasing after it. The sheep would run to one of the old gardens with a perimeter fence and many internal ones built by gardeners to shelter their crops from the Falklands winds.

In the sheep would go, followed by Lassie in hot pursuit. Fortunately for the sheep these fences were pretty frail and weak. It was like a cartoon and you would hear 'crash, bang, wallop' and occasionally see a few sticks of fencing sailing into the air. Amongst all this hullaballoo would be Toni shouting 'Lassie, Lassie, Lassie!' with some whistles followed by more shouting and the crashing and banging. At the end of these sessions the dog, sheep and Toni had all had their quota of daily exercise.

The club at Fox Bay West and Mel

As I have already mentioned the club at Fox Bay West was a bit of an attraction. In fact, it was a bar, which was called a club, and we used to crave its social amenities after cramming as many hours as we could into our working day and week. So we would tear around on Friday night and then afterwards go round to someone's house, usually Val and Mel's, and sleep it off and into a stonking hangover.

Mel was a bit of an entrepreneur, well before anyone knew what one was. He had got a series one Land Rover of 1950's vintage and doubled up all four wheels and then invited us all for a camp trip. This machine was amazing. The only thing that let it down was the horse power, although thinking about it if it had had a more powerful engine shoe horned in under the bonnet other 1950's vintage components would have probably started to fail. The gearbox, or diffs or half shafts probably. This lack of power didn't prevent Mel putting the vehicle through its paces and he would charge into some soft stuff encouraged by shouts from the back. He named this creation the Honey Bug and as it hit the soft peat and sank down in first, low range the engine would come to the verge of stalling as it fought against all the forces of sinking into sticky, thick, soft peat.

In the early days after the war there began a process where military vehicles came on to the local market. The military would have cast sales that had everything in them from some decent vehicles, surplus to requirements, with perhaps a small fault down to what would look like junk to many people. To enterprising Falkland Islanders, even the junk was offering them stuff that they would have only dreamed of before. So even a severely trashed vehicle that had a donor chassis was something really sought after. Many people in the 1980s had the ability to strip a Land Rover down to the last nut or bolt and rebuild it.

Get a good chassis and perhaps a good bulkhead and people would build their Rover's running gear into the army chassis and that was a good bit of business. It has to be said, to be fair, that the advantage was with people on the East where the sales were held.

Buying a farm

We were trying to buy a farm. A part of what was San Carlos farm and the section called Port Sussex to be precise. Although Colin Smith had driven the sale the government were putting up the money and so were involved with the process. We had an incredible interview that still seems unreal today 26 years later. (In fact the funding wasn't that straight forward with two farms getting no support from government and everyone else only getting part funding. Colin Smith loaned the two farms the total amount and the rest the outstanding sum although Falklands law makes it illegal to take out a second mortgage so it was an unsecured loan.)

We sat in a room with an old farm manager of a large farm, John Ferguson the head of the Agricultural Department who happened to be Toni's boss, and Alistair Cameron who was a senior government officer. Things were going okay until the farm manager suggested that we would struggle to survive on £2,000 for the first year. At that time £2,000 was a lot especially as everyone grew their own vegetables and cut their own peat, did most farm work on horseback and didn't have a phone. Neither of us smoked and I drank modestly but wouldn't if we were that poor. We said we were going to shear our own sheep and that we felt £2,000 was perfectly adequate.

The farm manager was obviously not living on such a meagre budget and begged to differ. Then this chap, warming to his task of demoralising us, said that three or four miles of fencing were flattened on the back of the mountain and what would we do. I said that I had spoken to the farm manager of San Carlos and he hadn't mentioned anything along those lines. I said we would go and stand it up. Oh, no it is completely finished. This turned out to be codswallop but he spoke with total authority. We then got on to how much we had in our bank account. I said that we had enough to cover the commitments outlined in our proposal but weren't prepared to divulge what actual money we had in our bank account. We thought that that was asking for a little too much information.

Although Alistair told Toni he thought we had done okay we got a letter back saying that we were unsuitable.

We lobbied all and sundry. In those days the Governor was all-powerful and Toni asked if we could see him. We spoke to Councillor Terry Peck who fought our corner. It was all in the balance when we went out to Fox Bay but we hoped that the earlier decision would be reversed.

Living in camp everyone was used to mail and communications not being instantaneous. No daily post, no Island-wide phones. One Friday night we are at Mel's warming up for the club with a few beers when the weekly news programme, the *Friday News Letter*, came on. During this programme one of the news items was our success in getting government funding to buy Port Sussex farm.

Velma

During the war people who were known to be politically opposed to the Argentines and leaders in the community were rounded up and flown to Fox Bay East. Toni's aunt was one of them. Velma had won a scholarship when she was a child and went to school in Montevideo, Uruguay.

I had no idea that she could speak Spanish although I should have guessed as much considering that she had attended school over in Latin America for a number of years. As they stood up at the airport during their forced exile out of Stanley she was listening to the Argentines who were guarding them. One of them said, 'I would like to kill that fat one.'

'I'd like to kill them all,' said the other.

At that time, they didn't know where they were going and feared it might be over to the mainland. In fact, they were off to Fox Bay East for some interesting times hosted by the amiable Cockwells.

One night while we worked at Fox Ray Richard and Grizelda invited Toni and I up for supper. We got on to the war stories, obviously stimulated by the fact that Velma was Toni's aunt. The only problem we had was following the story because whoever told the particular yarn the other would contest the finer detail, i.e. who was sitting in the front of the vehicle, how many in total were in said vehicle, which direction it was pointing, what time of the day. Toni and I nearly got ricked necks as we turned our heads to and fro like watching an endless tennis rally. It was an entertaining evening with some fascinating war stories but who was right about how many people were in the front of the Land Rover?

Tractor versus bike

As contractors we were allowed to use the Fox Bay East crappy Leyland tractor to go for miles to pick up sand from the beach for any cementing or concrete work. The bloody thing was nearly not worth using but the choice was either that or nothing.

So off we would go and get some sand and then try and get back. I don't know who in their right mind would want a two-wheel drive tractor in the Falklands but obviously someone did. It did have double wheels at the back, which was something.

Coming back the trailer was too heavy for the tractor which reared up until the draw bar jammed on the back of the tractor and we went up a couple of the hills with the front end in the air, steering with the individual back brakes. God knows why we didn't refuse to go because it was incredibly dangerous. We carried on going but we did reduce the loads.

On one such journey we were returning the tractor to its shed close to the mill. The lights were poor and about as effective as a candle in a jam jar. A hundred metres or so from the tractor shed there was a bit of a crunching noise and we pulled over and took a look. Dave had run over one of the Cockwell children's push bikes that had been left in the road. We hadn't seen it at all and the tractor had been right over it and the destructive weight had done its worst.

As foreman I went up to the big house, with Dave following closely behind. The place was heaving with loud music, talking, laughter and crockery noises. I knocked on the outside door. Nothing. I hammered on it. Nothing. Pounded on it even and then decided to have a try at the next one in.

'Come in, come in,' boomed Richard. 'Hello, hello, come in.' We ambled in in our boiler suits, grubby and unkempt after a day's slog which included hand loading a trailer with sand. Everyone there looked the complete opposite and stared at us as though we were some curiosity that they had never seen before. 'I wonder if I could have a quiet word Richard,' I asked.

'It's all right, we're all friends here,' said Richard. 'Spit it out. What can I do for you?'

'I would really like a private chat if I could Richard.'

'Okay, very well,' said Richard. 'If you insist but it's not necessary you know.'

'Thanks Richard,' I said as we tumbled out into the porch. I continued, 'I am really sorry Richard but coming back with the tractor tonight we ran over one of your son's bikes that was left on the track."

'Oh, no problem, should be able to straighten it out,' said the optimistic Richard. Dave handed him the mangled remains.

'Oh, oh, yes, well, I see what you mean.' An embarrassed pause lasted for a moment. 'It really is okay you know because they're both getting new bikes on the boat, don't worry.' With that we were sort of dismissed and Richard returned to his dinner party. I couldn't imagine Richard giving us a severe bollocking but I thought he would at least be cross.

'Contractors'

Fox Bay East was a strange place to be at that time because it was unlike any other settlement outside Stanley. Everywhere else the focal point was the farm manager's house and the manager. Admittedly other big farms that had split up had lost that hierarchy because all owners were equal but here at Fox Bay East there was the embryo of a self-declared village with a government agent, two owner occupiers, and the ex-manager who was setting up a wool processing business. Each element seemed to be jockeying for their sphere of influence.

We, on the other hand, were referred to as 'the contractors'. We all felt a collective hurt because we just saw ourselves as locals doing work in the community. The term contractors to most Falkland Islanders meant people that came down here from outside the Islands and were paid well, had an area set aside for their recreation and had a catering wing that kept them in a manner that they would never have had in their own homes. Yes, we got good wages in local terms at that time but that was it.

During our time at Fox Bay, Toni had asked Joyce Halliday if she would show her how to milk a cow. So each morning at 6am, Toni would join Joyce in the cowshed. Toni really warmed to the task of feeding the cows their morning hay and molasses and milking them by hand. It was great to hear how excited Toni was each day as she got more and more milk for her efforts. It went something like. 'I got enough for a cup of tea this morning,' 'Got half a jug,' 'Full jug,' 'Milked a cow,' as the days passed.

Les was a great boss to work for but he had his little ways, his customs and routines that could rub some of the gang the wrong way, but as you can see that wasn't difficult. One of the things that Les liked was a review with me when he came out. So I would walk around the settlement with Les pointing out the progress and trying to say which of the gang members were responsible for the work. We would then plan a priority for the next few weeks.

Giles and others thought it was a waste of my time but Les was the boss and I was happy to oblige. Perhaps some of the gang thought I was on a jolly but I was doing what my boss wanted me to do. I would try to speed the process up but it usually took a morning or an afternoon. Ultimately it was necessary to have Les recognise the progress and discuss the priorities of the continuing programme.

Every night Les would say, 'Got a lot done today, boys' and Giles would throw his eyes heavenwards and the rest of us would mumble agreement. With me doing this walkabout with Les it became a bit of an 'in joke' and then when Les was back in Stanley some wag would say, 'Got a lot done today, boys,' to which we would all shout, 'Yes and a fuck sight more when you're not here.' Thankfully, no one ever got sloshed enough to say it in Les's presence, which was always possible.

We put up acres of tin, hardboard, paint and a few chimneys, lots of pipe and earned a reasonable wage and we worked hard.

We did have fun as well. We had one dartboard and invited like-minded people in the settlement over for games. But there were only so many darts non-dart people can throw, so we would resort to cookhouse games like going through the broom etc.

During our time at Fox Bay, a Yorkshire man came to work for us. He was middle aged, doing labouring work and yet came to work in a collar and tie. Christ knows exactly where he came from but I have never been to a part of Yorkshire with that kind of dress sense.

After a few beers one night we decided we couldn't stomach another game of darts so decided to go through the repertoire of games. During this evening we tried the game where you stand with your heels against the wall and then with only two beer cans to stop you touching the ground reach out as far as you can and place one of them and then get back to an upright position using the one remaining can to keep you off the ground.

Charlie (please attempt Yorkshire accent when pronouncing his name) managed a spectacular collapse on the return to the upright position and trapped his little finger under the can momentarily. He gave a curse but under the general aesthetic of a few beers there wasn't much of a fuss made. One game led to another and probably in sequence to the cans of beer and our social evening of tomfoolery carried on until the early hours.

Next morning, feeling like homemade shit, we all sheepishly forced a coffee or tea down and then off to our various work. All of us, that is, apart from Charlie. At smoko I came back and checked on Charlie's progress. Nothing. Lunch, zero. Well after lunch Charlie surfaced claiming that he had hurt his little finger and was therefore incapacitated. Hungover more like, just like the rest of us, but to be fair to Charlie, as a newcomer he hadn't had the amount of practice the rest of us had had.

Giles versus mouse

During our time at Fox Bay East one had to make one's own amusement. In the early days a cheeky rodent had made his home behind the plaster just above the Rayburn peat stove. He/she was obviously delighted with us moving in and firing up the stove and making this mouse home warm and comfortable. In celebration, the mouse went into spring-cleaning overdrive and he would spend the evenings scratching out his hole and kicking the debris out onto the top of the stove; I don't think any of the stuff was flammable but the act of shovelling and scratching for hours on end infuriated Giles.

Giles found a huge meat knife in the kitchen and would stand, like a heron, over the hole for ages waiting for the mouse to show its contempt for us humans and kick out some more dirt. I don't know what it was but when Giles stood over the hole the mouse didn't even offer the smallest of scratches but the minute Giles sat down the mouse would heave out a quantity of dust. Of course, this would get Giles worked up and he would scream obscenities, in a way that only Giles could, and leap from his chair to thrust the knife into the wall with great enthusiasm but with zero results. Giles would, with great difficulty, change tactics and sneak up to the wall, but again this mouse had the beating of Giles and at the end of the evening Giles would leave the kitchen with some threat or reference to that f***ing mouse and stomp off to bed. You could imagine this type of thing going on for a couple of days and then I think most of us would have just accepted the scratching and invested in a couple of mouse traps. Giles took this animals existence as a personal affront and no goddamn mouse was going to beat him.

No one ever told Giles but the rest of us found this battle between Giles and the mouse quite entertaining without any alternative like TV or a video.

The war was in great danger of escalating, with Giles on the verge of a major flip and tearing down the wall behind the stove to get at least some kind of satisfaction from his foe.

Sadly, or fortunately whichever way you viewed this titanic mismatch, Giles was robbed of catching the mouse or stabbing an entry hole in the wall that he could have climbed into in pursuit of his friend. One morning Toni came down to find one mouse as flat as a pancake under Geoffrey our cat. Some believe that he killed the mouse and was so delighted with his first kill that he played with it for hours before finally falling to sleep on it thus robbing us of something far more entertaining than a Wii game or a million episodes of *Eastenders*.

Duck!

A young couple from the UK came to join the team at the Mill during our tenure at Fox Bay East. Unfortunately for them their timing was poor and they came while Giles was on his own and he decided that he would help break down barriers and make friends by taking them around for their inaugural trip to the Fox Bay West club. I'm not sure how much they had consumed at the club, but obviously Giles had had enough because he thought he would introduce Martin and Carol to some of Falklands' culture. This meant chasing some tame ducks on the green at Fox Bay East in a vehicle on their return home. Usually it is all loud quacks, some focused flapping and wasn't that good fun? With Giles's coordination a bit shot he misjudged a savage swerve and flattened a duck under the wheels. Instead of mumbling a few apologies Giles got out of the vehicle and manically blamed the duck for the incident and threw it into the night sky.

The sensitive Cant's sat stunned in the back of the Land Rover, eyes wide open and who knows what they were thinking but it probably went along the lines of 'Beam me up Scottie'. beam me back to the UK.

Goodbye Giles

Toni and I left before the end of the job but by then the back of the job had been broken. Les and his merry men went on to complete what was a large project in those days.

Back in Stanley, Giles left in a strop after some altercation with Les. He realised that he was the only one working for Les with a driving licence so he parked the firm's tractor in the road blocking the entrance to the workshop. Giles wasn't coming back and he showed his contempt by this final action. In a way, it was a shame and I feel that if I had still been about it might have had a better ending but that wouldn't have been guaranteed. The truth was Giles and Les were opposites. Giles did get through a phenomenal amount of work for the firm but it was always on his terms.

Giles was left some money in a trust fund by his parents that matured or he was able to access it while he was in the Islands. He decided to invest it in buying land and building houses. Like all countries, even in the Falklands, there are rules and regulations that you have to obey when you build a house. Admittedly some of the rules don't make sense but at the end of the day rules are rules and so you either bend them, ignore them, accept them or fight them.

Giles decided to fight them, which gave his expansive repertoire of confrontation a new focus. For a country that was supposedly crying out for entrepreneurs like Giles it was funny how the powers that be couldn't have tried to smooth the way, but equally if someone had, there is no saying how effective that would have been.

Despite taking on the world Giles managed to erect his own house and another three houses including a kit house from Chile which he got over to try.

Giles just wouldn't take no for an answer and he was prepared to go to the top for the definitive decision. He tried to see the government's chief executive for a couple of weeks but his secretary explained that he was busy or at a meeting. I think Giles thought he was being fobbed off because eventually he showed up at the man's house on a Saturday morning to discuss his grievances.

Eventually Giles and Christel decided to leave the Falklands for pastures green. I know he gave government grief and was a pain in the arse at times but he is the only house builder that actually invested his own money in buying and erecting houses and taking the risk so to speak.

Since that time many builders have come on the scene and probably a number of them more skilful than Giles, but few, if any, have risked their own money in building a number of properties for other people.

Giles parting shot was to plant daffodils in his front garden spelling out something offensive directed at the government and naming his road, which serviced the houses he built, Unaided Avenue. Today it has been civilised into something boring but pointed – Narrow View – which is government having the final say but hardly documents the struggle one independently minded person had with authority.

Wedding day

Toni and I went from working for Les to owning Port Sussex and I believe we left with his goodwill. I had also worked hard for Les and for about six months had a reminder of my dedication to the cause which was numb toes on my right foot where I had got so cold putting Agrilux on the doctor's house at Fox Bay in the middle of winter. Les's son James moved to Stanley from Port Howard to join the management team.

Although Les Lee and Son went on for a number of years I always thought fondly of Les in what I think of as his niche market – your friendly neighbourhood handyman who would come round and do a job and have a cuppa or a tot and comment on the local issues.

Between working for Les at Fox Bay East and moving to the farm Toni and I got married. It was in the middle of winter and so we were hoping for reasonable weather. I had asked Giles to be my best man but then I was worried about how things would go in the church. We had been living in sin for a while and the padre had been sounding Heather out about our intentions and we thought he might highlight our journey to our union before God. In the discussions, Giles felt that if this did happen he would probably say something.

So the day arrived and I was in the church and at the alter waiting for Toni to arrive. Funnily enough my legs began to shake and I had to keep my legs slightly bent to stop it.

God was certainly with us that day because the padre didn't mention our sinner's paradise at Rincon Cottage or our not-so-sinful abode at Fox Bay East. Giles was a reformed character for the day and didn't put a foot wrong.

The day was glorious. One of those winter days when it is calm and bright and perfect for our special day. We went back to the Police Cottages and had pictures taken of the wedding party.

Later that day we went to the Upland Goose for the reception and much later we had our wedding dance at the town hall.

Visiting our new home

We had won the battle to own Port Sussex farm and would join the other successful farmers for a season as a co-op working together to get the sheep in and shorn and then shared out on a percentage basis. For me this was a great period of time that cemented a number of lasting friendships.

One of the first jobs was to go out and have a look at the farm and our first trip was out in Toni's father's Land Rover. Myself and Heather were in the vehicle and Toni and her dad were on motorbikes. We had a fairly uneventful trip out until we got to the top of Sussex Mountain at a place called Gin Rock gate. Within one hundred yards of that we got bogged. The two Tony/is carried on, on their bikes and went down to the house and we arrived shortly after that.

The real epic though was after our wedding, in the middle of winter. My father was down for the wedding and was due to fly out in about a week from Stanley Airport. I have written this in less than thirty words but in those days it was an epic flight from Ascension Island in a noisy Hercules transport plane with numerous in-flight refuellings. Here the tanker flies in front of the Hercules, trailing a hose with a cone-shaped end that the Hercules has to push a probe into, which is fastened to the front of the aircraft. The whole operation was hardly commercial in all the risk and none too comfortable but well worth going through for the right reasons.

We thought it would be a good idea, in the middle of winter, to take Father out and show him our new home. Giles and Christel and the two girls, Katherine and Simone, decided to accompany us as the second Land Rover that made travelling in winter easier when a vehicle gets bogged.

We had bought a Land Rover in an army cast sale. It had a smashed gearbox but other than that it was in a really good condition for an army vehicle, especially the bodywork and the springs, which looked brand new. I managed to get another gearbox and we were able to put the vehicle onto the road. It had been a Land Rover used by the military police, which might be the reason why it was in fairly good shape. I was disappointed that the blue light had been removed along with the siren but cruelly they had left the switches in.

So we set out a day or so after our wedding. We had tall wide track grip tyres that had only been on the Islands a year or two. Giles had the smaller version.

It was all pretty plain sailing until we got to Bluff Cove, including a short piece of road that was being built back towards Pony's Pass from a place called Elephant Canyon. To the uninitiated, Elephant Canyon sounds like a very Falklands name and one might think connected to the elephant seal that you see around the Islands. Not so, because the elephants here at Elephant Canyon were the elephant beers made by Carlsberg that was consumed in vast quantities by some of the workforce building the road. After this piece of road, the track deteriorated and there were ditches, rutted out and soft camp to negotiate. Like a lot of winter trips, we would sink down and think this is it, but then just manage to crawl through and equally only just scrabble through a few passes as we made our way southwest.

It was pretty cold and the Land Rover heaters were inadequate to compensate for the draft coming in past the doors. There were a few moans about cold feet but we were well on our way.

It was while we were climbing Fitzroy Ridge that we had a small pointer that things weren't as they should be. A lot of the older Land Rovers would get hotter if you were ploughing through soft camp for a long period of time, but in Giles's vehicle the hand went past the 'getting a bit hot' into the red which is a bit more worrying. To demonstrate that the temperature gauge was working, steam started pouring out from under the bonnet.

It doesn't pay to put cold water into a very hot engine because it can lead to a damaged head or block. It isn't wise to take the radiator cap off straight away either because you can get easily scalded by boiling water and steam as the pressure is released.

Not a concern about the former because we couldn't find a container. By the time, Giles had decided that one of his wellington boots was a suitable receptacle and he had trudged and squelched to the nearest source of water, under a plethora of oaths and foul language, the Land Rover had cooled down enough for a boot-full of water.

We had all seemed incredibly focused before this momentary glitch, but this forced stop had dented our confidence and although we weren't lost – we were on Fitzroy bloody Ridge – we were no longer sure where the gate was in the fence we had just driven up to. Giles sought help on the 2 meter. Amazingly the gate was very close to the new road, which was to be built from MPA to Stanley. We seemed to cover the ground quite quickly up to Swan Inlet where an old wooden bridge spanned the Swan Inlet River, sitting on concrete supports sitting on the riverbed. One of these supports had obviously moved because there was an undulation a few yards onto the bridge from this side. Beside the bridge was a pass for larger vehicles that would damage the bridge. Most of the time, if driven through sensibly, the pass was fine but after heavy rain it became too deep for Land Rovers to cross safely. Another factor to affect the depth of the pass was if the tide was high after rain because this would back the water up to a certain degree.

It was the smaller bridges over the smaller ditches that caused the problems because over most camp tracks you can wander from one side to another looking for ground that hasn't been cut up, but to cross a bridge all the tracks come together turning the ground into slops. These treacherous bottlenecks used to get into some states over the winter months and be strewn with rope and debogging material and water-filled holes. The Guttery Pass was one of these bottlenecks and more by luck than judgement we slithered up and over the bridge. Some gates got like this too but the trick was to forget about the gate and to undo the fence from the standards and then lay it down and go over it. It is a last resort because it slackens up a fence and makes farmers cross, but if a gateway is impossible it is the best way.

We stopped a few times to congratulate ourselves and Father seemed to be enjoying his Falkland's answer to the Camel Trophy.

We were also lucky in having a guide, of many years' experience, Rab McRae, who we were looking to for his expertise as we closed in on San Carlos. The track to Goose Green was fairly clear with most of the tracks meandering across the white grass flats with the clay track somewhere pointing the way.

We turned off after Burnt Side and headed in the direction of San Carlos. The clay track was still clear although most of the traffic of recent times seemed to stay off it. We passed Camilla Creek that featured prominently in the attack by 2 Para on Goose Green. Giles and Christel had been the last people to live there when Giles was an outside shepherd in the 1970s. The house had suffered severe wear and tear during the war including a huge hole burnt in the kitchen floor. The house was still standing at this time, but Goose Green eventually took it down and moved the materials to the settlement.

After Camilla Creek, for us greenhorns, the track was more challenging because there were gaps in the clay track with some sticky little valleys that looked a bit suspect with the odd piece of broken rope and wood lying about.

The clay track was not fit to use apart from in the dry part of the year because driving on it in the winter was like driving in grinding paste and took a toll on all moving parts on your vehicle that it could get to.

We arrived at the Sussex boundary and headed directly towards the Sussex house that we could see in the distance. This meant going around the edge of the creek and past the clay track which left the beach in the northeast corner and coming off on a faint track heading parallel with the beach heading west. The track then goes slightly inland and drops into the arm of the sea that ends in what is called Hells Kitchen. Here there are two main options. Turn left, go 30 metres or so and cross the creek at the low pass if the tide is out. Or if the tide is halfway in, you turn right, go north a couple of hundred metres and then cross the creek at its head and climb up the steep slope in front of you. In the winter this climb is very dangerous and over the years, where the increase of traffic has removed the vegetation, it has become virtually impossible to climb unless it is relatively dry.

So here we are, arriving with our guide with at least 40 plus years of experience and oh bugger, although Rab has been through the Low Pass more times than he cares to admit, to our dismay he tells us it has always been on horseback. He is unable to tell us if it is too deep for Land Rovers. We decided to walk over to the house, which with the two young girls wasn't exactly an after-dinner stroll.

On arriving at Sussex we found that someone had lit the fire while the hot water system had been drained down, ruining the boiler in the back of the stove. I suppose you could describe this trip as our honeymoon and with all the romance one can muster in a cold house, without a fire, everyone decided to lay their sleeping bags out in one of the smallest upstairs rooms. I've read somewhere that an average human body generates 2 kilowatts an hour. What total codswallop – it was bloody freezing.

Next day Giles and I went over to see what the tide was doing and typically it didn't seem to be doing anything. Remembering it is July and bitter, which is equivalent to January in UK. We didn't have a clue how deep the water was or where it should be on the beach to be fordable. Giles, never the one to wait forever for some kind of pointer, stripped off his jeans and waded into the creek. Giles found out pragmatically that the creek is too deep and very cold.

Eventually we get the Land Rovers back to the house and we take Rab over to Kellys Garden, a military camp just outside San Carlos, where the Chinooks are stationed that will pop him over to Port San Carlos where he lives. The track was bloody awful. Toni is convinced that she will not travel to San Carlos in the winter unless it is an emergency when we come to live at Sussex. The track has been beaten up by constant military traffic notably the tracked BV which had been instructed to stay on the one track, because of its low pressure it would go across all but the softest terrain even when it was an impassable consistency to any wheeled vehicles. I always thought that if they had spread the use in the areas where it was possible it would have helped improve the ground and vegetation. Our honeymoon only lasted a couple of nights and it wasn't that romantic if the truth be told. Our trip back to town started with us going back through Hells kitchen but not through the Low Pass, which was being uncooperative once more. We came down the steep hill into the top part of the creek. It was easy coming down you just put your wheels in the ruts and sledged down. You could be flat out in reverse but once you were on your way you would still end up at the bottom.

Giles' Land Rover

I think even at this early stage of our travels, Giles realised there was something wrong with his Land Rover but, like the imitation pioneers we were, we carried on. We didn't have much choice. The Land Rover began to throw its fan belt off and then we found that it was fully adjusted and the fan belt was far too big. You could just about skip with the slack. Goose Green was the nearest place with a garage and so we made a small detour at Burnside and turned towards Goose Green through the Puzzle Gates.

The mechanics suggested changing the pulley, but the shaft size was different so they came up with a whole dynamo with pulley. Meanwhile Giles, the rough mechanic that he was, had pulled off one of the short metal pipes that the hoses slip on to while trying to remove a stubborn hose. They braised that on and then the new dynamo got knocked onto the ground and a lug broke off making it impossible to fit on the Land Rover, so it was back with the old and the likelihood of a slow trip back to Stanley.

It was a cold old night and we all spent it with welcoming members of the Goose Green community. Toni and I went and stayed with Andy Clarke in the school, Father with Gladys and Mike Robson and Giles and Christel somewhere else.

That night we met two of our new neighbours, Ron and Iris Dickson, although I had met Ron about seven years before at San Carlos when I was a teacher. We talked away about the farms and had a few beers.

The next morning it was freezing and there was a hard frost. We left Goose Green to the squealing of the Mercer's Land Rover, Giles at the wheel, his teeth gritted, and everyone else in with him, with expressions of tolerance. We had drained the radiator when they needed to braise up the damage that Giles had caused and the anti-freeze had not been replaced. The water pump was frozen solid and the slack fan belt was making a hell of a noise squealing an exit out of the settlement for all to hear.

It wasn't long before Giles had pulled over and was booting the vehicle in frustration and cussing, 'When I get back to Stanley I am going to buy a brand new fucking Rover. Christel, usually the peacemaker and calmer adult member of the Mercer family, chipped in with, 'with a hard top Giles?' That didn't help. 'Don't fucking push me, man,' said Giles, forgetting Christel is a woman, like Americans sometimes do.

Things were on a knife-edge especially after the threats to its future, the Land Rover spat out its fan belt every few hundred metres during the worst times. We stopped at the Stanley Gates, called that because most people from Goose Green, Lafonia and San Carlos went through them on the way to town. We stopped for a breather and to calm Giles out of the red zone. Father had been travelling with the Mercers because we didn't have seats in the back of our Land Rover. He confided in us that he thought things were getting better because we were off the 'Fs and Cs' and back on to the 'Ss and Bs'. Father really enjoyed his raw off-road experiences, but he was beginning to worry that we might not make it back to Stanley in time for his plane out of the Islands.

We carried on with the fan belt coming off more and more and tempers hovering in and just below the Fs and Cs. Although, if I am honest, Giles is only a heartbeat from this state in normal time. The weather began to close in and from being just cold it began to snow very heavily. Big fluffy flakes made it a white out and very difficult to drive. The snow began to build up on the windscreen wipers and then ice formed on the blades so they no longer wiped the windscreen very effectively. I hadn't been bogged until then but managed to drive into a swamp. It took some good jerks on the rope to get us out. After that we got disorientated and lost in the Fitzroy Horse Paddock, going around in circles. This was more than embarrassing for Giles and Christel who had worked there for a while.

By this time, we were heading into Fitzroy because we knew town was not going to happen. We didn't want to go further in the dark, with our limited experience, and get stuck out for the night.

Cold and grim we finally managed to find our way into Fitzroy. Some people had suggested that the settlement of Fitzroy wasn't that welcoming but we needed shelter for the night and we proceeded to the cookhouse with a little trepidation.

Ben and Fanny Ford lived in the galley. Fanny was the cook for the single men living in the bunkhouse at Fitzroy. Giles and I went down to the galley and knocked on the door. Fanny was very welcoming and told us to go down to the bunkhouse and she would knock us up a snack.

We went back and foolishly joked that we had been turned away. We were able to watch a human firework display. It took all of Giles's zero diplomatic skills to stop Christel and Toni charging down to the house and being exceedingly objectionable.

It wasn't long in the warm bunkhouse before we began to thaw out and Fanny brought in a feast of vast proportions that was very welcome. The participants of this trip have often reminisced about Fanny's kindness and generosity to us weary travellers who were at the end of our tethers.

The next day was sort of an anti-climax. We rolled out of Fitzroy and crawled up the south side of Fitzroy Ridge making heavy weather of it, but each yard was getting us all closer to our destination – Stanley. Of course, the fan belt began to fall off more frequently, which had Giles stomping and cursing, and I am sure with Christel and the girls dreaming of the new Land Rover with a hard top.

It had taken us a full day to get to Sussex, if you don't include the Land Rovers not making it through the Low Pass and three eventful days to get back. Giles didn't get a new Land Rover, he got a blue Suzuki jeep which the Mercer family filled to capacity. As one would expect Giles gave this vehicle a hard life, like tow starting his four-ton lorry and making the trip out to Sussex in the summer months a number of times. It did become less of a struggle in the mid-1990s when the roads began to roll out from Mount Pleasant towards Goose Green making it easier and easier as the roads got closer. Sadly, for us, Giles and Christel and by then three girls called it a day and left the Falklands before we got a road all the way to Sussex.

We had a lot of trips in and out in winter and summer, at night and during the day but this trip easily beats them all for events and duration.

Moving in

It wasn't long before we moved from Rincon cottage in Stanley, our home for a couple of years, to Port Sussex our new home in camp.

Years later, on one of our trips to town we come across a familiar Land Rover conked out in the middle of the L'Antioja. It was Giles and Christel's old beast and giving its present owners some more of the same challenges it gave to the Mercers. We offered to give them a tow out but our help was declined. They were just having so much fun perched on the wings out of the water with the bonnet open looking enquiringly at the engine and they didn't want us spoiling it.

There were inevitably a few loose ends as we made our move from the metropolis to our isolated farm. One of these loose ends was a wild cat that Toni had felt sorry for and fed for many months. It used to hide under a piece of corrugated iron in the back yard. It was taming down slowly but no one had laid a hand on it and it was still very flighty. Toni decided, quite rightly, that it wouldn't be fair to leave him behind because he had become used to and dependent on Toni's charity. The plan was to try and coax him into the back kitchen shut the door, catch him and put him in a cat cage, get him castrated for good measure and take him out to the farm.

The day came and Toni enticed him into the back kitchen and I shut the back door. The cat went completely bananas and did the feline wall of death around the kitchen. Stuff was sent flying from the benches and from the sideboard. After a period of time, that seemed ages but was probably at best a couple of minutes, I managed to catch him using big thick gardening gloves and put him in the cage. He took a trip up to the vets and then went into the Land Rover for the inaugural run to Sussex with all the essentials to set us up until our main stuff arrived.

We were soon off and everything seemed to be going well, including no continuous meowing that cats can create when confined for a trip. At one of the gates just outside Swan Inlet, about halfway, Toni checked the wild tabby only to find an empty box. Not the end of the world but our good intentions appeared to be dashed. It seemed to be pointless to backtrack because he could be anywhere and there weren't any other road users to ask if they had seen him bounce out. We carried on a little dispirited remembering how Toni had found him and fed him from a miserable runty thing into a reasonable animal.

We eventually pulled up at Sussex, following a successful crossing of the Low Pass, and discovered that there was a marker on both sides of the creek which you shouldn't go seaside of. If they are visible you can cross comfortably. We got the fire going had a drink and began unpacking the Land Rover. Toni's mum had packed our worldly goods because we were working at Fox Bay East right up to our departure. She was an expert packer and had things wrapped up and adequately protected for a rough ride in our Land Rover.

The last of our possessions were being removed from the Land Rover and out of the back, at warp-factor speed, came the tabby cat. We didn't see him for three months but over time he did tame down, although not enough to ever be a house cat.

A little while before we left town our house cat Geoffrey was knocked down by a car. A small boy from along the road was delighted for some reason and kept telling us that our cat had been run over as he tore up and down on his three-wheeler, the sort with the peddles on the front wheel. Geoffrey was twitching in the road so I went to finish him off with a knife, but from his reactions I realised he was far from dead. Geoffrey was in a hell of a state. Broken jaw, teeth missing and the vet Steve Whitley had to rebuild his face bringing his jaw back together.

He was just getting better when he disappeared. We put an announcement on the radio. Lost, one cat, answers to the name of Geoffrey. (Or any other name. The sound of a tin being opened etc.) No one phoned to report him found. Toni spoke to Steve who still did the vets programme, although a more sophisticated version than the earlier episode of pushing the pig's arse back in with a wooden spoon.

Steve did his vet programme and then at the end mentioned Geoffrey saying that he was still needing medication. The phone rang soon after and we went to the army camp and picked him up. He was having the life of Riley, stinking of Brute and obviously settling in to his new home. He was warm, well treated and spoilt and hadn't missed us one jot.

On another of those runs with the Land Rover full to the gunwales with our personal stuff, going passed what was going to be Mount Pleasant Airport, a chap working for the consortium Laing Mowlem ARC, flagged us down. Two guys working for Fitzroy farm were stuck on the beach in Swan Inlet and would we go and help. I was more than dubious because we had such a load but they needed our help. This guy had been down to help but with only road tyres, he had been unable to shift them.

So off we went down to where the Land Rover was stuck on the beach. Again it was a little worrying because if we went down there was no way we would get out before the tide came in. It was Gary Hewitt and Tootie Ford and they were well down on the passenger side. We put their rope onto the tow hitch, they fired up the farm Land Rover and off I went. With the weight of a fully loaded rover and the grip we got on the beach they came out no problem.

Now it was time to get back to the road. Going back, we had to go through this sharp little ditch and going out we had dragged a bit, but going this way we hung up and stopped. Fortunately, the contractor had stayed with us and was able to pull us out.

We never had a trip again like the one with Giles, Christel, Simone, Kathryn and my dad, but it was serious off road every time. You always left town or the farm, having checked the essentials. Bumper jack (high lift jack) and something to put the jack on – if you had bogged somewhere there was a good chance that the foot of the jack would sink into the ground without lifting your vehicle, so you had to have a decent plank of wood to spread the weight. Wood was better than metal because the jack wouldn't slip as easily as it does on metal. Bridges – once you got the Land Rover jacked up you needed to put something under the wheels. There weren't always rocks at a reasonable distance from your bogging to carry back and chuck under the wheels. A decent toolbox was also recommended to cope with any eventuality, and a 2 meter set. If you were very badly bogged or broken down, you called for help.

Here we were on the brink of another adventure. The start of a settled life. I couldn't help thinking of some of the veterans that I'd met when I worked at the Rose. They wanted to know what people would do now that the war was over. I thought, like many others, that we owed it to all those brave people that had liberated us to make a success of our future that they had secured, as individuals and as a country.

As individuals we had bought a farm nearly seventy miles from Stanley without any roads, no experience of sheep farming or being responsible for your own power and water supply. So it was in at the deep end, so to speak and sink or swim.

In the next book I will describe our challenges like bucking horses, stroppy bulls, taking down a large building, transporting it over the mountain and putting it up at Port Sussex Farm, raising two children, and much more.